Bernard Shaw's Remarkable Religion

THE FLORIDA BERNARD SHAW SERIES

Florida A&M University, Tallahassee
Florida Atlantic University, Boca Raton
Florida Gulf Coast University, Ft. Myers
Florida International University, Miami
Florida State University, Tallahassee
University of Central Florida, Orlando
University of Florida, Gainesville
University of North Florida, Jacksonville
University of South Florida, Tampa
University of West Florida, Pensacola

THE FLORIDA BERNARD SHAW SERIES

This series was made possible by a generous grant from
the David and Rachel Howie Foundation.

Edited by R. F. Dietrich

The Florida Bernard Shaw Series is devoted to works of and about Shaw, Shaw's literary
production, and Shavian topics of interest. While supportive of traditional approaches, the
series also aims to encourage scholars with new critical paradigms to engage Shaw's works.

Pygmalion's Wordplay: The Postmodern Shaw, by Jean Reynolds (1999)
Shaw's Theater, by Bernard F. Dukore (2000)
Bernard Shaw and the French, by Michel W. Pharand (2001)
The Matter with Ireland, second edition, edited by Dan H. Laurence
     and David H. Greene (2001)
Bernard Shaw's Remarkable Religion: A Faith That Fits the Facts, by Stuart E. Baker (2002)

Bernard Shaw's
Remarkable Religion

A Faith That Fits the Facts

Stuart E. Baker

University Press of Florida
GAINESVILLE · TALLAHASSEE · TAMPA · BOCA RATON
PENSACOLA · ORLANDO · MIAMI · JACKSONVILLE · FT. MYERS

Copyright 2002 by Stuart E. Baker
Printed in the U.S.A. on acid-free, TCF (totally chlorine-free) paper
All rights reserved

07 06 05 04 03 02   6 5 4 3 2 1

Library of Congress Cataloging-in-Publication Data
Baker, Stuart E. (Stuart Eddy)
Bernard Shaw's remarkable religion : a faith that fits the facts /
Stuart E. Baker.
p. cm.—(The Florida Bernard Shaw series)
Includes bibliographical references and index.
ISBN 0–8130–2432–3 (cloth : alk. paper)
1. Shaw, Bernard, 1856–1950—Religion. 2. Religious drama,
English—History and criticism. 3. Rationalism in literature.
4. Religion in literature. I. Title. II. Series.
PR5368.R4 B26 2002
822.'9129–dc21   2001043729

The University Press of Florida is the scholarly publishing
agency for the State University System of Florida, comprising
Florida A&M University, Florida Atlantic University, Florida Gulf
Coast University, Florida International University, Florida State
University, University of Central Florida, University of Florida,
University of North Florida, University of South Florida, and
University of West Florida.

University Press of Florida
15 Northwest 15th Street
Gainesville, FL 32611–2079
http://www.upf.com

For Jalma, who made it possible.

Contents

Foreword

"I believe *because* it is absurd," said Søren Kierkegaard, speaking for all those who think a religious belief unworthy unless it *can't* be proved and is even contrary to Nature. After all, they reason, the gap between God and man is so great that it must require a "leap of faith" to bridge it. But in an age of science such as ours, in which the gap has perhaps lessened, there are many who think that such leaps of faith may be from the factual to the factitious and therefore too often dangerous and destructive, both to the individual and to society. To those looking for a faith that better "fit the facts," Bernard Shaw for half a century offered a fascinating, seemingly new religion that attempted to answer the need for up-to-date factuality in its being based on evolution. Shaw's remarkable departure in theology, in fact, tempted some to try to explain his artistically and prophetically expressed religion in more conventional and literal terms and even to convert it into something more systematic and analytical, something more akin to formal philosophy and theology. The latest, and I believe most successful, attempt to explain and update Shaw is Stuart Baker's *Bernard Shaw's Remarkable Religion: A Faith That Fits the Facts,* which is all the more valuable because it shows the increasing relevance of Shaw's religious insights to this age of, on the one hand, fundamentalist backlash and rising religious intolerance and, on the other, a nihilistic rejection of all religion.

Baker presents Shaw as an original religious thinker, perilously asserting the unity of knowledge in the face of the dialectical tensions of the day between the extremes of skepticism and blind faith, naturalism and supernaturalism, materialism and spiritualism, summarized as the conflict between science and religion. The peril was in this "jesting apostle's" often inviting misunderstanding and sometimes outright hostility in the rather reckless and playful way he expressed himself. Shavian speech was typically a high-wire act, balancing between trying to make do with language as he found it and creating a new speech of his own that lacked familiarity. Our language often betrayed him in either case. For example, in arguing that religion must become scientific and science must become religious, he often found himself trapped in the sorts of semantic snarls and quandaries that our jerry-built but imperious language inevitably throws us into, and thus he was misunderstood by both scientists and the religious, the two camps he was trying to reconcile. Another cause of misunderstanding was in his sometimes being too free with language, too creative with it, for the tastes of many. Although Shaw said that "there is no question of a new religion but only of redistilling the eternal spirit of religion," this redistiller renewed the archetypes of religion in such paradoxical and ironic language that he appeared to the convention-bound and literal-minded as "antireligious," which defeated his own purpose. Thus Shaw became one of those prophets without honor in his own time who seems to need the help of explainers, translators, and updaters to make his case. I think you'll find that the case has never been made better than in the following, in which Shaw once again comes alive as a religious teacher, and perhaps none too soon.

R. F. Dietrich

Preface

The seed of this book can be found in an essay I published in 1989 called "Shavian Realism." I first developed and described there the ideas presented (very differently) in the first three chapters of this book. It occurred to me at that time that an understanding of Shaw's "*manner* of looking at the problems," as Warren Sylvester Smith put it, was really the key to understanding Shaw's religious or metaphysical views and, moreover, was the secret to understanding why those views were so valuable. I had planned to write another essay explaining this insight, which seemed to me at the time to be rather simple and straightforward. For Shaw, as for others of his time, *realism* meant the courage to see things as they are, not as one might wish them to be, but most self-declared realists had their gazes fixed rigidly outward, on the material, scientifically observable world; Shaw insisted on the reality of that which was within, on the irreducible reality of human will. He contrasted realism with "idealism," which projected our desires and fears onto abstract entities outside ourselves and thus evaded the pain of accepting responsibility for our own natures. Shaw's religion, I realized, was founded on the realization that the reality within was ineluctably nonmaterial and teleological, that realism inescapably entailed the recognition that "will" is an inherent aspect of the universe, and that we are all manifestations of that will. I imagined that this simple and straightforward idea could easily be expounded in a brief essay.

I could hardly have been more naive. As simple as Shaw's views in some sense are, they are so heterodox, so utterly at odds with the received, ingrained assumptions of our time, that a forthright exposition is met with bewilderment and often hostility. The core assumption of scientific materialism, that the universe is nothing but a giant machine performing its gyrations without point or purpose to the end of existence is accepted without question by most contemporary intellectuals regardless of the many other differences between them. The postmodernists' disdain for the notion of "progress" and their contempt for "essentialism" both derive from the belief that the universe is fundamentally without value or purpose. Ironically, some postmodernists have combined the dogmas of scientific materialism with the scientific reverence for systematic skepticism in order to attack science itself, insisting that science is but one way of understanding the world and is no more intrinsically valuable than any other. But as distrustful as they are of the scientific enterprise, they never question the validity of science's materialistic metaphysic. There is, of course, a sizable and powerful group that rejects both scientific atheism and postmodern relativism: the traditional religionists, who nevertheless betray their awe of science by attempting to construct "scientific" theories like Creationism in an attempt to enlist science in support of their received religious beliefs. But science makes them uncomfortable, and they are highly suspicious of reason and logic.

As hostile as these three groups are to one another, they have in common an inclination to regard Shaw as a dangerous crackpot. The traditionalists suspect him of atheism, the fashionable postmodernists dismiss him as an antiquated, essentialist believer in the naive concept of "progress," and the scientists accuse him of wishful thinking and fuzzy-brained balderdash. While it seemed clear to me that Shaw offered the means to reconcile these warring groups, it became increasingly obvious that it would be no easy task. The Shavian metaphysic provides the orderliness and systematic approach to knowing the universe that is so precious to the scientists, the assurance that there is something reasonably called divine purpose at the heart of things which is demanded by the traditional religionists, and an antidote to the pointlessness and lack of purpose that is the despair of the postmodernists. Yet to accept these benefits, each group would have to relinquish cherished assumptions. They all feel besieged by enemy ideology, and accepting a challenge to their precious dogmas seems akin to opening the city gates and lowering the drawbridge. To tear down these defenses is a slow and painstaking process because one must convince the combatants at each step of the disarmament that the benefits outweigh the risks. The defenses built up include many rather involved philosophical arguments, and it became obvious that my exegesis of Shaw's religion was going to have to address much of the reasoning at the foundation of contemporary orthodoxy. A book, not an essay, was demanded.

So while the principal audience I wish to address is the community of scholars and enthusiasts who value Shaw as a thinker as well as an artist, I hope to reach some of the many others who are interested in these vital issues. Philosophers, scientists, and theologians as well as most thoughtful members of the lay public are endlessly debating the relationship of science and religion, the place of human volition in the universe, and the possibility of a religion that is intellectually honest and a reliable guide to daily life. I have attempted to present the issues in a manner acceptable to specialists but without the jargon that might put off the general public unless it seemed essential, and then I have tried to provide clear and simple explanations. One more thing: I have not attempted to hide my belief that these issues are momentous and Shaw's answers to them vastly superior to the various orthodoxies. This is consequently a rather more passionate book than one is apt to find in the lists of a scholarly press. I offer that as a warning, not an apology. I find myself more deeply engaged with a work I am reading if the author is honestly committed to a point of view, even if that is not a view I share, and I hope my readers will have a similar experience with this book.

Acknowledgments

Whatever virtue this book possesses owes much to many people, including many such committed writers whom I have never met. Of course, Shaw himself is foremost among those; I thank the British Museum Press for permission to reprint excerpts from Shaw's *Fragments of a Fabian Lecture*. But there are many others whose clarity of vision and incisive gaze have provided the illumination I needed for my own timid efforts. David Hume and Bertrand Russell provided me with the philosophical foundations necessary to attempt the metaphysical interpretation of Shaw, and John Searle's more recent efforts to rehabilitate the idea of mind in respectable philosophical circles gave me courage and inspiration. My debts to the interpreters of Shaw who have preceded me are endless and uncountable. Shavian critics are by and large wonderfully open, pragmatic, and flexible, as one might expect given their subject. They willingly explore new approaches and ideas and are refreshingly free of the attitudinizing and ideological cant that clogs so much of academic writing these days. Of the many who have enlightened me purely through their writings I would have to call especial attention to Eric Bentley, whose book on Shaw is still a classic after so many years; G. K. Chesterton, who understood Shaw far better than any of his other contemporaries; Louis Crompton, whose solid research and penetrating insights still provide the best available reading of many of Shaw's plays; and Charles Berst and Warren Sylvester Smith for their insights into Shaw's spiritual side.

Of those who have so generously aided this project with their time and intelligence, I especially thank Bernard F. Dukore for his unflagging encouragement, meticulous reading of the manuscript, and copious and illuminating suggestions. Richard F. Dietrich, Daniel Leary, and Alfred Turco, by their careful reading and often brilliant suggestions, have helped me to understand what my book was actually all about. There are many others. I will always be grateful to the late Fred Crawford for his encouragement and support and to Dan Laurence, the dean of Shavian scholars, to whom we all owe endless respect and something that approaches awe. I am grateful to Michael Holroyd for elusive facts I was unable to ascertain for myself.

And I owe a debt that cannot be expressed to my students, who have engaged me in lively and loving dialogue over the years. In particular, I thank Leah Lowe, Page Rozelle, Georgia Brown, Phyllis Woodard, and Judith Sebesta for their research and suggestions.

The editorial staff at the University Press of Florida has been as generous and helpful as any author could wish, but I am especially indebted to Amy Gorelick, who helped me to stand back from the work and really see it after years of my being immersed in it, Jacqueline Kinghorn Brown, for her assistance in making my rough offspring presentable to the public, and Trudie Calvert, the copy editor, whose meticulous care and eagle eye saved me from many embarrassing errors. Their help was indispensable.

Finally, this book would not have been possible without the unfailing support and criticism of my wife, Jalma, who has been my navigator, coach, and cheerleader for the ten years and more of its gestation.

I am certain to have omitted others. To those, my profoundest apologies as well as belated thanks. Shaw was fond of quoting St. Paul: "We are members one of another." No one does anything without the assistance of all others.

Introduction

Here we have what is for me the paradox of Shaw's career: A man of Shaw's profound understanding and personal shrewdness gave, for the last thirty-five years of his life, the wrong answers to almost all the questions that have perplexed our age.

—Julian B. Kaye

The librarians and the teachers have begun to run to the planetariums. It is hard to get in, however. The places are crammed with children who know what to read in order to know what to see.

And Shaw's ghost is in there with them, asking their advice on books that he should scan in order to catch up. Catch up, hell, he's been ahead of us all of our lives. It is we who must do the running.

—Ray Bradbury

This book will contend that in the matters truly most important to our age Kaye is wrong and Bradbury is right. Kaye, unable to reconcile his admiration of Shaw's prime with his distaste for the political pronouncements of Shaw's final years, concludes that Shaw was intellectually stuck in the Victorian era. Having made a brilliant synthesis of the best thought of the nineteenth century, he never was able to comprehend the very different world of the twentieth. Obviously there is at least some truth in such an assertion; no one ever completely transcends one's own age, and Shaw was fifty-eight years old at the outset of World War I, when that extraordinary experiment in cultural and intellectual upheaval called the twentieth century began in earnest. But if Kaye is right to the extent that he claims to be, Shaw the thinker is essentially irrelevant to our own age. I believe that Shaw's ideas—both in general and in their specifics—are as urgently needed today as they ever were. This book is an attempt to show why this is so.

There are a number of obstacles in the way of such an endeavor. Although I disagree with Kaye's conclusions, it cannot be denied that the objections he raises are serious, for he is hardly the only critic who has been dismayed at Shaw's opinions of Mussolini, Hitler, and Stalin. Any defense of Shaw's relevance to our times must confront the later as well as the earlier Shaw. An even more serious obstacle is his apparent lack of influence. While the plays continue to be revived, often with great success, Shaw the thinker is still commonly dismissed as an egomaniacal crackpot. Darwinism is triumphant after a long period of obscurity, and Creative Evolution is alive only in the minds of a ragged little band of cranks who are too cowardly to face the truth of their biological existence. The superman has degenerated into a child's cartoon fantasy, and the future promises only more of the same degraded humanity that produced the ovens of Auschwitz. The dream of Lilith has been replaced by the stone of Sisyphus. Shaw performed a valuable service, back then, when he so wittily punched Victorian hypocrisy in its self-righteous nose, but that is long over now. Such, at any rate, is the common view.

The common view is wrong. We applaud the Shaw who saw through the self-congratulatory delusions of the nineteenth-century bourgeoisie and censure the Shaw who failed to comprehend the bitter realities we hardheaded postmodernists so courageously face, and so we see him as an iconoclast and not a prophet. The truth is that we have our own self-serving delusions, our own pompous egotism, and Shaw could still help us see beyond them. Some of us, at any rate, flatter ourselves that we see the universe as it is, a cold and mindless machine, spinning on in utter indifference to our needs or desires. Shaw, we imagine, did not have the courage to accept that truth. Of course not every thinking person at the opening of the twenty-first century sees herself or himself as a hardheaded materialist, but even the adherents of New Age thought feel estranged from Shaw. While the materialists and Social Darwinists see him as a fuzzy-minded sentimentalist, the spiritual liberals loosely gathered under the label of "New Age" recoil from him as coldly cerebral, overly logical, and even cynical. In a curious way, both groups suspect him of belonging to the enemy camp.

Those assumptions are not entirely unreasonable. Shaw believed vitally in both science and religion, but, more radically, he insisted that they be part of each other and not merely avoid conflict. He wanted a scientific religion and a religious science. A scientific religion would be one based on logic and honest observation. It would be glad to change when reason and

the facts asked it to. A religious science, he was convinced, would acknowledge that the Holy Ghost was an observable fact. That both camps view
him as an eccentric heretic is not surprising. It is common in religious
circles to hear shepherds warning their flocks of the dangers of trusting too
much in reason, and even those scientists who are devout churchgoers regard questions of the spirit as belonging to a realm of understanding entirely separate from that of science. Those peacemakers who insist that
there is no necessary conflict between science and religion assume they
occupy different and mutually exclusive domains; they seek to maintain
peace through total segregation. Unfortunately, this is not a way to satisfy
those who believe in the unity of knowledge—a category that includes
most careful thinkers in both camps.

The most common way to explain Shaw's paradoxical refusal to fit into
our accepted categories is to declare him intellectually inconsistent. His
philosophy was, in this view, a pastiche of various incompatible and ill-
digested ideas, chosen more for effect than for content and patched together with a cheerful arrogance that imagined it could plaster over jagged
discontinuities with bloated rhetoric and irreverent wit. Liberals who
could not reconcile his socialism and feminism with his harsher political
pronouncements after World War I found the inconsistent Shaw to be the
only Shaw they could understand or stomach. The Shaw who endorsed
capital punishment (euthanasia of the criminally unfit would be a more
accurate description of his view) and had good things to say about
Mussolini and Hitler was, they are sure, merely trying to shock, like a child
whose naughtiness is a bid for attention.

Shaw has always had a sizable following of loyal fans, most of whom
felt that these assessments were at best superficial, but none has satisfacto-
rily answered all of the critics. Shaw hoped to provide a religion for the
twentieth century, and in this he failed. That the twentieth century failed
Shaw may be closer to the truth, for the spiritual and intellectual bank-
ruptcy of contemporary nihilism, popularly called postmodernism, is leading us ever closer to the rocks. The reckless irresponsibility of the intellectuals is worse now than when Shaw exposed it in *Heartbreak House*
eighty-five years ago. The skipper is not drunk; he has abandoned the helm
on principle because his philosophy teaches him there is nowhere to go.
The people who accuse Shaw of inconsistency are progressives who deny
the possibility of progress. Perhaps there is hope for the twenty-first century. There is certainly hope in one small but astonishing fact: Shaw was
right and the perennially fashionable nihilists are wrong. The critics who

see in Shaw only confusion and pastiche are victims of their own acute astigmatism. Shaw was a consistently logical mystic, an original philosopher whose very constancy leads people to think him contradictory, and a radical so far beyond his age as to be incomprehensible despite his own voluminous self-exegesis. All this because he took two of our most venerable ideals—human equality and Christian charity—down from their golden altars and treated them as commonsense precepts for everyday living and practical social organization.

None of this is obvious. The best of the critics who thus dismissed Shaw are intelligent and perceptive women and men who were misled only by the preconceptions of their age. That is not folly, merely an infirmity of mind from which we all suffer in varying degrees. The cure can be painful at first, as Major Barbara discovered when she watched her father write that check in the Salvation Army shelter. To her it seemed an earthquake that cruelly razed her magnificent faith to the ground, but when she later understood what she had learned in that frightening moment, she figuratively ascended into the clouds.

Shaw still has much to teach us, much that is worth an even greater price than Barbara's profound but temporary heartbreak.

A Note on the Text

All references to Shaw's plays and their prefaces are to *The Bodley Head Bernard Shaw* unless otherwise noted.

I

Foundations of Faith

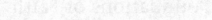

1

A Creed for Living
A Faith That Fits the Facts

UNITY

Bernard Shaw aspired to give the world a new religion, a faith suitable for a new age. But a religion requires a congregation, which his faith has not found, and so he failed—at least for now. He did create something more remarkable and rarer: a creed that is a reasonable and practical guide to living in the real world, a faith that is completely compatible with the facts, a religion consistent with itself. No one seems to have noticed.

We all know that he *professed* the need for unity of facts and faith. His most fundamental belief was, in Major Barbara's words, that "life is all one" (3:183). We cannot put our various beliefs into separate watertight compartments called "philosophy," "science," and "religion," any more than we can segregate religion and daily business or divide the world into saints and scoundrels. He called for a "faith proof against science" and declared that there was "not a single credible established religion in the whole world" (Pref. *Saint Joan* 6:57; Pref. *Major Barbara* 3:63). Most people imagine that he failed to provide the "intellectually honest" creed he demanded. The consensus is that his religious, philosophical, and political ideas were inconsistent, impractical, and unoriginal: a hodgepodge of notions patched together from other, more consistent and original, thinkers. In fact, his originality is attested to by the persistence with which he is misunderstood, and one of the most original traits of his philosophy is its astounding consistency.

A Patchwork Philosopher?

Shaw has not been understood. There is no difficulty about his specific opinions on the many concrete issues about which he expressed himself—except perhaps where critics still find his recommendations too outrageous to be taken seriously. Rather, he is most profoundly misunderstood at the very core of his philosophy, in the fundamental assumptions on which he based his entire approach to life. As eloquent as he was and as garrulous as he could be, Shaw could not make clear the heart of his philosophy. Sometimes, the rhetorical strategies he used to promote acceptance of a particular objective obscured the principle behind the objective. At times Shaw seemed as successful in demolishing his own ideas as in attacking those of others. There is much truth in Bertrand Russell's assertion that Shaw was most effective as an iconoclast, as the exposer of false and conventional ideas, but was unable effectively to convey his own version of the truth (*Portraits from Memory* 79). Many doubt he had one. Friends and foes both believe that however brilliantly he may have played with the ideas advanced by others, he was neither an original nor particularly profound thinker. Max Beerbohm satirized Shaw in a famous cartoon in which an audacious Shaw demands immortality in return for intellectual "garments" taken from the great thinkers of the nineteenth century. Confronted with the secondhand nature of the goods he is trying to sell, Shaw points with pride to the patches (Gassner 291).

Even friendly critics concur. William Archer, in virtually his last words on his friend's ideas, said that Shaw's thought was not "in its essence original—for the main ideas of the Shaw philosophy are borrowed from a dozen different quarters" ("The Psychology of G.B.S." 301–2). Eric Bentley echoes this judgment: "Shaw may not have been an original thinker; he tried, rather, to make a synthesis of what certain others had thought" (Foreword to Signet Shaw, xix). "Synthesis" is often used to characterize Shaw's thought. Julian Kaye's highest praise is that Shaw created a "brilliant synthesis of nineteenth-century thought" (xi). Whether the critic is sympathetic or hostile, whether the Shavian philosophy is called a synthesis or a hodgepodge, the verdict is that Shaw was not a systematic thinker but an eclectic who lacked a foundation of basic principles.

This judgment is superficially true and profoundly false. Shaw was a consistent and logical thinker whose every pronouncement harmonized with fundamental principles on which his philosophy, his playwriting, his fiction, his polemics, indeed his whole life, were based. The confusion stems in part from those very principles, which include an open-eyed skepticism toward a priorist values and judgments. In this Shaw is perfectly in accord with much of modern philosophy, particularly the philosophy of science. But science is concerned with the structure of the physical world, and Shaw devoted his life to the moral and social world; while science asks, "What is?" and "How does it happen?" Shaw was concerned with "What should we do about it?" and "How can we make it better?" Philosophy has always been less certain about such questions. While still far from achieving consensus, it has been moving in Shaw's direction here as well. Difficult as it may be for many to believe, moral philosophy is still trying to catch up with Bernard Shaw. Equally surprising, and just as true, is that philosophers are beginning to regard science as Shaw did. Shaw is still far ahead of our time, as well as his. Our civilization is, to cite one of his favorite passages from Scripture, rushing down a steep place to drown in the sea (Mark 5:13). He knew the way to save us and devoted his life to showing us the way, but we have not understood. Why?

The heart of the difficulty is that Shaw, though he knew that religion, philosophy, and science were one, did not think or speak in a way to be understood by theologians, philosophers, or scientists. He was really a prophet. Like many prophets, Shaw did not articulate in a systematic and analytical way the fundamental assumptions forming the platform from which he viewed the world. To make sense of Shaw—to reconcile the apparent contradictions and finally see as he saw—we must systematically reconstruct the intellectual foundation that came spontaneously to him.

Consistency or Contradiction?

To what extent did Shaw's thinking change or evolve during the course of his long career? Many explain the seeming contradictions by maintaining that the Shavian philosophy can be understood only as a long evolution over the course of his lifetime. Samuel Yorks devotes a book to this view. J. L. Wisenthal argues that in the 1890s Shaw's thinking underwent important changes that are evident in the plays of that period and, more significantly, in revisions Shaw made in earlier works—especially *The Quintessence of Ibsenism* (29–37). In contrast, Louis Crompton writes: "When he sat down to write the first act of *Widowers' Houses* in 1885, he was a man whose opinions and judgment were fully mature" (1). Charles Carpenter declares that Shaw's fundamental philosophical convictions had been formed by 1881 and remained unchanged until his death (28). Pressed to choose between these opinions, it would be much wiser to go with the latter because there is nothing in Shaw's later work that violates the principles laid out in 1891, and many of the pronouncements people find disturbing about the later Shaw are implicit in the writings of the early 1890s. As Lloyd Hubenka suggests, the apparent changes in Shaw's philosophy are really natural developments of a viewpoint established early in Shaw's intellectual life (ix–xxiv). It is not that his principles changed, or that he lacked any guiding principles, but that the principles on which his thought was based themselves provide for intellectual flexibility. The seeming changes are natural outgrowths of a few basic assumptions that came to Shaw quite early and which he never abandoned throughout his long life.

Many obstacles to understanding Shaw were created by the very strategies he used in his incessant attempts to make the world see things as he did. His ideas are thought to be pieced together from bits of Nietzsche, Ibsen, and Bergson because he deliberately associated himself with those giants. Even when he denies their influence, as in the preface to *Major Barbara*, he calls attention to his affinity with their ideas. In point of fact, he owes those particular thinkers little more than a phrase or two, but those phrases were borrowed in an apparent attempt to present his views as part of a larger intellectual wave of the future. "My business," he declared, "is to incarnate the Zeitgeist" (*Collected Letters* 1:222). Shaw actually went out of his way to present his ideas as unoriginal: clever young people in his plays, such as Ellie Dunn and Savvy Barnabas, talk about Shavian ideas as notions well established—even old-fashioned—among their contemporaries. He tried to establish his ideas in the minds of his audience by subtly trying to seduce them into thinking the ideas had already been established. And then there is the fact that two of the most important statements of his philosophy were presented as critical commentaries on other artists: *The Quintessence of Ibsenism* and *The Perfect Wagnerite*. Under such circumstances it is not surprising he is considered unoriginal.

Shavian Misdirections

There is also the matter of the style in which he presented his ideas. The contentiousness with which he attacked cherished icons was enough to convince many that his views were both simple and extreme. He is widely thought, for example, to be an enemy of both science and democracy. Neither is a remotely reasonable statement of his views. He was certainly opposed to the idolatry of science and democracy (and anything else, for that matter), but the simpler and more shocking view has made the lasting impression. Shaw once chided a "man of genius" for his lack of temper and diplomacy in dealing with those of inferior vision, but he could well have heeded the admonition himself (Pref. *Apple Cart* 6:276).

He seems to have concluded very early on that there was such a gap between the way he saw things and the way the rest of humanity saw them that straightforward communication would be impossible. Writing of the hazards of autobiography in an early autobiographical essay he declared that the difference between the way he saw the world and the way the rest of humanity saw it was so great that he could not be certain whether he was mad or sane (*Sixteen Self Sketches* 74).

In the preface to the *Pleasant Plays* (written in the same year, 1898) Shaw again refers to the inability of the public to understand him. "I could explain the matter easily enough if I chose; but the result would be that the people who misunderstand the plays would misunderstand the explanation ten times more" (1:383). Convinced that a straightforward exposition of his ideas was impossible, he invented strategies to provoke the public, not into accepting his view of the world but merely into looking in his direction, into starting along a path that might someday lead them there. By and large success evaded him.

The conviction that the public was incapable of understanding his ideas may be at the root of one of the more curious Shavian contradictions. Although Shaw was to use many farcical elements in his own plays, he strongly objected to the conventional "farcical comedies" of the late nineteenth century as being mechanical and fundamentally inhuman. He complained of the Savoy Operas on much the same grounds but also objected specifically to Gilbert's "paradoxical wit," declaring that he was "cursed" with the same ability, and "could paradox Mr Gilbert's head off were I not convinced that such trifling is morally unjustifiable" (*London Music in 1888–89* 283).

Shaw was aware, of course, that his public would savor this remark as a particularly exquisite paradox coming as it did from the pen of one of the most extravagant paradoxers around. It *is* exquisite since the paradox is used to explain the reason for Shavian paradox. His jests, he is saying, are intensely serious. He is so serious as to be impatient with frivolous jesting because of its moral irresponsibility. He even claimed that his paradoxical wit was involuntary, a consequence of the intellectual gulf separating him from the public:

All I had to do was to open my ... eyes, and with my utmost literary
skill put the case exactly as it struck me, or describe the thing exactly
as I saw it, to be applauded as the most humorously extravagant paradoxer in London. The only reproach with which I became familiar
was the everlasting "Why can you not be serious?" (Pref. *Unpleasant
Plays* 1:14)

In 1913, Shaw added a new chapter to *The Quintessence of Ibsenism* in
which he asks, essentially, "How are Ibsen and Strindberg different from
Molière and Dickens?" The answer is very revealing both of Shaw's own
estimate of his place in the history of ideas and of the style that has made
it so easy to misunderstand him:

> The explanation is to be found in what I believe to be a general law of
> the evolution of ideas. 'Every jest is an earnest in the womb of time'
> says Peter Keegan in John Bull's Other Island. 'There's many a true
> word spoken in jest' says the first villager you engage in philosophi-
> cal discussion. All very serious revolutionary propositions begin as
> huge jokes. Otherwise they would be stamped out by the lynching of
> their first exponents. (*Shaw and Ibsen* 202–3)[1]

Not even his enemies have noticed that this "general law of the evolution
of ideas" implies that Shaw, the jester and buffoon, is a more advanced
thinker than Ibsen, Strindberg, and Tolstoy. He is saying that his ideas are
so far ahead of his time as to be unthinkable except as jokes. But the reason
jokes are privileged and jesters have the ear of the king while heretics are
burned at the stake is that the jester can always be dismissed as a fool and
his jokes laughed away. Personal safety is purchased with intellectual danger: the danger that you will never be taken seriously. Martyrdom has
obvious disadvantages, but it also has its own, not insubstantial, way of
influencing the history of ideas. But as General Burgoyne points out in
The Devil's Disciple, "Martyrdom ... is the only way in which a man can
become famous without ability" (2:115). The public is impressed, even
awed, by someone who is willing to suffer a horrible death for the sake of
his ideas; and since most people are far more interested in courageous
people who suffer horrendous fates than in brilliant ideas that might re-
shape our fates, martyrdom is another, and perhaps more immediate, way
of focusing the attention of the public on an idea. Its principal advantage is
that it impresses on the minds of all that such ideas, ideas worth dying for,
are serious things indeed. Shaw, no doubt inevitably, chose to be a buffoon
rather than a martyr. He bought longevity—both figuratively and liter-

ally—at the price of never being taken completely seriously. It is now time, more than one hundred years after the *Quintessence of Ibsenism*, to probe beneath the jester's mask and take Shaw utterly seriously. It will not be easy, for much of the essential Shaw will still be shocking and repellent even to those who admire Shaw; even—no, especially—to those who idolize him. In fact, although he never did drop the clown's mask completely, he let it slip rather carelessly after he became famous and relatively invulnerable. The result is that the most enthusiastic admirers of the jester who laughed the nineteenth century out of court and strewed the way with witticisms for the entrance of the twentieth, are the most unhappy with the ancient sage who earnestly tried to explain that brave new century to them.

Shavian Eyesight

Warren Sylvester Smith wisely tells us that Shaw's real value is not in the answers he provided "but in his *manner* of looking at the problems. The special quality of the light he throws is unique and likely to remain so" (*Shaw on Religion* 10). The greatest difficulty in understanding Shaw's philosophy is finally the difficulty of describing his way of looking at the world. As eloquent as he was, he could not overcome that difficulty himself. Shaw did not indulge in deliberate mystification. He wrote in the original *Quintessence* that "no great writer uses his skill to conceal his meaning" (194), yet, in that very essay, generally regarded as the essential statement of Shavian thought, he is unable or unwilling to define the difference between the type of person he calls an idealist and the one he deems a realist. He admits that a realist can in some ways be appropriately called an idealist but avoids clarifying the difference with a clever yet unsatisfying evasion. The omission is momentous; the difference between a realist and an idealist is not the difference between a sensible, rational person and a wild-eyed fanatic; it is the difference between Shaw and the enlightened, progressive, educated, sensitive, and thoughtful persons who were—and still are—his natural allies. To be sure, there are conservative idealists as well as progressive ones; the point is that the crucial difference is not that between progressive and conservative but something more important and far more elusive.

Shaw is not very helpful in defining that difference. He offers us parables, such as the well-known anecdote about his visit with an optometrist who told him that his eyesight was "normal" and thus unusual, "normal sight conferring the power of seeing things accurately, and being enjoyed by only about ten percent of the population, the remaining ninety percent being abnormal. I immediately perceived the explanation of my want of success in fiction. My mind's eye, like my body's was 'normal': it saw things differently from other people's eyes, and saw them better" (1:12–13). He goes on to tell how his abnormally normal vision finally gave him employment and profitable notoriety in the capacity of jester. Later, in one of his many generous attempts to assist his biographers by telling them what to say about Shaw, he wrote:

> There is a cutting edge to Shaw that everybody dreads. He has in an extreme degree the mercurial mind that recognizes the inevitable instantly and faces it and adapts itself to it accordingly. . . . An Indian prince's favorite wife, when banqueting with him, caught fire and was burnt to ashes before she could be extinguished. The prince took in the situation at once and faced it. "Sweep up your missus" he said to his weeping staff "and bring in the roast pheasant." That prince was an oriental Shaw. (*Sixteen Self Sketches* 203–4)

These are important hints as to how he saw the world. They sketch a portrait of Shaw the realist, suggesting that a certain cold-bloodedness is a requisite feature of realism, but they are far from satisfactory or conclusive. After all, who could object to seeing the world as it is and not through some distorting lens? Do not we all think that we see things as they are? If someone else sees them differently, it does not help our understanding in the least to be told merely that he sees straight and we see crooked. William Archer, one of Shaw's oldest and most sympathetic friends, remained convinced until he died that Shaw was one of the least objective and clear-sighted of human beings. Referring in 1899 to Shaw's parable of his eccentrically accurate vision, Archer wrote:

> He looks at life through an exceedingly abnormal temperament, and has convinced himself that it is the one absolutely normal temperament in the world. . . . How far Mr. Shaw is from possessing that objectivity of vision which he claims may be judged from the ease with which any reader of the least critical faculty could reconstruct from these plays [*Pleasant and Unpleasant*] the character and opinions of their author. (*Study and Stage* 3)

A quarter-century later, in a thoughtful, sympathetic, and sincere assessment of his friend's career, Archer maintained the same view of Shaw's objectivity. In the context, it is a touching article; Archer had had premonitions of death which, in the event, were true: he died shortly after the article appeared. It had been Archer who had given Shaw his start, who had provided the eccentric Irishman his first opportunity to take the stage as Punch—otherwise G.B.S., the absurdly paradoxical critic of London's art world. By this time, however, Shaw was enjoying the success of *Saint Joan*, thought by many the crowning achievement of his career and by others the last flare of his dying genius. Archer salutes his old friend as "the Grand Old Man of literary Europe" but then goes on to say that Shaw's mind "is concave, convex, corrugated, many-faceted—anything you like except plane and objective" and that "his perceptions are warped by the intensity of his feelings: the mirror of his mind does not accurately image the external object." Archer continues:

> Mr. Shaw is the most complete and instinctive apriorist of recorded time. He does not live in the real world, but in a world of his own construction. No doubt this is in some measure true of all of us, but it is the inmost secret of Mr. Shaw's whole psychology. His perception of fact is absolutely at the mercy of his will. The world without has no existence for him, except in so far as it can be, and is, fitted into the pre-existent scheme of his world within. The result is that he can seldom or never make a perfectly accurate statement of fact. The most honourable of men, the most incapable of telling a falsehood for his own advantage, or even in furtherance of a cause or an argument, he is equally incapable of seeing, reflecting, expressing things as they objectively or historically are. He sees them through the distorting, systematising medium of his own personality; whereas the man who is to be an effective force in this world must either have the clearest insight into things as they are, or, if he sees them awry, must do so by reason of a common and popular obliquity of vision. ("The Psychology of G.B.S." 300, 301, 303)

One must beware here of succumbing to the inevitable temptation to dismiss Archer, since, after all, who is William Archer now, except a name peripheral to those of Ibsen and Shaw? Archer was a perceptive and intelligent critic; it would be dangerously presumptuous for us to condescend to him from what we may perceive to be the summit of our postmodern wisdom. It is wonderfully flattering to agree with Shaw about the follies of the Victorian era; we all see through them now, of course, and when we imagine ourselves in Shaw's place, looking at them through *Shaw's* eyes, we can identify with the solitary crusader against pomposity and falsehood. But it does not follow that we would have seen things as he saw them had we been born when he was. Nor is it necessarily true that Western civilization was submerged then in a dense fog of delusion that has since lifted. It would be comforting to think that we can now see clearly because the civilization in which we live has risen above the clouds of error and superstition, so that we ordinary mortals may now see the truth that was then visible only to the select few. But that is precisely what the educated spirits of the nineteenth century thought of *themselves*, and it is one of the principal delusions attacked by Shaw. And then again, are we not being rather self-servingly select when we choose to identify with the Shaw who saw through the illusions of the nineteenth century while repudiating the Shaw who (as many see it) so abysmally misunderstood our own century? If we are as critical of the twentieth-century Shaw as his intimate friends and supporters were of the nineteenth-century Shaw, it must remain an open question whether we really understand the way Shaw saw the world. We should hesitate before presuming to understand him better than one, like Archer, who knew him as intimately and fondly as anyone in the world.

COMPLEXITY FROM SIMPLICITY

It was not easy to understand Shaw then, and it is not easy now. But it is not impossible. On the one hand, Shaw appears a mass of contradictions. He repudiated rationalism, called himself a mystic, and derided logic as a tool for dealing with human problems; yet others have thought him so rational and logical as to be coldly devoid of human feeling. A man of such refined personal sensitivity and fastidiousness as to verge on hysteria, he passionately opposed vivisection, meat-eating (which he called cannibalism), vaccination, imprisonment, and capitalism; yet he declared himself the enemy of idealism and morality. As a critic he denounced farce as heartless, complaining of inhumanity in such an apparently innocuous piece as The Importance of Being Earnest, while praising melodrama as "simple and sincere drama of passion and feeling" (Drama Observed 1:313); yet as a playwright he used the techniques of farce to attack the moral dichotomies that are the most telling feature of melodrama. He was a lifelong and passionate socialist; yet he lived a life of such eccentric nonconformity as to be the embodiment of what he approvingly called the "spirit of Anarchism."

For many the essence of Shaw's greatness is just such complexity and ambiguity, and they may be loathe to simplify or clarify his thought, as that, they might feel, would reduce his stature. For Eric Bentley the essence of the Shavian approach is "not Either/Or but Both/And" (*Bernard Shaw* 58). Colin Wilson regards Shaw as a product of extreme romanticism tempered by exceptional objectivity (xii–xiii). But complexity and ambiguity, despite popular aesthetic theories, do not themselves make greatness. They are too easily produced by sloppiness, confusion, and incoherence. We are drawn to them when we sense that they are the manifestation of a deeper and truer reality, a more profound harmony, a more subtle and elegant order. The essential difference between Shaw's enemies and his friends lies in their perception of his ambiguities. Those who dislike and reject Shaw (and there are many) see his complexity as contradiction and willfulness; those who admire him sense the deeper order and understanding.

Shaw's philosophy is in fact simple, consistent, and—despite what has been said here so far—capable of being made quite lucid. Its simplicity is one of its greatest strengths: it avoids the questionable speculation that makes so many philosophical systems so vulnerable. The Shavian worldview sticks to essentials and rests on a very firm base. While he understood that a consistent philosophy had to rest on a consistent metaphysics, his philosophy is concerned first and last with the question of human purpose: "How should we act in this world, both individually and collectively?" He approaches that question with heartbreaking, horrifying, cold-blooded honesty. But another part of the strength of this view of the world is that it frankly acknowledges that it is in large part unprovable; it owns that it is a "faith," albeit a faith unlike most others. People find it hard to understand because, first, stated simply and straightforwardly, it seems obvious and uncontroversial—indeed, almost trivial. Second, some of the logical consequences of this philosophy are so at odds with conventional thinking that they strike many—if not most—people as eccentric, bizarre, or outrageous. People cannot believe that such unobjectionable premises could lead to such outrageous conclusions, so they fail or refuse to make the connection. The final paradox of Shaw's thinking is that he appears arbitrary and capricious precisely because he is so meticulously consistent. Moreover, and most important, he was right. Although he was unquestionably in error about many specifics, the basic principles that guided him are still powerful and difficult to refute.

Logic and Faith

He stressed the unprovable part of his beliefs: the need for faith. During most of his career, Shaw presented himself not as a philosopher but as the prophet of a new religion, one who rejected the rationalism of philosophy for the mysticism of revelation. The emphasis is important but misleading. Shaw demanded much more of religion than do most people. For him a religion must meet two unusual requirements. The first is consistency. He concludes the preface to *Major Barbara* with three requirements for the salvation of civilization. The last of these, added almost as an afterthought but essential to the play that follows and to Shaw's profoundest convictions, is that religious creeds must be consistent, both within themselves and with all of one's life. A creed that is not a guide to living, that must be kept in a watertight compartment, separate from one's business activities, is simply not honest. The other requirement for a credible religion, in Shaw's view, is that it must be proof against science. Shaw's creed, in other words, had to be, first, a faith to live by and, second, consistent with both the facts and logic. It must be real. So when Shaw declared himself to be a "mystic," he did not mean quite what others do. For many people a mystic is one who abandons the rigor of logic and reason in a leap of faith that admits of no justification besides itself. In calling himself a mystic, Shaw was emphasizing what he regarded as the heart of his belief, the part that was beyond reason. But hearts do not live by themselves; they need bones and muscle and digestive systems and all sorts of less poetic support systems. The mystical part of Shaw's religion is its reason for existing; it is life and hope and purpose, but it must not be mere wishful thinking or a cowardly evasion of reality. It is an easy matter to develop a creed that is only a projection of the heart's desire, a castle in the air without foundation; it is a different chore to build such a faith on a solid basis of fact and to use it as a guide for living in a real and heartbreakingly imperfect world. Judged by these rigorous requirements, Shaw's religion was a success. That is surely a valuable legacy. We have certainly felt the need for religion in this age of nihilism and despair, but the intellectually honest cannot accept a religion that must wear heavy and conspicuous blinders to hide itself both from the world and from its own behavior in the world.

In another and important sense, Shaw's religion was, or at least is so far, an utter failure. If a religion is a social organization devoted to shared spiritual principles and ritual practices, as it is often taken to be, then Shaw failed completely to establish a new creed. That failure is significant because it was not enough for him simply to find an individually soul-satisfying faith. Believing as he did that "men without religion have no courage" and that no social or political change is possible unless it is rooted in the values and goals of the citizens, he naturally saw a religion based in equality and progress as the prerequisite to social equality and progressive politics (*Collected Letters* 2:670). His efforts, however futile in their ultimate goal, produced two notable successes. The first was that it was the inspiration for his prodigious literary and dramatic work. Indeed, as the established religions come slowly and reluctantly around to his way of seeing the divine, he may eventually succeed in his aim of providing fables for a new faith. The second success is the subject of this book. Shaw demanded consistency and honesty of religion, and he got it. Undershaft tells his daughter Barbara, former major in the Salvation Army: "You have made for yourself something that you call a morality or a religion or what not. It doesnt fit the facts. Well, scrap it. Scrap it and get one that does fit" (3:170–71). People pay a high price for professing beliefs that do not fit the facts. They have to shut their eyes, a condition that inclines one to stumble. Still, most do shut them, for fear of the terrible pain that loss of faith and the search for a new faith entails. Major Barbara has the courage to choose pain over blindness, thus showing she understands that anyone who hides from the facts for fear of losing her faith has not only locked the barn door after the horse has been stolen but has replaced the living animal with a dummy so as to pretend that it was not stolen at all. A faith that is terrified to be lost is no faith at all. The central tenet of what has become the twentieth-century creed is that no such faith is possible—that the horse has been not only stolen but butchered. "God is dead," and the facts have killed Him. Shaw showed that this is not true, that faith in something reasonably called a divine power can be self-consistent and consistent with modern scientific knowledge. Yet the proponents of the "scientific" view dismiss Shaw has fuzzy-headed and his Life Force as blind wishful thinking, while the few who support Creative Evolution do so from a traditionally mystical and nonrational point of view. No one has shown how thoroughly consistent and genuinely scientific his faith really is.

We have come to take for granted that religion requires a leap of faith, that one embraces religion in spite of the facts, that religion involves an entirely different way of knowing the universe from that provided by science and reason. Shaw's faith was not a blind leap into the unknown but the pinnacle of a solid pyramid build with stones of fact and logic. For him, religion, metaphysics, science, politics, and the day-to-day business of living were all one. A religion that had to be kept separate was not credible, and it was not of any real use in the world. Most examinations of Shaw's religious ideas look primarily at those points where they resemble more conventional theology and so fail to appreciate its foundations. They confine themselves to the tip of the iceberg. To truly understand the Shavian religion we must start from the bottom and work up. We must start with the difficult task of defining the Shavian way of seeing the world, show how this view of the world leads to fundamental premises about our relations with each other and with the universe, and see how these premises shaped Bernard Shaw's thinking in every arena, both artistic and practical. We can then realize how they determined the form and style as well as the content of his plays and gave necessary shape to his ethical, political, and economic ideas, as Shaw demanded of his faith that it be the foundation on which everyday living must rest, not pious platitudes to be evaded.

I will finally examine the most difficult question of all: How can the assertion that Divine Will permeates the universe possibly be consistent with anything that can be called science? It is a particularly difficult question because science has become more, not less, materialistic, more, not less, arrogant in its assumptions of omniscience, more, not less, contemptuous and intolerant of any attempt to interpret the nature of the universe as spiritual or teleological. Any suggestion that the universe is other than just a giant machine is treated as dangerous heresy and those who make the suggestion as enemies of science and progress. At the same time, however, voices are being heard that call attention to the areas of our experience that science leaves unexplained and ignored and to the gaps it leaves in our understanding. There are now two broad camps that increasingly are drawn into a mode of battle rather than discussion and dialectic: the traditional materialistic scientists and the traditionally unscientific religionists. Like most armies, they instinctively assume that all who are not enlisted on their side are of the enemy, yet a courageous few stand apart from the combatants and point out both the flaws of each side and the advantages of reconciliation. None of these has yet presented the case as simply and clearly as Shaw did, but they are actually moving in his direction. The heated contest of science and religion is useful to anyone who can step out of the smoke of the battle for a moment because each has been very effective at showing the weaknesses of the other side. They have, that is, shown to anyone who can observe impartially how it is possible to have what Shaw demanded of his creed: a faith that is both spiritual aspiration for the future and practical guide for the present. We will see how that is possible.

We have inescapably returned to the first and most important task: defining the Shavian way of looking at the world. It must be defined and clarified or we are lost, for it is the foundation of everything else: his individualistic socialism, his belief in equality in morals and money, his assertion of the primacy of the will, his approach to social organization, his rational mysticism, his skeptical faith, his unswerving and obstinate flexibility, his unscrupulous morality, and his puritanical immoralism. I will refer to this fundamentally Shavian outlook by the somewhat unsatisfactory title of realism—or Shavian realism. It is a distinctly unsatisfactory term because it has been used in so many conflicting ways, and Shaw himself, as Dietrich points out, plays on the slipperiness of its meaning (20). But there is really no better term, and its use is demanded by the terms used in that quintessentially Shavian document, *The Quintessence of Ibsenism*. To understand this way of seeing, to analyze it, to break this spontaneous vision of the way things are into a systematic philosophical method, we will have to heed a precept of "The Revolutionist's Handbook": "What a man believes may be ascertained, not from his creed, but from the assumptions on which he habitually acts" (2:788). Once understood, the principles of this special realism will be clearly seen as the simple pillars on which all of Shaw's seeming complexity is based.

2

Realism

The Shavian approach to philosophy can be seen at its most general in a review, published in the *Saturday Review* in 1896, of an English translation of Nietzsche's works. The English, Shaw tells us, do not like or understand philosophy because they imagine it to be dry, abstract, and dull. They have learned from bad examples. "Any studious, timorously ambitious bookworm can run away from the world with a few shelvesful of history, essays, descriptions and criticisms, and, having pieced an illusory humanity and art out of the effects produced by his library on his imagination, build some silly systematization of his worthless ideas over the abyss of his own nescience" (*Drama Observed* 2:568).

True philosophy is quite different and far more interesting. If you wish to derive philosophy from art, the trick "is to look at pictures until you have acquired the power of seeing them." The same is true in the case of music, arts, and humanity. To understand these things you must be involved with them in a direct and participatory way.

And you must transact business, wirepull politics, discuss religion, give and receive hate, love, and friendship with all sorts of people before you can acquire the sense of humanity. If you are to acquire the sense sufficiently to be a philosopher, you must do all these things unconditionally. You must not say that you will be a gentleman and limit your intercourse to this class or that class; or that you will be a virtuous person and generalize about the affections from a single instance: unless, indeed, you have the rare happiness to stumble at first upon an all-enlightening instance. You must have no convictions, because, as Nietzsche puts it, "convictions are prisons."

> Thus, I blush to add, you cannot be a philosopher and a good man,
> though you may be a philosopher and a great one. (568–69)

This is not what one would expect from "the most complete and instinctive apriorist of recorded time," as Archer was pleased to call him; rather it would seem a radical statement of the empiricist faith: you must start with no principles or convictions of any kind, including moral or ethical ones, but must learn all in the school of experience. Shaw goes on to berate Nietzsche precisely for the "professorial folly" of proclaiming about art from bookish imaginings rather than direct observation. Shaw is here revealing his intellectual roots, roots that surprisingly have been neglected by Shavian scholars. If the core of Shaw's thinking has been misunderstood, its germination has simply been ignored.

SHAW AND NINETEENTH-CENTURY RATIONALISM

Again, Shaw has misled us. His plays (especially the early ones) are filled with unflattering references to the passé radicalism of the mid-nineteenth century, represented by the likes of John Tyndall, T. H. Huxley, Charles Darwin, and George Eliot. But of these at least Tyndall, Huxley, and Eliot were Shaw's heroes too, when he was young. He implies that he has since thrown them over and acquired an entirely new outlook, dumping rationalism and materialism for mysticism and the Life Force. The impressions of adolescence, however, are apt to be more indelible than we, in our mature recollection, are inclined to believe. The fact is that Shaw did not abandon rationalism as much as he enlarged upon it. He did not embrace its opposite but created something new, something that included many of the basic assumptions of rationalism. In a sense he developed a Hegelian synthesis of scientific materialism and mystical idealism, but he never fully articulated it as such. Rather, he presented himself as a mystic who repudiated rationalism. In Hegelian terms, he insisted that he was fighting for the antithesis of rationalism (or at least of materialism), while in truth his philosophy accepted what was valid of nineteenth-century materialism and rejected the false.

To understand Shaw's roots in materialism we must first revise our view of nineteenth-century science and its way of seeing the world. Shaw has helped us to see Victorian scientists as dogmatic, materialistic, antihumanitarian fact worshipers, of whom Charles Dickens's notorious Gradgrind is only a slight caricature, but Shaw was not alone. The conventional view that Victorian science was "a dreary and dehumanizing Mechanism and Materialism which threatened the destruction of Faith or Imagination or Feeling, or all three" has been only recently challenged (Cosslett 1). In truth, the new world of science presented by John Tyndall (and to a lesser extent, Huxley) was filled with wonder, delight, beauty, and poetry. And as a young man Shaw thought Tyndall and the others were ushering in a "glorious period" in history ("The Case for Equality" 141).

John Tyndall

Numerous references to his countryman John Tyndall make it clear that the Irish physicist and popularizer of science was a major influence on the youthful Shaw. Despite his later repudiation, there are interesting echoes of Tyndall in the writings of the mature Shaw. When Shaw observes that after Tyndall and the other materialists "have taught you all they know, you are still as utterly at a loss to explain the fact of consciousness as you would have been in the days when you were instructed from The Child's Guide to Knowledge" (*Quintessence* 114), he is saying nothing that Tyndall himself did not explicitly point out in his essays and lectures (for example, "Scientific Materialism" 93–95, "The Belfast Address" 179, 208, and "Science and Man" 373). Tyndall, like Shaw, regarded religion as indispensable and deemed it necessary to satisfy the religious appetite in ways compatible with science ("Belfast Address" 209). He also spoke against the intellectual arrogance of science. While he maintained with other materialists that we must have the courage to face facts and follow them wherever they lead us, he insisted that "the man of science equally dare to confess ignorance where it prevails" ("Science and Man" 373).

He was a remarkably open-minded and thoughtful materialist. He was also forthright and lucid in his materialism, so it is not surprising that traditionalists regarded him with distrust and hostility. His address in Belfast to the British Association in 1874 seemed to many as menacing intellectually as the French Revolution had been politically. As Mrs. Whitefield says in *Man and Superman:* "Nothing has been right since that speech that Professor Tyndall made at Belfast" (2:720). "That speech" shocked the traditionalists by asserting that knowledge of the physical world is the exclusive domain of science: "The impregnable position of science may be described in a few words. We claim, and we shall wrest from theology, the entire domain of cosmological theory. All schemes and systems which thus infringe upon the domain of science must, in so far as they do this, submit to its control, and relinquish all thought of controlling it" (210). Despite the peremptory tone of this declaration, the address was evenhanded. Tyndall presented an imaginary debate between a disciple of Lucretius (the proponent of Matter) and the eighteenth-century theologian and philosopher Bishop Butler (the champion of Spirit). Both, Tyndall contended, present unanswerable arguments. He particularly stressed his endorsement of the words he put into the mouth of the bishop: "You cannot satisfy the human understanding in its demand for logical continuity between molecular processes and the phenomena of consciousness. This is a rock on which Materialism must inevitably split whenever it pretends to be a complete philosophy of life" (180). For Tyndall the answer to the difficulty lay in a radical revision of our conception of matter. Matter has been unjustly maligned. We have been taught to think of spirit as the epitome of goodness and matter as the essence of baseness, when we should regard them both as "essentially mystical and transcendental" ("Vitality" 57). We should not think of "brute matter" but of "the living garment of God" ("Scientific Use of the Imagination" 141). Shaw rightly observed that Tyndall's "materialism" reveals "a nobility which produces poetry" (Pref. Methuselah 5:317). But Shaw neglects to mention that Tyndall is candidly open to the demands of the spirit and humble in confessing his ignorance when confronting its mystery.

George Eliot

Regarding George Eliot as the literary exponent of the 1860s scientific viewpoint, Shaw confessed that he "almost venerated" Eliot's masterpiece, Middlemarch, as a young man ("Postscript: After Twenty-five Years" 702). That veneration appears unconsciously in Shaw's earliest known literary effort, an ironical guide to growing up titled "My Dear Dorothea"—for Eliot's heroine is named Dorothea and the phrase "my dear Dorothea" occurs often in the novel. There are other echoes in Shaw. Indeed, the thematic core of Middlemarch, the education and spiritual development of a young woman, is one of Shaw's most persistent dramatic themes. (The older male in the role of teacher and mentor, nearly inevitable in Shaw, is significantly absent in Eliot's novel.) It is easier to understand why he admired Eliot than why he later renounced her. There is a clear puritan streak in both writers. Both have been criticized for being overly intellectual and for allowing ideas to intrude upon or overwhelm pure character development. Eliot unquestionably identified herself with the rationalist and scientific movement of the period, but she did not present science as an infallible beacon of wisdom trying to penetrate the darkness of religious superstition; she even anticipates Shaw's contention that belief, whether in electrons or angels, is mostly a matter of fashion ("The Influence of Rationalism" 399–400; Pref. *Androcles* 4:510– 11; Pref. *Joan* 6:58).

Middlemarch is particularly rich in observations and instances that resonate in Shaw. There is the faith in the inevitability of gradual political improvement that was the hallmark of the early Fabians. Eliot's Caleb Garth, although mistrusted by those with inferior vision, is given responsibilities because even selfish people prefer to trust their affairs to one concerned with doing things right (even if more expensively than they would like) than to someone interested only in his own betterment. This is the manner in which Shaw hoped that genuine democracy could work, with superior people rising to the top, despite the suspicions of lesser beings, simply because people prefer that things be done well. One of the clearest links between the two writers is the conviction, intense in both, that we are all members one of another and that an individual's integrity is inseparable from that of society. Dorothea's ardent desire to improve the world and her inability to enjoy the beauties of art while there is filth, misery, and ugliness in the villages of her uncle's estate are as characteristic of Shaw as they are of Eliot (378). And when Shaw, in "The Womanly Woman" chapter of the *Quintessence,* describes the way a woman's perception of marriage changes after the nuptials, he could have found all his evidence in the marriages of Dorothea, Rosemond, and Celia and in Eliot's ironic observations about them. There are other curious resonances. The "sequel" Shaw tacked onto *Pygmalion* sounds remarkably like Eliot's "Finale," for example. But if one had to find a single reason why Shaw would "venerate" *Middlemarch* and its author, it would probably have to be the fine impartiality with which she treats her characters. No matter how mean, petty, or coarse the characters may be, she always portrays them from their own point of view. Two of the most moving moments in the novel involve crises in the lives of characters with whom Eliot would be likely to have the least sympathy. Bulstrode is Eliot's Macbeth, a man whose tragedy is that he is gradually drawn into evil despite his better nature and moral ambitions; yet unlike Macbeth he is petty, pompous, self-righteous, and hypocritical. Rosemond is a shallow, trivial, spoiled, and stubborn beauty incapable of any goal deeper than a rich and lovely setting in which she may be admired by wealthy and important men, yet we are touched when her meretricious castle of glass shatters around her. Both of these characters could be targets of satire and bitter denunciation because they either soil or destroy the lives of much better people, but Eliot insists that we understand the world they see and the pain they suffer. There are no villains or heroes, or, in the words of Major Barbara, no good men and no scoundrels. A similar strict impartiality, based on his conviction that we are all moral equals, became a religious principle with Shaw, one which he maintained to the end of his life, even in the face of the evidence presented to his declining years in the shape of Hitler and Mussolini.

Why, then, did Shaw so emphatically reject Eliot? He accuses her of "fatalism."

> "George Eliot" (Marion Evans) who, incredible as it now seems, was during my boyhood ranked in literature as England's greatest mind, was broken by the fatalism that ensued when she discarded God. In her most famous novel Middlemarch, which I read in my teens and almost venerated, there is not a ray of hope: the characters have no more volition than billiard balls: they are moved only by circumstances and heredity. "As flies to wanton boys are we to the gods: they kill us for their sport" was Shakespear's anticipation of George Eliot. ("Postscript: After Twenty-five Years" 702)

It is true that most of the characters in the novel are extremely limited in both vision and ability and that the aspirations of those with greater aims are constantly reduced by their circumstances. There are several references to the "force of circumstance" and the "modest nature" of goodness (335, 314). One of the clear lessons of the book is that one cannot safely ignore the forces of heredity and environment. But it is not hopelessly pessimistic. These are the final words of the novel, George Eliot's closing observations on her heroine:

> Her full nature, like that river of which Cyrus broke the strength, spent itself in channels which had no great name on the earth. But the effect of her being on those around her was incalculably diffusive, for the growing good of the world is partly dependent on unhistoric acts, and that things are not so ill with you and me as they might have been is half owing to the number who lived faithfully a hidden life and rest in unvisited tombs. (811)

To a generation for whom Samuel Beckett's "They give birth astride a grave" is as familiar as a proverb, this is positively sunny; it may even strike contemporary pessimists as skirting the verge of Pollyannaism.

Beyond, Not Against, Rationalism

Shaw's judgment on Eliot and *Middlemarch* is surely too harsh, and the same could be said of his reaction to Tyndall. Tyndall's confident and exuberant prose justifies Shaw's perception of a glorious new age, and Eliot, though less bright and enthusiastic, sees slow but steady progress through these limited creatures called human beings. There is nothing in Eliot comparable to Samuel Beckett's religious devotion to despair. We all take from literature only what we can, and Shaw's immaturity may not have seen the optimistic side of the scientific rationalism of Tyndall and Eliot. It is difficult to avoid the conclusion that in rejecting them Shaw was in reality discarding his former self—the limitations of his own adolescent materialism. If the young Shaw saw only despair in Eliot, why did he so admire her? The answer is suggested by Shaw's often repeated version of the intellectual history of the nineteenth century, which is much more credible as the growth of Shaw's own mind. Rationalism, according to Shaw, freed us from the cruel whims of a capricious and vindictive deity; it dethroned and banished the tyrant Shelley called the "Almighty Fiend" and William Blake scorned as "Nobodaddy." Science and reason delivered grateful humanitarians from incomprehensible caprice and willfulness into the arms of a knowable order and a predictable universe.

But for the maturing Shaw, this new order of science revealed terrors of its own, terrors to which he believed Eliot had succumbed: "George Eliot was like the released Bastille prisoners: she was rescued from the chains of Evangelical religion & immediately became lost, numbed & hypnotized by 'Science'" (Collected Letters 2:77). Was Shaw moved to reject Eliot because he felt himself "numbed & hypnotized" by scientific materialism? There is an irrational horror in Shaw's rejection of the materialism of Tyndall and Eliot; it is a reaction with distinct parallels to Shaw's personal fastidiousness. He had an almost hysterical aversion to the grosser aspects of the human body. He understood intellectually, along with his sensible female protagonists like Ellie Dunn and Barbara Undershaft, that we cannot achieve spiritual goals by repudiating matter, but his squeamish soul deeply distrusted the material world, in particular the indelicate details of sex and elimination. This may have produced a curious and unfortunate blindness that kept him from seeing himself how close his basic ideas were to those of Tyndall and Eliot and is probably the main reason finally why he failed to present a convincing statement of his own faith. Rather than showing how we can go beyond materialism, he seemed to be returning to irrationality and wishful thinking. For apart from Shaw's squeamish aversion to things physical, Tyndall's view of matter as "the living garment of God" is perfectly in harmony with the Shavian metaphysic. Although Shaw's *philosophy* is perfectly consistent, the sometimes intense conflicts of his emotional life have done much to obscure his message and confuse and dismay his audience. It is, unfortunately, not the only way in which the emotional Shaw (however vital a component of Shaw the dramatist) blinded both us and himself to the practical implications of his fundamental philosophy. He was blind to the spiritual promise in Tyndall and the careful optimism of Eliot, and both could have been useful to him.

Shaw was not deceived about one thing: Eliot was unquestionably a determinist. Science, she said, is not incompatible with the revelations of divine inspiration: "The master key to this revelation, is the recognition of the presence of undeviating law in the material and moral world—of the invariability of sequence which is acknowledged to be the basis of physical science, but which is still perversely ignored in our social organization, our ethics and our religion" ("Progress of the Intellect" 31). Elsewhere she stresses the central importance of the concept of "established law" governing all phenomena "without partiality and without caprice" ("Influence of Rationalism" 413). For Shaw, the reduction of everything to scientific law had an unacceptable consequence, made clear by Darwin's theory of natural selection. Shaw said Darwin "had shewn that many of the evolutionary developments ascribed to a divine creator could have been produced accidentally without purpose or even consciousness" (*Sixteen Self Sketches* 122). Shaw may have encountered this logical result of Darwinism in Samuel Butler's *Luck or Cunning?* (1886), but Huxley, one of Shaw's early intellectual guides, made the connection startlingly apparent in his 1874 essay "On the Hypothesis That Animals Are Automata." Huxley rejected the idea that animals lack consciousness but concluded that all animals, ourselves included, "are conscious automata" (142). This doctrine, which has come to be known as "epiphenomenalism," holds that physical events cause mental events, but mental events are powerless to affect the body. Consciousness is an epiphenomenon; in Huxley's words, consciousness is related to the mechanism of the physical body "simply as a collateral product of its working" (140). This is the idea Butler objects to when he accuses the Darwinians of "pitchforking . . . mind out of the universe" (18). For if epiphenomenalism is true, there is no such thing as design in the universe; nothing that has happened, is happening, or ever will happen requires the existence of consciousness. Houses are built, wars waged, cities constructed, and art created by processes that are purely physical in nature and require only physical laws for explanation. Our awareness is along for the ride but is helpless to change a thing. It would be more accurate to say that will, rather than mind, was banished from the universe. Not surprisingly, this doctrine was and still is highly controversial, even among Darwinians and other scientists; Tyndall, for example, emphatically rejected it ("Apology for the Belfast Address" 236).

Despite the controversy, epiphenomenalism still lingers on. And with good reason, for if you are convinced that all physical events are the result of physical laws, there does not appear to be any place for something as ephemeral as consciousness. If mind can abrogate physical law, the world ceases to be the orderly, inevitable place Eliot and the nineteenth-century scientists believed that it must be (see Cosslett 15–17). An intolerable element of caprice would have entered into the orderly world of physical law.

For Shaw this very idea of order introduced an intolerable idea: not disorder but mindless determinism. The world of rational materialism was a world without a soul. The materialists saw free will as a capricious and cruel devil, an unacceptable agent of chance that would destroy their beautifully ordered world. Scientific law was their savior. For Shaw this meant escape from an arbitrary tyrant into the clutches of a blind and indifferent one. Shaw avoided the difficulty feared by the scientists by redefining determinism; he was a determinist but not a materialist. He, like Tyndall and Eliot, believed in an orderly universe. Theirs was materialistic and mechanistic; his was teleological. The rule of scientific law is the rule of efficient causes. It leaves no room for teleology, for final causes; it eliminates the need and possibility of will. If Eliot was more optimistic than Shaw gives her credit for being, it could be that he understood the logical implications of her fatalistic philosophy better than she did. Are we then caught between a cruelly arbitrary God and one that is blind, stupid, and indifferent? Are we forced to choose a monster or a machine? For Shaw this was unendurable, and he frankly said so. The determinists, latching onto this admission, contemptuously accuse him of wishful thinking. He was realist enough to know that "every man sees what he looks for, and hears what he listens for, and nothing else" (*Collected Letters* 1:301), but he insisted that the *facts* were on his side, that if materialistic fatalism were true, "if it were scientific—if it were common sense, I should say let us face it, let us say Amen. But it isn't" (*Collected Letters* 2:828).

The Law of Will

What—besides wishful thinking—led Shaw to believe that materialism wasn't true? Two things: the first is a simple commonsense observation and the second an unwarranted assumption on the part of the materialists. In the first place, consciousness and will both undeniably exist and scien-

tific materialism is utterly incapable of accounting for them. If our conscious desires make no difference in the world, if all our actions can be
accounted for by strict physical laws that have no need for conscious will,
then why should will exist at all? The second reason is that will need not be
capricious, as the materialists assumed. It might represent the working out
of a universal principle, the equivalent of what, before the rationalists, was
called Divine Providence. Shaw encapsulated this viewpoint in the first
chapter of *The Quintessence of Ibsenism*. The essential message there is
that reason need not be and has not been abandoned; it has merely been
put into the service of the will. The rationalists substituted universal principles for the whims of a vindictive deity and insisted on the scrupulous
regard for fact. Shaw merely insisted that the universal principles were
teleological and manifested in human will. The universe is orderly, human
reason is capable of understanding it, and will can change it. Will is not
caprice but the working out of universal principles. All will is Divine Will.

If that were all there were to it, there would be no end to human
progress. Unfortunately, divine purpose has an enemy that blinds reason
and perverts will. The enemy is not original sin or human wickedness; it is
not a conspiracy of evil tyrants or malicious devils. It is something unexpected. Shaw called it idealism.

IDEALS AND IDEALISTS

If there is confusion about Shaw's repudiation of reason in the first chapter
of the *Quintessence*, it is nothing compared to that produced by his attack
on idealism in the next. But anyone who wishes to obtain the secret of the
Shavian philosophy must, like the fabled suitors compelled to solve an
impossible riddle for the hand of a beautiful princess, unravel the mystery
at the heart of *The Quintessence:* the conundrum of the 700 Philistines,
299 idealists, and one realist.[1]

The question seems simple: What, in this parable, is a realist? The
simple answer, "One who sees things as they are, not as he wishes them,"
is not satisfactory. Few think of themselves as deluded by wishful thinking.
Shaw is not helpful. The realist is not defined except as something different from a Philistine or an idealist—and something both above and beyond them. Shaw asks us to "imagine a community of a thousand persons,

> organized for the perpetuation of the species on the basis of the Brit-
> ish family as we know it at present. Seven hundred of them, we will
> suppose, find the British family arrangement quite good enough for

them. Two hundred and ninety-nine find it a failure, but must put up with it since they are in a minority. The remaining person occupies a position to be explained presently. The 299 failures will not have the courage to face the fact that they are failures—irremediable failures, since they cannot prevent the 700 satisfied ones from coercing them into conformity with the marriage law. They will accordingly try to persuade themselves that, whatever their own particular domestic arrangements may be, the family is a beautiful and holy natural institution. . . . The family as a beautiful and holy natural institution is only a fancy picture of what every family would have to be if everybody was to be suited, invented by the minority as a mask for the reality, which in its nakedness is intolerable to them. We call this sort of fancy picture an IDEAL; and the policy of forcing individuals to act on the assumption that all ideals are real, and to recognize and accept such action as standard moral conduct, absolutely valid under all circumstances, contrary conduct or any advocacy of it being discountenanced and punished as immoral, may therefore be described as the policy of IDEALISM. . . . We then have our society classified as 700 Philistines and 299 idealists, leaving one man unclassified. He is the man who is strong enough to face the truth that the idealists are shirking. . . . What will be the attitude of the rest to this outspoken man? The Philistines will simply think him mad. But the idealists will be terrified beyond measure at the proclamation of their hidden thought—at the presence of the traitor among the conspirators of silence—at the rending of the beautiful veil they and their poets have woven to hide the unbearable face of the truth. . . . How far they will proceed against him depends on how far his courage exceeds theirs. At his worst, they call him cynic and paradoxer: at his best they do their utmost to ruin him if not to take his life. (*Selected Non-Dramatic Writings* 219–20)

Like most parables, this seems far simpler than it is. Shaw acknowledges the complexity, first, by asserting that a realist is in some way a higher type than the idealist and even is in some sense himself an idealist, and second, by hinting at unfathomable complexities in the relations among these three groups. He ends the chapter by summoning up all his considerable eloquence and brilliance to present us with an intense if abstract confrontation between an idealist and a realist. The realist appears as a Rousseau-like moral anarchist who knows that he (and presumably each of his fellows) is naturally good if only the moralists would leave him alone; the idealist appears as a coward terrified of his own baseness and potential depravity.

> The realist at last loses patience with ideals altogether, and sees in them only something to blind us, something to numb us, something to murder self in us, something whereby, instead of resisting death, we can disarm it by committing suicide. The idealist, who has taken refuge with the ideals because he hates himself and is ashamed of himself, thinks that all this is so much the better. The realist, who has come to have a deep respect for himself and faith in the validity of his own will, thinks it so much the worse. To the one, human nature, naturally corrupt, is only held back from the excesses of the last years of the Roman empire by self-denying conformity to the ideals. To the other these ideals are only swaddling clothes which man has out-grown, and which insufferably impede his movements. No wonder the two cannot agree. The idealist says, "realism means egotism; and egotism means depravity." The realist declares that when a man ab-negates the will to live and be free in a world of the living and free, seeking only to conform to ideals for the sake of being, not himself, but "a good man," then he is morally dead and rotten, and must be left unheeded to abide his resurrection, if that by good luck arrive before his bodily death. (222–23)

Then, after having put forth this final burst of eloquent passion and con-viction, Shaw's brilliance collapses with a resigned sigh: "Unfortunately, this is the sort of speech that nobody but a realist understands." In it all, the only explicit definition of realism we were given came from the mouth of the idealist.

We are left with several unanswered questions: Why is the idealist, who seems a destructive fanatic, superior to the Philistine, who at least can claim a balanced psyche? And in what sense is a realist also an idealist? One seductively simple interpretation of the parable is that the realist is Jean Jacques Rousseau, the idealist is Saint Augustine, and the Philistine is Mrs. Grundy. One thinks that we are all naturally good, one is sure we are all quite bad, and the other does not understand the question but is certain it is bad taste to ask it. There is truth in this interpretation but only a partial truth. For one thing, there is more to the idealist than guilt and self-hatred. An idealist is so called because he strives for something beyond and (he hopes) *above* what actually is; that something is his ideal. Nobody uses the word "ideal" to denote everyday, prosaic reality. A realist is also unsatisfied with what is, yet he repudiates ideals. So what are ideals, and what can possibly be so wrong with them?

Ideals and Standards of Conduct

Shaw's clearest statement on the nature of idealism is in the notes for the lecture on Ibsen from which the *Quintessence* was born: "If a definition of idealism as a sense of obligation to conform to an abstract conception of absolute fitness of conduct is of any use to any member of the audience, he or she may quote it as the one given by myself" ("Fragments of a Fabian Lecture" 95). This is certainly clear enough, but it contains a vaguely implied disclaimer, as though he provided this definition only with great reluctance. Then, in the ensuing paragraph, he virtually withdraws it altogether: "Having concluded with a definition, I must add that if my critics expect me to be bound by it, or feel apprehensive of being bound to it by me, they do me a double injustice. As it is impossible to say exactly what one means, it follows that it is impossible to mean exactly what one says" (95–96). Surely Shaw is not being coy or mysterious, particularly since he maintains flatly in what was originally the final chapter of the *Quintessence* that no "great writer uses his skill to conceal his meaning" (194). We must take him at his word and conclude that he finds himself unable to say *exactly* what a realist or an idealist is. The definition is pointedly omitted from the *Quintessence*, although everything said there (with one important exception) is in harmony with it. Instead, there is a strange evasion and somewhat misleading hint about the apparent idealism of the realist: "If the term realist is objected to on account of some of its modern associations, I can only recommend you, if you must associate it with something else than my own description of its meaning (I do not deal in definitions), to associate it, not with Zola and Maupassant, but with Plato" (122).

SHAW AND PLATO

This questionable reference, which Shaw makes so casually, greatly annoys professional philosophers and leads them to dismiss Shaw. It seems to contradict Shaw's remarks in connection with Nietzsche, as well as much of the rest of *The Quintessence*, which suggests that Shavian realism is quite different from Platonic realism. Whatever else it may be, it would appear to be firmly rooted in nominalism and empiricism, generally thought of as the polar opposite of Platonic realism. Shaw clearly disdained to be tied down to textbook definitions. One may get a better idea of what Shaw means by this oblique allusion to "Platonism" from his preface to *Three Plays by Brieux*, where he discusses the nature and purpose of dramatic realism. He thinks that Zola's naturalism is self-defeating: Zola, he says, added gratuitous elements to his fiction to make it appear more like real events—that is, like things one might read in newspaper crime stories. "To all artists and Platonists he made it thereby very unreal; for to the Platonist all accidents are unreal and negligible; but to the people he wanted to get at—the anti-artistic people—he made it readable" (xii). How a "Platonist" artist would proceed we may gather from Shaw's praise of Brieux, whose method he contrasts to the true crime technique of Zola:

> But the great dramatist has . . . to interpret life. . . . Life as it occurs is senseless: a policeman may watch it . . . without learning as much of it or from it as a child or a nun may learn from a single play by Brieux. For it is the business of Brieux to pick out the significant incidents from the chaos of daily happenings, and arrange them so that their relation to one another becomes significant, thus changing us from bewildered spectators of a monstrous confusion to men intelligently conscious of the world and its destinies. (xxiv–xxv)

Thus the sense one gets from this preface (written in 1909) is that "Platonism" for Shaw is a belief that the universe is orderly and comprehensible and that it is the business of the artist-philosopher to describe the order, not the accidents, of the world. *The Quintessence* and the comments about Nietzsche tell us that one can come to understand that order only through experience—through unreserved, intimate, and unqualified involvement. Order must be derived totally *from* experience and must never be imposed *on* experience. The task of the artist- philosopher is to get at those concrete facts that reveal the essential and avoid those that are merely incidental and accidental. Ideas are important, but their origin must be empirical, not *a priori*. To insist that this is nothing of what Plato had in mind would doubtless not give Shaw the least concern.

The question that should concern us is whether Shaw had already adopted this particular form of "Platonism" in 1890 when he drafted what was to become *The Quintessence of Ibsenism*. Several critics have maintained that he had not. Wisenthal, Alfred Turco Jr., and others have argued that, in Wisenthal's words, "the general tendency in the 1891 *Quintessence* is to dismiss or attack all of those who live in a world of ideas" but that his attitude toward ideas, ideals, and idealists became increasingly favorable as evidenced by both his later works and his subsequent revisions of *The Quintessence* (30). There is no doubt that Shaw changed his mind about many things—as we all do if we are at all flexible and open-minded—but I think it is a mistake to believe that Shaw ever became even slightly favorable to what he calls "idealism" in his 1891 essay. He acknowledges there—indeed, he stresses—that there are aspects of the "realist" that could be called "idealistic," but he is emphatic that they are not the same. Shaw changed, I believe, not by coming to accept or endorse the idealism he criticized in 1891 but by emphasizing the prophetic side of the realist's vision. The Shaw of 1909 or 1913 is the fruition, not the repudiation, of the Shaw of 1891.

In 1891 Shaw was not attempting to repudiate either the world of ideas or the aspirations of those who want to make this a better world: those with a vision of a higher world. First, it is clear from the original Ibsen lecture that Shaw was not attacking ideas and was certainly not endorsing a kind of Gradgrindism that declares only hard, cold "facts" to be of any value. He explicitly told his Fabian audience:

> One or two persons with whom I have discussed the matter seem to have supposed that idealism stands and falls with generalization, abstraction, typification, and cognate methods of thought. This of course would be absurd, although no doubt it is in trying to work these methods that people fall into the mistakings which I call idealism. For instance, it would be interesting to obtain a generalization of feminine beauty of the English type by making a composite photograph from all the pretty women in the country. But if you proceeded to denounce as ugly every woman who did not resemble the photograph, and to take exception to her taste in dress on the ground that her bonnet, however becoming to herself, was unsuited to the face in the photograph, that would be idealism; but obviously a denunciation of such idealism would not be a denunciation of composite photography. ("Fragments" 95)

So while it is true that ideals start out as abstractions or generalizations, that is not all there is to them, and—more important—it is not what makes them dangerous. It is certainly not what Shaw objects to, as his insistence on his own form of "Platonism" makes clear. Abstractions are in fact the part of ideals even realists find absolutely necessary; they are indispensable, Shaw says, to thinking about moral subjects ("How to Become a Man of Genius" 345–46). There is a sense in which all abstractions are illusory, as they do not denote anything that actually exists, but interest and enthusiasm for a moral or political goal "must be followed by theory in order that people may think it as well as feel and imagine it ("The Illusions of Socialism" 412). So the pernicious part of ideals is somewhere in the region that goes beyond mere abstraction.

Unfortunately, in that murky region especially, Shaw is much more clear about what idealism is *not* than about what it unambiguously *is*. Most of the time the context suggests Shaw's retracted definition: an arbitrary standard of behavior, particularly one imposed in opposition to the individual will. But if that is all he meant, it is hard to imagine why he did not just say so. Shaw was not one to write obscurely merely to appear mysterious.

That he had more in mind is clear at the beginning of the chapter on ideals and idealists. Ideals are described as "masks" with which man "in his infancy of helplessness and terror" covers inexorable facts which he could not bear to face in their naked reality. The chief of these "ideals" was established when "he fixed the mask of personal immortality on the face of Death" (118). Obviously, belief in personal immortality does not constitute an arbitrary standard of behavior. Illusion, not the violation of individual will, is the essential trait of idealism. It is the crucial difference between the realist and the idealist. Both may have the same aspirations, be social and moral reformers, and be reaching for the same noble goals; but one is willing to look at the facts without illusion and the other is not. Both, in some sense, can be called idealists. The resulting linguistic confusion is justified by the fact that the eternal indictment of the realist is that he is assaulting sacred ideals. We can call them "realists" and "idealists" respectively because that is what they call themselves.

To minimize the confusion, I will henceforth talk of the realist's *vision* and leave ideals to the idealist. For to further complicate the matter, a person can be a realist on one subject and an idealist on another; and the progress toward a kind of realism can take the form of a successive discarding of old ideals and their replacement by new ones.

Ibsen and Shaw on Ideals

Ibsen's position, according to Shaw, is a progressive and skeptical idealism rather than pure realism. He told the Fabian Society that Ibsen

> admits freely that he is an idealist like his fellowmen; and that all he
> wants to insist on is the need for constantly renewing our ideals,

throwing out the stale as we take in the fresh; recognizing that the truth of yesterday is the superstition of today. . . . But I, being more Ibsenite than Ibsen, do not admit that every unfulfilled intention is an aspiration towards an ideal. I do not consider London Bridge the ideal of the Bayswater omnibus; nor do I regard my umbrella as a stepping stone to my ideal of a dry hat. ("Fragments" 94–95)

It is important when looking at the *Quintessence* to remember that Shaw really was writing about Ibsenism, not Shavianism, and to be careful in distilling pure Shaw out of Shaw's Ibsen. Shaw agrees with Ibsen that ideals can be useful and even progressive. The *Quintessence* has references to the positive side of ideals. "Ideals," he says, "are sometimes beneficent, and their repudiation sometimes cruel. For ideals are in practice not so much matters of conscience as excuses for doing what we like"("Little Eyolf" 177). This passage was written for the 1913 edition, but it is not a recantation of 1891. In fact, Shaw had explained the paradox a year earlier, in 1890. The process by which a beneficial, revolutionary ideal becomes a conventional and tyrannous one is described in the original Ibsen lecture:

Some day a man says 'I will not fight a duel.' 'You are bound to' reply the neighbors. 'I dont care: I dont want to; and I wont' says the man; and when the neighbors discover that he is not struck dead for his temerity, nor Society dissolved by it, they follow his example, and presently persuade themselves that they abstain from duelling on principle. Again, there comes a time when the young lady whose mother would rather see her die than working for a living, faces that contingency and applies herself to mathematics with a view to teaching in a High School. And no sooner has she thus driven her will clean through her duty to her parents and to her sex, than she tries to impose the same method of self assertion on all other women as a matter of principle, whether they have any bent towards mathematics or not. ("Fragments" 83)

Shaw wrote in 1913 that because ideals could be both beneficial and mischievous it may happen "that of two people worshipping the same ideals, one will be a detestable tyrant and the other a kindly and helpful friend of mankind," but in 1890 he had shown how the tyrant and the friend could be the same person. In Shaw's example, the rebelling female mathematician is a friend to women like herself and a potential tyrant to women who may detest mathematics. The feminist movement of our own era has provided copious examples of similar tyrannical liberators: for example, career women who disparage homemakers. I am personally acquainted with an idealistic feminist who punished her ten-year-old daughter for playing with dolls instead of toy cars and trucks. So although ideals may start—indeed might always start—as tools of the will, they easily become its mortal enemy. We start out finding "reasons" and "principles" for what we want to do but may end by doing what we hate because we have persuaded ourselves that we must be ruled by principle. We triumphantly tear down one idol only to put up another in its place.

IDOLATRY

Ideals, indeed, are idols. In the 1913 preface Shaw claims even to have been tempted to revise his book by substituting "the words idol and idolatry for ideal and idealism" (101). He is quite serious; he means that an ideal is not merely an abstraction or a principle but something in which people inappropriately invest a certain kind of emotional energy, the kind that goes by names like "reverence," "veneration," and "worship," and which is typically accompanied by adjectives such as "sacred," "holy," "inviolable," and the like. An important aspect of Shaw's way of seeing the world is his almost total immunity to such affective disorders. It is a reason this intensely passionate man was thought by many to be emotionless and coldly cerebral. A well-known anecdote tells how Shaw was informed by a phrenologist that he had a hole where his "bump of veneration" ought to be (Pearson 105). That cranial depression might well be called the "well of realism," for to a realist veneration is a form of spiritual self-abnegation and ideals are a species of false gods.

Illusion and veneration are the diagnostics of ideals. Shaw insists on their illusory quality even when the ideals in question are close to home. In "The Illusions of Socialism," he hints that the illusions of the title are actually ideals when he explains that illusions are often "useful incentives to men to strive after still better realities" (407). He describes two particular types: flattering illusions and necessary ones. It becomes clear that they overlap. They flatter socialists by portraying them as morally superior to their enemies but are necessary to stimulate people's interest in the cause sufficiently to work hard for it. These illusions are as fiercely defended as the ideals of marriage, for when those under the spell of socialist illusions are confronted with a piece of socialism as a "raw reality" they react much as does the idealist of marriage when presented with the truth about that holy institution. Some (the Philistine socialists) merely dismiss the concrete step toward socialism as fraudulent because it does not resemble their dreams, but others "will violently denounce it, and brand its advocates as frauds, traitors, and so on" (407). To "maintain the purity of their faith, they begin to set up rigid tests of orthodoxy; to excommunicate the genuinely scientific Socialist; to entrust the leadership of their organizations to orators and preachers" (417). In short, they make a sacred idol of their orthodoxy. Like the moral idealist, the political idealist sees anything short of his ideal as hopelessly degraded and corrupt. Some of the confusion created by Shaw's parable is because the real distinction between Philistines and idealists is not the propensity to objectify their aspirations and passions as "ideals," but because the idealists have more sensitive consciences, deeper passions, and higher aspirations: they care more and are not easily satisfied. That is why the idealist is a higher type than the Philistine. But the ability to see things as they really are is the possession of the realist alone.

Semantics

Ideals are abstractions that are regarded in a special way, a way that transforms them from indispensable intellectual tools into illusory idols. They are illusions when (despite Shaw's identification of himself as a Platonist) they are seen as Plato saw them, as independent and superior realities rather than merely as useful fictions. In rejecting the idealist view of abstraction, Shaw was very much in the mainstream of Western philosophy, especially English analytical philosophy. He also instinctively understood something that has particularly absorbed twentieth-century philosophy: the immense power of language to distort our understanding of the world. Shavian realism is a close sibling to the study of what in the decades of the mid-century was called the field of semantics. The fundamental insight of writers such as C. K. Ogden and I. A. Richards, S. I. Hayakawa, and Stuart Chase was that we often confuse words with things, treating empty phrases as if they were concrete realities. The confusion is particularly destructive when we endow abstractions with deep emotional significance and confound judgment with observation. The essence of Shavian realism is that it avoids such errors. A good introductory course in realist vision can be found in Chase's The Tyranny of Words or S. I. Hayakawa's Language in Thought and Action. The fundamental delusion of idealism is a misuse of language, a way of confusing words with realities. In particular it is a consequence of "confusing what is inside our head with what is outside," as Hayakawa succinctly puts it (200). Ideals are empty phantoms woven out of words and inflated with wishes or fears; they are given the illusion of substance when they are blown up with our longings. They begin with the simple mistaking of word for thing, but that alone is not enough to sustain them. We cling to ideals because they are the crutches and the shields of our enfeebled wills; we dare not face the world and say "I want that such and such be done," or "I wish thus and that," or "I detest and abhor this or the other" on our own authority: we must give our desires and fears a foreign habitation and a name—one apart from and superior to our own tremulous souls.

The wishes and fears are real. What is inside is not only real but is vital. Shaw realized that the idealists have a valid point when they protest that most of the exhortations to see things as they are, to avoid the distortions of sentimentality and emotion, whether in the name of objectivity, naturalism, realism, or science, are the commandments of death: they ask us to eliminate all that is most vital. They seek to gain cold, objective truth at the price of life itself, to deny or destroy what is inside for the sake of what is outside. Shaw does not make that mistake; he insists only that we not confuse the two, that we not confound the outside with the inside. He recognizes that the idealist is a higher type than the Philistine because he will not settle for mere bovine contentment; he cannot live without his aspiration for something greater.

The Objectification of Desire

In the closing sentences of his preface to the *Pleasant Plays*, Shaw suggests that his business is to dramatize the consequences "of our persistent attempts to found our institutions on the ideals suggested to our imaginations by our half-satisfied passions" (1:385). Ideals are illusions that are either self-imposed or else clung to as if they had been. They are dangerous because we invest in them our desires and fears; they are manufactured receptacles for our passions: idols, in a word. The passions themselves are real, are important, and must be acknowledged. Idealism errs to the extent that it is the inclination to act as if our passions—our values and desires—had *objective* as well as *subjective* reality. At heart, the realist's secret is a simple knack for always making the distinction between what is inside and what is outside without also making the mistake of dismissing the *inside* as mere contamination of objectivity. What is inside is life itself.

Realism is as simple as it is uncommon. Shaw's estimate of one realist in a thousand is probably generous. We can all claim to be realists with respect to those ideals we happen not to share. We can, that is, if we forget that those seven hundred "Philistines" are quite as free from deluding ideals as is the one realist. That should warn us to beware of feeling smugly superior to nineteenth-century ideals. It is as easy to laugh at antiquated ideals as at discarded fashions, but our children will laugh as heartily and as justly at our own intellectual as well as physical garments. We wear our clothes and our morals more loosely now than then, and that is no doubt a good thing, but idealism is by no means dead; and an age in which presidential elections are decided by the intensity of a candidate's commitment to flag worship should pause before condemning another age as idolatrous. Realism, in Shaw's sense, is as distinctly abnormal today as it was one hundred years ago.

Idealism is seductive because it provides masks for realities we dare not face. This is true of liberating ideals as well as enslaving ones; it is true for the woman who made an ideal of her will to become a mathematician as well as for the moralist who idealizes matrimony because he cannot face the failure of his own marriage. Idealism is a mask whether it is used to deny our wills or to liberate them. In the former case it allows us to hide from our sense of failure and inadequacy. In the latter it provides a hedge against responsibility. It allows us to avoid saying, "I will do it because I want to." Thus both forms of idealism are a denial of self and of responsibility. Whether we thwart our wills or enable them, ideals provide a barrier between ourselves and our wills. That is why they are pernicious.

Shaw's rejection of idealism is inseparable from his belief in the inevitable primacy of the individual will. It led as well to something he called "moral equality." On those three solid columns—realism, individualism, and equality—his entire philosophy was carefully and logically built. For all their logic and inevitability, however, some of those developments still have the power to startle and even to shock.

The Will and Its Responsibilities

CONSISTENCY

G. K. Chesterton dismissed Shaw's early exposition of his philosophy as "Schopenhauer standing on his head" (186). His witticism neatly summed up the popular view that Shaw took a complex and recondite metaphysic, reduced it to a frivolous formula, and converted the scowl of pessimism into a grin of anarchism by turning it upside down. Schopenhauer on his head is ridiculous, and the easiest way to trivialize something is to identify it with something preposterous. The image of the irrepressibly cheerful Shaw as a topsy-turvy parody of the eternally gloomy Schopenhauer seems appealingly right but is actually misleadingly wrong. Realism, not Schopenhauer, led Shaw to his belief in the primacy of the will.

Despite his attacks on Shaw, Chesterton understood him better than most. He said so. The introduction to his book on Shaw, obviously intended as an object lesson for its subject, consists entirely of two sentences: "Most people either say that they agree with Bernard Shaw or that they do not understand him. I am the only person who understands him, and I do not agree with him." Despite his disagreement, Chesterton hit upon the fundamental truth that Shaw knew nothing of genuine paradox and that all "his splendid vistas and startling suggestions arise from carrying some clear principle further than it has yet been carried. His madness is all consistency, not inconsistency" (173).

Shaw universalized his logical development as a thinker by presenting it as a historical progression. He repeated this tale numerous times but most clearly in the treatises collected in *Major Critical Essays*. Religious belief, Shaw said, gave way to rationalism, which then succumbed to Schopenhauer's "will." As intellectual history it is unconvincing and has received little attention. Actually, it is a description of Shaw's intellectual development seen as a dialectical argument.

Shaw's Intellectual Development

The realist (Shaw), although brought up in an environment of conventional hypocritical piety, sees through such sham as soon as his critical faculties develop. He recognizes that many of the institutions revered by those around him are nothing but illusions. He sees that Falstaff was right, and "honor" is nothing but a word; there is nothing in the objective, observable world that corresponds to the word "honor." He recognizes the childishness of Bible-worship and the inconsistencies and improbabilities of conventional religion. He becomes aware of an unconventional belief system that proposes to be consistent and honest. It is based vaguely in something called science; Shaw calls it rationalism and materialism. It is a very refreshing religion for a disillusioned realist who thirsts most of all for things as they are, not simply as we might cravenly wish them to be. It has one glaring flaw: in confusing "objectivity" with "realism," it fails to acknowledge what is inside as well as what is outside.

Rationalism, for Shaw, is virtually indistinguishable from what philosophers call utilitarian ethics. "Rationalists" attempted to discard superstition and live entirely by the principles of reason. They concluded that a rationally developed value system could be derived entirely through a simple calculus of pain and pleasure. Schopenhauer's great insight—that will, not reason, was the source of human action—was hopelessly contaminated in Shaw's view by his acceptance of the "Rationalist-Mercantilist error of valuing life according to its individual profits in pleasure" (Major Critical Essays 310).[1] Shaw saw that Schopenhauer did not understand the significance of his own insight, for will is not merely motive power but the source of all values: the pessimistic conclusion that will is a malign force is unjustified and self-contradictory. You cannot declare that will is bad because will is the foundation of all value: as Bertrand Russell put it, "Outside human desires there is no moral standard" ("What I Believe" 62). Shaw instinctively understood that all our values come not from outside but from inside ourselves; and in this he was in complete accord with recent philosophy: A. J. Ayer claims that one of the few twentieth-century notions on which philosophers now agree is that "there is no such thing as an authoritative guide to moral judgement" (15). Both ethical judgments and those longings we think of as immoral or selfish come from the same place, from within ourselves; they are aspects of what we want—of our

wills—and they are both beyond the reach of reason. In short, Schopenhauer was right to believe that reason is the servant of will because it cannot tell us what to desire, only how to achieve it, and he was wrong in his
"conviction that the will was the devil and the intellect the divine saviour"
(*Collected Letters* 1:317). The interior conflicts that so obsess the duty-
bound idealist (and afflict us all from time to time) are not struggles between Evil and Good (our base instincts and the principles of virtue) but
symptoms of the uneven development of the will.

Thus long before he began to promote Creative Evolution, Shaw believed in the evolution of the will from something "lower" into something
"higher," and he realized that these can exist together in the same soul ("A
Degenerate's View of Nordau" 356). Ultimately we do what we do because
we want the action we take more than we want the one we reject. It may be
that we choose out of cowardice, fearing the opprobrium of our peers, and
take refuge in moral ideals, in which case we substitute the will of others
for our own. Conceivably this could be done realistically, rather than idealistically: you might dislike clothing yet abstain from public nudity because
your distaste for garments is not stronger than your wish to avoid offend-
ing your neighbors. It is not necessary to appeal to an ideal of decency. In
such a case it is not cowardice to defer to others but a judgment based on
the rational weighing of different aspects of your own desires. "An ideal,
pious or secular, is practically used as a standard of conduct; and whilst it
remains unquestioned, the simple rule of right is to conform to it" (*Quintessence* 238).

So far from being thwarted by his unfettered will, a man's spiritual
growth depends on his doing "what he likes instead of doing what, on secondhand principles, he ought" (*Collected Letters* 1:228). Those who think
Shaw inconsistent in trying to reconcile egoism and altruism, or individualism and socialism, fail to see that the will embraces both. Whether we
declare with Andrew Undershaft that "thou shalt starve ere I starve," or
we risk our lives to save the life of a stranger, we are responding to "appe-
tites" that are "simply primitive facts, so far utterly unaccountable, unreasonable, miraculous, and mystical" (*Everybody's Political What's What?*
236). The distinction between egoism and altruism vanishes when the will
is truly heeded:

> It is indeed a staring fact in history and contemporary life that noth-
> ing is so gregarious as selfishness, and nothing so solitary as the self-
> lessness that loathes the word Altruism because to it there are no
> 'others': it sees and feels in every man's case the image of its own.

'Inasmuch as ye have done it unto one of the least of these my breth-
ren ye have done it unto me' is not Altruism or Othersism . . . it
accepts entire identification of 'me' with 'the least of these.' (*Quintessence* [1913] 181–82)

If Shaw seems at times to follow a utilitarian road, it is because, like the
utilitarians, he rejected external moral codes; he was not concerned with
whether a given action conformed to some ethical principle but with "its
effect on happiness" (*Quintessence* 292). The word "happiness" is misleading, and Shaw changed it in 1913 to "life," perhaps to avoid precisely
the confusion of his views with what he had called in the 1891 edition the
"mechanical utilitarian ethic . . . which treats Man as the sport of every
circumstance, and ignores his will altogether" (238).[2] Shaw's observation
that the utilitarian ethic ignores man's will is revealing, for it shows that
he saw that the utilitarian, blindly following his calculus of pain and pleasure, is as much the victim of hallucinatory ideals as is the conventional
moralist. The will cannot be reduced to pleasure and pain. It follows its
own road and is the ultimate source of both sin and salvation.

Utilitarian Idealism

I became personally aware of the folly of utilitarian idealism when I wit-
nessed a friend of mine in a heated dispute with his wife about leaving a
bird feeder untended while they went on vacation. The wife was greatly
distressed at the idea of leaving the birds unprovided for, while her husband insisted that the purpose of the bird feeder was to "provide for our
pleasure, not the birds!" His pleasure principle ultimately won out, leaving
both husband and wife forlorn: she because of the distress of the birds; he
owing to his wife's unhappiness.

Now this is a strange sort of Calvinist hedonism indeed, its unswerving
tenet being that you must strive to be selfish no matter how miserable it
makes you. Of course, the utilitarian illusion that all values can be reduced
to the relative measurement of pleasure and pain is given the lie, as Shaw
was fond of pointing out, by the observation that "if you test life by striking a balance between the pleasures and the pains of living, you will go
straight . . . and commit suicide" (*Practical Politics* 2). When you perversely choose instead to live, the utilitarian idealist may try to convince
you that you are the victim of superstition and illusion, but he fails to see
that the will to live, to help others, or even to provide for small hungry
birds is no more irrational than the will to avoid pain. Pain and pleasure
may be in some way more primitive expressions of the will, but they are

not in any way expressions of the rational. In fact, the scrupulous application of reason reveals that a world composed of matter alone has no more room in it for pain and pleasure than for spiritual transport or religious ecstasy. The world of matter, as matter is conventionally understood, is a world indifferent to its own state. The existence of pain and pleasure in our world means that we are part of a universe that is capable of preferring one state of existence to another. Pain is a teleological principle quite as much as is the will to live or to nurture other living things. All such manifestations of the world-will are of an entirely different order than the cold, blind laws of physics.

THE WILL TO BELIEVE

Shaw's objection to what he called rationalism was not limited to distaste for the idolatry of egoism implicit in the utilitarian ethic; he disputed it on epistemological as well as ethical grounds, and in so doing he attacked the very reasonableness of rationalism. Shaw insisted that the will determines belief as well as behavior. This is a direct assault on the rationalist's cardinal point of honor, which is that he follows where the facts and logical thinking lead rather than along the easy path of wishful thinking. Shaw wrote in 1891 to the secularist E. C. Chapman:

> I agree with you that the motto "We seek for Truth" sufficiently indicated the distinction between the old positive method of the Secularist and the theological method of the Christian. But that does not dispose of my objection that we do not seek for truth in the abstract. The Rev. Benjamin Waugh seeks for facts that will support his will-to-believe that secularists are worse men than Christians. Our friend John Robertson seeks for facts that support his will-to-believe that Materialist-Rationalists are the only honest Secularists, and that all others are hypocrites and time servers. The result is that neither Waugh or Robertson have ever discovered one of the glaring facts that contradict them. . . . They have made statements which are false, with the rebutting facts staring them in the face. . . . Therefore all I ask both men to do is to give up pretending that they "seek for Truth." Every man sees what he looks for, and hears what he listens for, and nothing else. (*Collected Letters* 1:301)[3]

Thus the will not only determines values but governs, or at least guides, belief. Shaw goes on to make an even stronger statement, asserting that

we have no more case against theism than theists have against atheism. Newman shewed that our line of argument led to an insufferably repugnant conclusion. When we replied that we found the conclusion congenial, he had nothing more to say. Similarly, all we can do
is to shew that his reasoning led to insufferably repugnant conclusions. The Newmanite replies that the conclusions appear to him to
be perfectly satisfactory. What more have we to say? The irresistibil-
ity of a chain of logic lies, not in the logic, but in the acceptability of
the conclusion to the person addressed. (302)

Shaw used similar arguments throughout his life against the claims of
those, particularly scientists, who claimed strict objectivity for their views,
but here his position is particularly strong and general. Here is another
apparent case of Shavian inconsistency, for this extreme subjectivist viewpoint coincides almost exactly with the publication of the *Quintessence*,
yet the realist Shaw describes there would appear to be quite immune to
the criticism that he "sees what he looks for, and hears what he listens for,
and nothing else." And Shaw had written two years earlier that "we have
had in this century a stern series of lessons on the folly of believing anything for no better reason than that it is pleasant to believe it" ("The Economic Basis of Socialism" 26). Contradiction seems inherent in the very
presentation of the argument, as anyone who could point out, as Shaw
does, that his own side's logic is no stronger than that of his opponent
would not seem to be seeing and hearing only what desire dictated. But
does the realist's immunity to this subjective blindness really invalidate
the argument?

Realism and Wishful Thinking

In a paradoxical way it actually helps to confirm it, for the realist's faith in
the sufficiency of his own will is precisely what frees him from the blinders imposed by his "will-to-believe." Even liberating ideals are the refuges
of cowardice; they are masks we use to pretend that the objects of our wills
have greater authority than our mere desire. Only the realist is strong-
minded enough to drop

the pessimism, the rationalism, the theology, and all the other subter-
fuges to which we cling because we are afraid to look life straight in
the face and see in it, not the fulfilment of a moral law or of the
deductions of reason, but the satisfaction of a passion in us of which
we can give no account whatever. It is natural for man to shrink from

the terrible responsibility thrown on him by this inexorable fact. All his stock excuses vanish before it—"The woman tempted me," "The serpent tempted me," "I was not myself at the time," "I meant well," "My passion got the better of my reason," "It was my duty to do it," "The Bible says that we should do it," "Everybody does it," and so on. Nothing is left but the frank avowal: "I did it because I am built that way." Every man hates to say that. ("A Degenerate's View of Nordau" 359–60)

Every man, that is, except the realist. Because he is ready both to satisfy and to take responsibility for his will, the realist has no need to disguise it in the robes of external authority; he feels no need to claim that reason, Scripture, or any other divine oracle entails the conclusion he seeks; he confesses honestly that he believes because he wants to and that frank avowal is his liberation from self-deceit. The courage to face unpleasant facts goes hand in hand with the courage to accept that the desire to change them has no authority but one's unadorned will. The strength of mind that can say "I believe it because I will to" is sister to the courage unflinchingly to face facts that say "It is not so." Bereft of subterfuge, the realist has no option but to change the facts. The realist is always a reformer, if not a revolutionist.

The Universal and Individual Will

Shaw's realist is not a simple egoist, although in a strict and limited sense of the word, an egoist can be a realist, provided he is unashamed of his own selfishness and does not seek to justify it with rationalist-materialist ideals—or any other sort. But for Shaw such a person was "literally an idiot" (*Quintessence* [1913] 275). Etymologically an "idiot" is a "private person," which made it a perfect epithet from Shaw's perspective for persons who fail to see that "we are members one of another."[4] The realist Shaw describes has a larger soul, one that grows as the will is fed. For such a soul, egoism leads logically and spiritually beyond itself. Ibsen's *Emperor and Galilean* is for Shaw primarily a tragedy of a mighty soul who fails to see that his own powerful will is part of something larger. That drama receives far more attention than any other play discussed in the *Quintessence*.

It was something for Julian to have seen that the power which he found stronger than his individual will was itself will; but inasmuch as he conceived it, not as the whole of which his will was but a part, but as a rival will, he was not the man to found the third empire. He had felt the godhead in himself, but not in others. Being only able to say, with half conviction, "The kingdom of heaven is within ME," he had been utterly vanquished by the Galilean who had been able to say, "The kingdom of heaven is within YOU." But he was on the way to that full truth. A man cannot believe in others until he believes in himself; for his conviction of the equal worth of his fellows must be filled by the overflow of his conviction of his own worth. (*Quintessence* 242)

Realism and Moral Equality

The spiritual augmentation of the will, which Shaw presents in mystical terms, can be understood in a perfectly rational way. The growth and transcendence of the individual will proceeds in two different but related ways. Easiest to understand is that the road to the appreciation of others lies through the recognition of our own worth. The strength of our will emboldens us to abandon ideals and imposed moral codes; then, having satisfied our will, we cease "to be selfish" (*Quintessence* 217). What happens next depends on our courage and the grasp of our intellect. We could, like the young female mathematician in Shaw's illustration, substitute congenial ideals for those that thwarted us, declaring, in effect, "The Idol is dead; long live the Idol." Or we could see that all moral codes, principles, and ideals are artificial and unnecessary and that all that matters is the individual will. Then the waxing generosity of our newly satiated wills is supported by our reason, which perceives that, in the absence of absolute standards, all wills must be presumed equal. Casual observation forces us to realize that individual wills differ, but we have no basis for thinking that some are good and others evil. Such a consideration compels us to respect even those individual wills that conflict with our own. Having become realists, we have lost the right to denounce anyone else as wicked, no matter how uncongenial, even hateful, the aspirations of such an individual may be to us.

The second way in which the will transcends itself is more profound but just as rational. It is the recognition that the "world-will," which Julian thought to be his opponent, is actually "the whole of which his will was but a part." For it is an observable fact that as people become secure in the fulfillment of their wills they often (although not always) tend as well to become generous, giving, and sensitive to the needs of others. Where does such generosity come from? Why do we will to help others, sometimes at considerable cost to ourselves? These are questions that the materialist-rationalists have always been hard-pressed to answer, although they cannot be faulted for want of trying. They have striven mightily to maintain that all motivation can be reduced to pain and pleasure, which in turn must be derived ultimately from a few inescapable laws of physics. Shaw took the commonsense line that both consciousness and will are primitive and irreducible, but he did not assume that they were therefore incomprehensible. Can will have its own law, its own governing principles, despite the obvious fact that individuals are not alike and that nothing is more common than conflict of wills? Is the difference in wills a matter of caprice? Even if we subscribe to something we call free will, we do not imagine that the alternative to strict determinism is blind chance. But what, then, do we mean when we assert that our wills are free?

The Truth About Free Will

This question, although far from simple, must be addressed if we are to comprehend Shaw's belief in a world-will of which each individual's will is but an expression. Although Shaw defended the idea of free will against the materialistic determinists, he recognized the conceptual difficulties that the phrase involves. As early as 1888 he refers to the "insoluble problem (or unsolved problem, let us say) of free will" (Holroyd 1:117, 4:155).[5] By this he meant that in a very real sense our wills control us, not we our wills. We cannot arbitrarily change our own wills. When our wills are particularly strong, we feel ourselves under their compunction. Shaw detested the way moralists use the idea of free will to excuse cruelty to violators of social norms. It is no use to claim that the criminal could freely choose to obey the law; none of us are free to be other than ourselves. Our wills are just as compelling when they represent a spiritual retreat as when they are in the van of moral progress. There are men who beat their wives and can no more help themselves than could Huck Finn bring himself to turn in a runaway slave, although he "knew" how terribly wicked he was being. In the end we must all stand and say, with Martin Luther, "I can do no other; God help me."

So in an important sense, no one really believes in total freedom of the will. As Bertrand Russell points out, we never actually think that other people have free will; we always assume that their actions have causes and, in particular, that we can influence them (*Philosophical Essays* 43–44). Of course the believer in free will could rightly protest that she never imagined will to be *that* free. It would be small comfort to rescue our choices from the iron vice of strict determinism only to deliver them up to the whim of the roulette table. If our wills are not capricious, our actions can to that extent be predicted; insofar as our behavior can be predicted it would then appear to be determined.

The materialist position appeals to many for its simplicity and logic, which it achieves at the expense of excluding consciousness. Marvin Minsky, a vocal advocate of the view that the brain is *nothing but* a computer and the mind *nothing but* a computer program, put the argument clearly in his book on minds and brains: "Everything that happens in our universe is either completely determined by what's already happened in the past or else depends, in part, on random chance" (306). If it is not determined, to the extent that it is not, it is random. People find both of these unacceptable, so to "save our belief in the freedom of will from the fateful grasps of Cause and Chance, people simply postulate an empty, third alternative" (307). This third alternative is empty for inexorably logical reasons: the categories of Cause and Chance exhaust all possibilities. Another way to put this is to say that Chance = Not-Cause. This is a powerful argument. Indeed, if you accept that free will is incompatible with determinism, it is unanswerable.

The usual answer to arguments for simple determinism is a doctrine called "compatibilism," outlined originally by David Hume. The thesis is that determinism is compatible with free will so long as we understand freedom correctly. Our behavior is determined by the nature of our characters, but we can say that we are free if we are not *constrained*—if, in Hume's phrase, we are not in prison and in chains. Modern compatibilists would include such things as psychological compulsions as forms of "constraint." The philosopher John Searle, an opponent of reductionism, objects that compatibilism does not really address the question. "Compatibilism, in short, denies the substance of free will while maintaining its verbal shell" (*Minds, Brains* 89). It becomes clear in his discussion that his difficulty stems from his acceptance of the mechanistic worldview of modern science. "Since all of the surface features of the world are entirely caused by and realised in systems of micro-elements, the behaviour of micro-elements is sufficient to determine everything that happens" (94). He rejects the idea that our wills could possibly be "capable of making molecules swerve from their paths" and doubts that the idea is "even intelligible" (92). But the reason that the argument Hume found acceptable seems sophistical to Searle is that they are operating with different sets of assumptions. There is nothing in Hume's chapter "Liberty and Necessity" or the rest of his *Enquiry Concerning Human Understanding* to suggest that he endorsed a purely mechanical determinism or at all doubts the efficacy of the human will. For Hume, a man's behavior was indeed determined but not (at least exclusively) by the "behavior of the micro-elements," rather by such things as character, breeding, and education.

A sensible response to mechanistic determinism was provided in 1958 by Brand Blanchard. He insisted that he was a determinist, but his thinking was closer to that of Hume than to either Minsky or Searle. His answer is that there are different kinds or levels of causation. Will is free, in other words, in that it is not determined by mechanical causation but by its own rules and laws and "that in the realm of reflection and choice there operates a different kind of causality from any we know in the realm of bodies." The higher levels of causality may supervene on the lower levels, and "when causality of the highest level is at work, we have precisely what the indeterminists, without knowing it, want" (11). He does not say so, but the obvious inference is that the highest level is teleological: it is purposeful, not blind.

This is a view of the freedom of the will that accords perfectly with Shaw's metaphysics: freedom of the will is a misnomer to the extent that it does not deny all forms of determinism; it rejects only *materialistic* determinism.[6] The will operates according to its own principles and is independent of what have been thought of as purely physical laws. Actually, since both types of principles cause physical events, a more precise way of saying this would be to use the Aristotelian terms: *final* causes are independent of, and coexist with, *efficient* causes. Physical events influence volitional events as well as the reverse, but volitional causes cannot be reduced to materialistic ones. The two causal categories interact with each other much as different materialistic laws interact, depending on the circumstances in which they exist. But they are not the same. Beating a horse with a stick or bribing it with a carrot is not the same, in principle, as turning a key to start a gasoline engine. Final causes as well as efficient causes exist in the universe; they exist, at least in part, in our minds, and are to a significant extent identical with what we think of as our "selves," our egos. In everyday language: Things can happen because *I want them to happen;* I have some power, feeble though it may be, to change the physical world in accordance with my wishes. To maintain that volition can be reduced to, and explained entirely in terms of, mechanical causation is to render the will impotent. For the mechanical world, understood in purely materialistic terms, is blind and indifferent. That is, efficient causes, understood as such, are both unaware and uncaring of their effects. If my pleasures, pains,

longings, and aspirations can be explained entirely in terms of a blind ca-
cophony of indifferent forces and if they are impotent to change the world
in any way, then my seeing and caring about the state of the world is func-
tionally irrelevant. This is what the materialistic determinists maintain
and what the vitalists, with Shaw in their vanguard, so intensely deny. Yet
volition—if it *is* genuinely efficacious—is clearly not capricious. It follows
that there exists some kind of will-principle, that there is a force in the
world, following its own rules, that is not blind or indifferent to the state of
the universe. Shaw called it the Life Force.

SHAW'S RELIGION: WHAT IT IS AND IS NOT

Most studies of Shaw's religious ideas stress its harmonies with traditional
religion, but Shaw came to religion in a roundabout way, through science
and rationalism. He insisted that religion must be both rational and practical. His belief in Creative Evolution required a leap of faith but one that
sprang from a solid rational foundation. It was not a leap away from reason, not a defiance of logic and evidence, but a calculated leap into the
unknown under the guidance of good sense. Religion must respect facts
and reason; "the law of God in any sense of the word which can now command a faith proof against science is a law of evolution" (Pref. *Saint Joan*
6:57).

Shaw sometimes spoke of religion as a means to an end, which could
lead one to suspect the sincerity of his "religious" commitment. He felt
that society desperately needs religion, declaring that he had become "a
religious agitator because I have observed that men without religion have
no courage" (*Collected Letters* 2:672). He elaborated on this observation in
the preface to *Back to Methuselah*, where he implied that social progress is
dependent on a positive religion. In 1948, looking back on the manifestations of moral and political chaos that erupted during the first half of the
twentieth century, he declared that they were "all the aberrations that can
occur in the absence of a common faith and code of honor" (Preface, *Miraculous Birth* 18). But if he stressed the *social* need for a religion, his
insistence on a faith that could be subscribed to by intelligent, thoughtful,
and skeptical people, together with his persistent devotion to religious issues, make it impossible to believe that he was not sincere.

Shaw's religion was no opiate; it was a call to realism and responsibility.
When he declared that the Holy Ghost was the "sole survivor" of the

Trinity, he banished the very Persons of the Trinity who have traditionally made the Christian religion attractive ("Revolutionist's Handbook" 2:742). The Father, who can always be trusted to make all hurts well no matter how bad things seem, is as firmly expelled as the Son, in His role as Divine Whipping Boy. Only the Spirit is left: inchoate, imperfect, and immanent. That last attribute makes the others particularly terrifying, a fact that Shaw seems alone in understanding. He told the Cambridge Heretics that we must "drive into the heads of men the full consciousness of moral responsibility that comes to men with the knowledge that there never will be a God unless we make one" (*Religious Speeches* 35). That is a sobering responsibility. Not only can we not run to Daddy to save us from the terrors of the dark, or wash away our manifold sins in the blood of His Son, but we are given the awesome task of creating—no, becoming—God. Imperfect, we must create perfection, without guidance from One who knows the way or absolution for our failures. This is not a religion for cowards or comfort seekers.

Shaw's religion is simple. Unfortunately, as with other aspects of his beliefs, the core of his "faith" has become confused with the elaborations he provided as examples and illustrations, rather than as fundamental tenets. For him the will was a simple fact of nature. It exists. It is a causal agent, different from and superior to the purely mechanical forces which the physicists understand. To deny this, as the materialists did (and do), was to talk nonsense. His "faith" consisted in the belief that this will is a fundamental and progressive force leading the universe toward something we cannot begin really to understand but which we can reasonably call Godhead. The Life Force is only the will conceived as a general vital force that animates all life. It is not appropriate to speak of the Life Force as something that manifests itself in Ann Whitefield but not Violet Robinson, in Father Keegan but not Tom Broadbent. We all incarnate the Life Force. Some are closer to its goal than others, but Shaw always cautioned us not to be too confident that we know who they are. In *Back to Methuselah*, when the seed of the Gospel of the Brothers Barnabas is sown, few would guess the soil in which it comes to flourish. Shaw even suggested that he himself might be one of the utter failures (Pref. *Farfetched Fables* 7:386). It is incorrect, if common, to talk of Joan, Caesar, Undershaft, King Magnus, and similarly dynamic characters as Shavian Superwomen and Supermen. The Superman does not exist. We do not even know what he will be like; the Life Force does not know either, or we would not be muddling along in this disastrously inadequate manner.

Shaw's Religion: The Essence and the Argument

The clearest and most straightforward statement of Shaw's religious philosophy is in his speeches, conveniently compiled by Warren Sylvester
Smith. The message is much the same as in the preface to *Back to Methuselah* but more succinct and lucid. The core ideas are in several of the
speeches, notably "The New Theology," "The Religion of the Future,"
"Modern Religion I," and "Modern Religion II." In his usual misleading
fashion, he disclaims logic and reason: "I do not address myself to your
logical faculties, but as one human mind trying to put himself in contact
with other human minds" (10). He then expounds his religious ideas logically and rationally. While insisting on what might be called sentimental
premises, he develops them in a logically sound manner. He comes close to
the ideal of Thomas Aquinas, who declared that religious truth must transcend reason without ever violating it. This logical development is clear in
an outline of his core ideas:

(1) When humane, thoughtful people begin to think seriously about
traditional religion they are forced to reject much of it because the Old
Testament's "tribal idol," who is feared and obeyed because he is wicked,
petty, and vindictive, is morally inconceivable. Kind and caring people cannot conceive of a God who is more cruel, petty, and mean-spirited than
they are. The identification of this "Almighty Fiend," as Shelley called
Him, with "religion" makes kindly people declare themselves atheists.
Humane sentiment leads thoughtful people to reject God.

(2) Unfortunately, there are good reasons for believing in a ferocious
God. One is the argument from design: the complexity of living things
seems to serve a purpose; it enables them to live. The organs of the body so
admirably serve their various functions that they must have been ex-
pressly designed. The existence of design implies the existence of a designer, that is, God. But if God "designed" the world, He must have designed all of it, including suffering, stupidity, and wickedness. If God is in
charge, He must have caused it.

(3) This produces a dilemma: the argument from design concludes there
is a God, but observation says He must be Shelley's Almighty Fiend. Attempts to deny this logical conclusion only succeed in highlighting it.
When Gottfried Leibniz tried logically to demonstrate the omnipotence,
omniscience, and benevolence of God, he was forced to conclude that there
is no evil in the world. Maintaining both religious premises and logical
procedure forced him into blatant violation of common sense, as Voltaire
so wittily demonstrated in *Candide*. Shaw saw the omnipotent and be-

nevolent God of tradition as an inconsistent idol: "Now you cannot prove that [the] force [behind the universe] is at once omnipotent and benevolent" (17).

(4) Darwin was welcomed so enthusiastically because he offered a way out: design was unnecessary; blind chance, in the shape of "natural selection," could account for everything. Darwin loomed so large in the minds of the late nineteenth century because, as Shaw makes clear in the preface to *Back to Methuselah*, he offered deliverance to almost anyone with a complaint against the established order. The humanitarians embraced him because they saw in him salvation from a cruel and capricious god. The Almighty Fiend was an unnecessary hypothesis.

(5) There was a dark side to the theory of natural selection: it did away with the need for a designer, but it also did away with the necessity of consciousness and will. Nevertheless, consciousness, intelligence, will, and design do exist. We all are aware of their existence in ourselves. Altruism also exists; people do work that does not benefit them, and natural selection cannot account for that. This is the crux of Shaw's argument with the Darwinians. It is a two-part argument: the first attacks the premises of Darwinism and the second provides the "rational" foundation of his "faith" in the Life Force. Here are Shaw's words:

> Men were able to demonstrate that, according to the theory of natural selection, it was perfectly possible that all the books in the British Museum might have been written, all the pictures in the National Gallery might have been painted, all the cathedrals of Europe might have been built, automatically, without one person concerned in the process having been conscious of what he was doing. Some of the natural selectionists used to make the demonstration themselves with a certain pride in doing so. But the common sense of mankind said, "If all the operations of the species can be accounted for without consciousness, intelligence, or design, you have still got to account for the consciousness, intelligence, and design that undoubtedly exist in man." The religious people naturally turn this argument to account, saying, "It is all very well to say that life is a mere pursuit of pleasure and gain, but many men do not live in order to get a balance of pleasure over pain; you see everywhere men doing work that does not benefit them—they call it God's work; natural selection cannot account for that. There is behind the universe an intelligent and driving force of which we ourselves are a part—a divine spark. (16–17)

The Darwinians simply ignore the first part or the argument, which enables them to dismiss the second as wishful thinking. Since this controversy is at the heart of Shaw's claim that his religion was proof against science, it is a crux of his dispute with most modern scientists.

(6) While the Darwinians find salvation from the specter of a malicious and capricious deity in a mindless and indifferent universe, the religious people are unsatisfied. The way out of their dilemma, Shaw says, is Creative Evolution. God cannot be both omnipotent and benevolent. But the assumption that God must be omnipotent is gratuitous. Why would an omnipotent God create something inferior and imperfect: us? If you combine the evidence for evolution with the plain fact that will and consciousness exist in each of us, you have the argument that we are all part of God, that God is Becoming rather than Being, and that God is in the process of manifestation. Evil is no longer problematic because it is not the deliberate mischief of a malicious deity, only the mistakes of a yet imperfect one.

Two Syllogisms; Two Denials

Thus Shaw's religion is based on the logical denial of the foundations of the two major competing metaphysical systems of the modern world: the traditional religious cosmos governed by an omnipotent, omniscient, and benevolent deity and the scientific materialist universe conceived as a mindless, purposeless machine. The first argument is familiar: attempts to deny it refer to it as "the problem of Evil." It has been formulated in many ways, but a simple version goes like this:

A God who was omnipotent, omniscient, and benevolent could not create an imperfect world, a world soiled by evil.

Our world is imperfect and rife with evil.

Therefore, if a god created our world, she or he is not omnipotent, omniscient, or benevolent.

Scientific materialism concludes that God does not exist. But scientific materialism provides a faith of its own. It declares that the universe is orderly and knowable and that the laws of physical science provide the keys to all its mysteries. "Faith in the inerrancy of the Bible is childish, ignorant superstition," it boldly declares, "and the one true faith is in the inerrancy of the laws of physics." The universe is a giant machine. Shaw's refutation of this metaphysic is equally logical. Although Shaw disdained formal logic, it might be phrased as a syllogism thus:

If the universe is mindless and purposeless, every part of the universe
is mindless and purposeless.

I have a mind (I am aware of something) and I have purposes.

Therefore, I am either not a part of the universe, or the universe has
mind and purpose.

The first alternative is absurd, but the second seems equally absurd to
materialists (a category that includes most contemporary intellectuals). As
a result, they attempt contemptuously to dismiss the argument rather
than actually addressing it. When they do address it, they attack it by
denying the minor premise (although they do not always admit that is
what they are doing). As infuriating as many find this syllogism, however,
the argument is sound. It is essential to understanding Shaw's religious
metaphysic, so we will consider it in detail later.

The Appearance of Chance in a World of Law

Shaw's faith is terrifying in its denial of precisely what is reassuring in
both traditional faiths. Theism insists that God is in charge and will take
care of everything; materialism declares the universe to be indifferent to
our impotent desires. In either case there is nothing to be done. Shaw's
religion charges us with the responsibility to manifest Godhead, to set the
world right, to expel evil and enthrone good. But it also affirms things
which are important to the adherents of both alternative faiths. It assures
the champions of spirit that there is Divine purpose in the world, and it
maintains with the adherents of matter that the universe is orderly, understandable, and governed by law. It is not capricious. The Life Force, or will-
principle, is like any other "law" of the universe: its manifestations differ
because they are conditioned by circumstances. The law of gravity may
operate equally on a cannon ball and a feather, but the one will fall more
swiftly because other factors have their influence.

The existence of different manifestations of the will-principle can be
accounted for just as the different manifestations of physical law are: by
the existence of different circumstances and impinging forces. For Shaw,
the product of an age pervaded by ideas of growth, progress, and evolution,
it was natural to imagine the possibility of a "spontaneous growth of the
will" (*Quintessence* 238). Many philosophers today would argue with this
metaphysical system, but it is not a hodgepodge of undigested and unas-
similated scraps and pieces. It is a single, coherent, and consistent set of
principles from which the rest of the Shavian platform follows with logic

and something close to inevitability. Thus it is a short hop from the primacy of the will to Creative Evolution, and Shaw's insistence that "the way to Communism lies through the most resolute and uncompromising Individualism" appears as a strictly logical development rather than an inconsistent eccentricity (*Quintessence* 276).[7] Shavian moral principles are also an inescapable consequence of his metaphysic. The metaphysical principle that each individual's will is the manifestation of a larger will-principle or Life Force leads directly to the ethical principle of moral equality, the conviction that, as Barbara Undershaft puts it, "There are neither good men nor scoundrels: there are just children of one Father; and the sooner they stop calling one another names the better" (*Major Barbara* 3:90, and Preface 48). The will manifests itself in many ways, depending on the circumstances in which it appears, but each manifestation is the result of a consistent, universal principle.

A religion, of course, needs more than a consistent metaphysical principle. A creed is, at least ostensibly, a guide for living. In the case of Shaw's religion, that "guidance" comes from accepting the responsibility of one's own will. That is why what he called realism is as important to his religious ideas as is the primacy of the will. Most religions are founded on the masks he called ideals, the imaginary forms into which we project our fears and longings. We idealize the sources of our hates and fears as evil and comfort ourselves with absolute morality, which both legitimizes our hatred and absolves us of the awful responsibility of ever choosing the lesser of two dreadful evils, for we can always idealize the evil we choose as a positive good. Realism demands embracing a relativistic morality and accepting responsibility for our own actions. An absolute morality leads to the division of men and women into saints and scoundrels; relativism forces one to conclude that we are all brothers and sisters. In the second part of this book I will explore more fully how Shaw translated that aspect of his creed into action in the world.

The Apostolic Attitude

Shaw's approach to ethical persuasion is thus not obvious. At first glance it may appear that, in this view, moral persuasion is impossible, or at least inconsistent. How can you convince others to change their ethical beliefs (presumably to make them closer to your own) without violating your own principle that you are moral equals? Are you condemned to moral inertia, forced to wait quietly for the wills of others spontaneously to grow into a stature commensurate with your own (for we must be convinced that ours is the more advanced manifestation of the world-will)? How is moral progress possible? If we lapse into passivity on the grounds that one person's will is as good as another's and that despite our differences we are all condemned to be who we are, do we not invite irresponsibility in the way feared by Erasmus and other opponents of determinism? They argue that if we give up an inch of the individual's free will, whether to God's unknowable decree, the laws of physics, or a "will of which I am a part," we provide the shirker with the unanswerable excuse that "I cannot help myself, that is just the way I am made." But individual wills, although expressions of something larger, are to a significant extent identical with our "selves." We cannot blame our wills on anyone or anything else; we are our wills. For Shaw, the highest responsibility was responsibility to oneself; this does not tell us how we may influence the ethical perceptions of *others*, but it does point the way, which is to awaken that higher self in others and expose it to those facts that have sensitized our own. We can only adopt what Shaw called the apostolic rather than the Athanasian attitude. The former is a desire to convert others to our beliefs for the sake of sympathy and light; the latter is an impulse to murder people who do not agree with us (Pref. *Misalliance* 4:70). That is all we can do.

On inspection, it turns out to be quite a bit. The simplest technique is just to expose people to the facts. Some of what we think of as immoral behavior is based on ignorance of the facts. The difficulty arises when such ignorance is willful self-deception designed to help people hide from their own consciences. Realist moral persuasion depends, then, on rending the veils of illusion and forcing the self-deceived to face the truth. This is never easy, for we hate to stand naked before our consciences, but it is possible when the objects of persuasion are hiding from their own ideals. Then one may say: "This is what you profess; that is what you actually do. Prove that you truly believe what you say by changing your actions to comply with your protestations." That is the essence of the nonviolent technique used by Gandhi and Martin Luther King Jr. Despite the unflattering things that Shaw said about ideals, moral progress often results when actions catch up with ideals: American society is still reluctantly moving toward the ideals professed in the Declaration of Independence, goaded from time to time by the likes of Martin Luther King Jr. But the methods of Gandhi and King would not have worked in places such as Nazi Germany or the South Africa of apartheid, where racist exploitation and brutality were supported by popular ideals rather than unacknowledged violations of them. Where slavery is sanctified as religion and genocide as science, quiet moral persuasion appears a frail straw indeed.

The Uses of Ideals

Since ideals are such effective tools for social pioneers like King and Gandhi, it is worth reconsidering what Shaw regarded as the Ibsenist position: that ideals should constantly be examined and questioned, with the new replacing the old in pace with the growth of human consciousness. What can be so wrong with ideals so long as they are not allowed to stagnate and become a hindrance rather than a help to the human spirit? The creation of new ideals allows us to resolve conflicts between higher and lower manifestations of the will in the direction of spiritual progress. Instead of scorning Thomas Jefferson as a hypocrite for owning slaves while expounding the ideal of human equality, would it not be more sensible (and safer, lest anyone inquire too closely into the correspondence between our own actions and ideals) to rejoice that ideals exceed actuality, for they are spiritual aspirations. We should think of them as unfulfilled goals, as food on which our spirits can grow until we can shed the old ideals as a snake sheds its skin, recognizing that what had protected our ethical growth in former stages now serves only to constrict it. Shaw, on whom the lesson of *The Wild Duck* was not lost, would agree that for the majority of the human population this argument was inescapable. Those who cannot think in moral terms without ideals must of course have them, but that some people cannot move without wheelchairs is no reason to compel universal use of them. It is always better, says the realist, to face the truth than to hide from it. But part of the truth is that many will not face it under any compunction, and we could well ask, as Relling might have Gregors Werle, "What harm does this dishonesty do?"

The answer to that question is the heart of the Shavian ethical position. It has to do with the reason that such dishonesty is so universally tempting. What is the source of its seductive power? Ideals come in many guises. The most pernicious, at least from Shaw's point of view, is the arbitrary standard of behavior self-righteously imposed by the powerful and cravenly accepted by the weak. But what of the progressive idealist, the one who stands up for a new ideal, such as the woman who abandons ideal femininity to espouse the ideal of sexual equality? Can we fault her for moral cowardice? Yes, says the realist, for although she has the (not inconsiderable) courage to defy conventional ideals, she lacks the courage to do it on her own; she quails before the act of saying "I did it because I wanted to do it." Her failure is the failure to take full responsibility for her actions. The battle of ideals is at heart a battle between different expressions of the will; only when it is fought honestly, when each appeals to no higher authority than the promptings of his own soul, will spiritual growth proceed at its proper pace. The charge against all ideals, progressive and retrogressive, is that they evade responsibility. For a realist, that is sufficient to condemn them.

AN EXAMPLE OF REALIST MORAL PERSUASION

Ideals are pernicious to the realist, even if she acknowledges their necessity as crutches for crippled souls, because she has no other method of ethical persuasion than to appeal to an individual's own unprotected conscience. Ideals serve more often to shield tender eyes from the glare of conscience than to protect a higher conscience from outmoded duties. The limited tools of a moral realist can be seen clearly whenever Shaw undertook to persuade his readers on an issue that was confined purely to values. There is no question that moved him more passionately than the humane treatment of animals, yet he never let his passion move him to idealism; he remained always a realist. A short time before he died he looked back on a lifetime of impassioned opposition to vivisection. In characteristic fashion, he is impelled to point out first of all what one *cannot* say against vivisection. It is a mistake to argue that vivisection does not produce useful results. "I had long discarded this defense, pointing out that even if every claim made by the vivisectors were completely disproved, some real discoveries might be made at any moment." And he was not an enemy of research. "Progress depends on experiments: without them we can neither learn anything nor, what is often more important, forget anything. But experiments, like other human activities, must be lawful and humane." He claimed the right, nevertheless, to call the vivisector a "scoundrel."

> The vivisector, I declared, is actually that worst of scoundrels, a scoundrel on principle; for no thief nor murderer attempts to justify theft or murder as such and claims not only impunity but respect and protection for them, whereas the vivisector maintains that knowledge as such is so supremely sacred that in its pursuit the professional man of science may commit the most revolting atrocities merely to satisfy his curiosity. (*Shaw on Vivisection* 55–56)

The vivisector's ideals are a most effective bulwark against his own conscience.

Nowhere, however, can one find a better picture of a realist as moral persuader than in the preface Shaw wrote for *Killing for Sport*, edited by his friend Henry S. Salt. Shaw begins by acknowledging his difficulties: "Sport is a difficult subject to deal with honestly. It is easy for the humanitarian to moralize against; and any fool on its side can gush about its glorious breezy pleasures and the virtues it nourishes. But neither the moralizings nor the gushings are supported by fact: indeed they are mostly violently contradicted by them. Humanitarians are not more humane than other people." Thus the first point: When the issue is values, it is irrelevant to argue from "facts." Indeed, on the point of ferocity, sportsmen are not in the same league with the humanitarians. "I know many sportsmen; and none of them are ferocious. I know several humanitarians; and they are all ferocious. No book of sport breathes such a wrathful spirit as this book of humanity. No sportsman wants to kill the fox or the pheasant as I want to kill him when I see him doing it." So much for the cruelty of the sportsman. Shaw goes out of his way not to be vituperative (after having cheerfully admitted the murderous passion which the killing of animals inspires in him): "Therefore let no sportsman who reads these pages accuse me of hypocrisy, or of claiming to be a more amiable person than he. And let him excuse me, if he will be so good, for beginning with an attempt to describe how I feel about sport." And he thus starts to explain, in as objective a manner as possible, the utterly subjective and sentimental nature of his attitudes. After mentioning, with impelling feeling, his revulsion at the description of a dog being shot for food during an Arctic expedition, he hastens to add that it "was necessary to shoot the dog: I should have shot it myself under the same circumstances." It was the callous attitude to that exigency that so appalled him. It is a matter, essentially, of "fellow feeling," which, he is quick to add, is an emotion beyond all reason and comprehension in its inconsistencies. Fellow feeling for animals means essentially that you treat them as you would other men and women rather than as you might a machine; you might hate them as well as love them.

Then he returns to attacking the rationalizations, not of the sportsman but of the humanitarian. You cannot simply say that one must not kill one's fellow creatures, as killing is necessary: the farmer must kill the rodent or he loses his livelihood, and if "you hold the life of a mosquito sacred, malaria and yellow fever will not return the compliment." Our very existence entails not merely the death of other animals but the actual extinction of their species. He even maintains that fox hunting is good for the preservation of the foxes, who would suffer more from the combination of neglect and the pressure of civilization than they do now from the dogs and guns. Even in the midst of describing his horror at the killing frenzy of much sport, he admits that he admires the skill of the marksman and is even fascinated by shooting "because killing by craft from a distance is a power that makes a man divine rather than human." He warns the humanitarians among his readers to beware of self-righteousness and self-deceit: do not "pretend that war does not interest and excite you more than printing, or that the thought of bringing down a springing tiger with a well-aimed shot does not interest you more than the thought of cleaning your teeth."

And then he turns it all around. Having absolved the sportsman of all charges of cruelty, barbarity, and ferocity, he makes us realize that the very normality of the killing sports and the casualness of the killers is the most horrible indictment that can be made against them. Their activity dehumanizes both them and us.

> To have one's fellow-feeling corrupted and perverted into a lust for cruelty and murder is hideous; but to have no fellow-feeling at all is to be something less than even a murderer. The man who sees red is more complete than the man who is blind. . . . To kill as the poacher does, to sell or eat the victim, is at least to behave passionately. To kill in gratification of a lust for death is at least to behave villainously. Reason, passion, and villainy are all human. But to kill, being all the time quite a good sort of fellow, merely to pass away the time when there are a dozen harmless ways of doing it equally available, is to behave like an idiot or a silly imitative sheep. (Preface to *Killing for Sport* 925–41)

It is a remarkable essay. Humanitarians as well as sportsmen are called to conscience. To many of the humanitarian idealists who first read it, it must have been bewildering or maddening. If it made any of them think of the opening of the seventh chapter of Matthew, it did some good; but it was clearly intended for the sportsmen, and it is doubtful that many have read it. They would have expected to be castigated and vilified, and no one invites abuse. Instead, they would have been asked, in a spirit of fellow feeling, to examine their own souls. That would surely have been a beneficial experience, whether or not they gave up the sport of killing as a result.

There is no more solid, thorough, or unanswerable foundation for the injunction to "judge not, that ye be not judged," than what Shaw called realism. Idealism—even at its most advanced, progressive, humane, and enlightened—is moral arrogance, which is why the worst of evils are always committed in its name. But realism, despite its humility, is always terrifying and shocking when it confronts our most cherished ideals.

THE IDEAL OF FAIR WAGES

We are less blinded by ideals today than one hundred years ago, but there are still realist propositions that have the power to bewilder and amaze— even to shock. We look upon outdated Victorian ideals with condescending amusement, for the illusory nature of unfashionable ideals is more obvious even than the absurdity of outmoded clothing. Currently held ideals are different: nothing seems more inevitable, natural, and logical than an unquestioned ideal. Economic justice is such an ideal. It is difficult to find anyone who does not subscribe to some version of the ideal of economic justice. It pervades our social life; it is the underpinning of our economic system; it is even the foundation of our sense of self-worth. There is hardly a more pervasive illusion than the notion that we should all be rewarded on the basis of what we deserve. It does no good to point out that if you insist on a difference in individual deserts you must give up all logical pretension to a belief in human equality. We are not identical, varying widely in all manner of skills and abilities, in attractiveness, in wit and charm, and in any other human quality you can name. If human equality does not mean equality of worth, it means nothing at all. Yet most people are convinced that they are underpaid. (It is more difficult to find someone who believes himself overpaid.) On inquiry it never turns out that they believe that everyone who is paid as little or less than themselves is underpaid; on the contrary, they will tell you that some of those more meagerly remunerated are shamefully overpaid. What can this mean but a hierarchy of human worth? What does this leave of the ideal of human equality? As the Reverend James Morell sadly admits: "Everybody says it: nobody believes it: nobody" (*Candida* 1:519). If you suggest to these people that they do not in fact endorse the idea of human equality, they will be shocked and insulted. Nothing is more sacred than an ideal which everybody professes and nobody believes, and nothing is more horrifying than the frank avowal that this is so. One could easily adapt G. K. Chesterton's aphorism about the Christian ideal to the ideal of equality and declare that it has not been tried and found wanting but found difficult and left untried. Like the

Christian ideal, it is not only unobserved in practice; it is not even honestly believed.

Some may protest here that this argument confuses true human worth with market value, but that charge recoils onto the accusers. In simple economic terms, when market value is the criterion, no one is ever overpaid or underpaid except through carelessness. The market values any commodity—human, animal, or inanimate—at whatever price someone is willing to pay. Market value is only a useful fiction; there is never any one market price for anything, even at the same moment in the same community. When someone says that he is underpaid, he does not mean that he could get more if he tried; he means that he is intrinsically *worth* more. Such a person subscribes to the notion that there is such a thing as a "fair" market price. The illusion that the market is nature's divine plan for sorting the wheat from the chaff (when it is not being sabotaged by meddling do-gooders) is one of the central pillars of capitalist ideology. The Social Darwinists who endorse this theory ignore the fact that the market is both unavoidably capricious and perpetually manipulated, but they are at least honest; the socialists have no such excuse. Anyone who maintains that some people should be paid more than others is assuming that there is such a thing as a fair or correct wage for different forms of labor. Such a one who also rejects the caprice of the marketplace as the court of last appeal must believe that people should be paid what they "deserve." Thus personal worth becomes equated with the "fair" price of one's labor. And not insignificantly, money becomes the final yardstick of human worth.

The realist knows that none of us deserves anything, that the notion of personal desert is only an idealist illusion, however satisfying to the economically fortunate. All systems of social hierarchy that claim a basis in intrinsic worth, whether hereditary aristocracy, socialist bureaucracy, or Darwinian plutocracy, are arbitrary and illusory. When Shaw proclaimed the natural truth of human equality, he was justified by the patent falsity of all claims to the contrary. The social idealists were pleased with that declaration, conforming as it did to their ideals, but Shaw went on to insist that they take it literally and act upon it. Unfortunately, although people are shocked when a favorite ideal is attacked, they may be panicked and bewildered when told to behave in strict accordance with it. Capitalists smiled and socialists stared when Shaw stated what he saw as the essential truth of socialism. He observed that once you have taken the decision away from the caprice of the marketplace there is no sensible reason why any one individual should get any more than any other, no matter how offensive that might be to those whose sense of worth depends on financial advantage. Thus he declared that socialism is "a state of society in which the entire income of the country is divided between all the people in exactly equal shares, without regard to their industry, their character, or any other consideration except the consideration that they are living human beings" ("The Simple Truth" 155). For Shaw human equality was a realist rather than an idealist proposition. He did not pretend that human beings were all equally talented, attractive, or even admirable. They are not equally suited to the task of telling other people what they must do, although someone must govern. Such talents are, in common parlance, "gifts," and there is no logic in rewarding anyone for being especially lucky. Sidney Trefusis, in *An Unsocial Socialist*, dismisses the idea that genius should be rewarded, declaring that it "cost its possessor nothing; that it was the inheritance of the whole race incidentally vested in a single individual" (106). Trefusis goes to some lengths "to illustrate the natural inequality of man, and the failure of our artificial inequality to correspond with it" (160). Although "you cannot equalize anything about human beings except their incomes" ("The Case for Equality" 122), failure to do so is not only dishonest but socially pernicious. Shaw put the case for eliminating artificial distinctions most succinctly in *The Intelligent Woman's Guide*:

> Between persons of equal income there is no social distinction except the distinction of merit. Money is nothing: character, conduct, and capacity are everything. Instead of all the workers being levelled down to low wage standards and all the rich levelled up to fashionable income standards, everybody under a system of equal incomes would find her and his own natural level. There would be great people and ordinary people and little people; but the great would always be those who had done great things, and never the idiots whose mothers had spoiled them and whose fathers had left them a hundred thousand a year; and the little would be persons of small minds and mean characters, and not poor creatures who had never had a chance. That is why idiots are always in favor of inequality of income (their only chance of eminence), and the really great in favor of equality. (102)

The final sentence reveals at least one source of the resistance to socialism among those who should most favor it: the poor. Nowhere is that resistance more glaring than in the United States, the land built on the myth that anyone can strike it rich. Socialism was once thought inevitable because the poor would certainly favor it, and they had the advantage of numbers. History has given the lie to that comforting illusion. As the American dream has come more and more to be the dream of something for nothing, its power over the imaginations of the poor has increased. In this country the poor reject equality in favor of meretricious fantasies, and the most popular method of redistributing income is the lottery.

Worse, the artificial distinctions created by unequal income have the malignant effect of becoming real distinctions. The illusion that certain people must get more because they deserve more is a self-fulfilling prophecy: those with more become better and those with less become worse. Society as a whole suffers because its average level has been artificially suppressed. The irony is complex. First, what Shaw called "the Anarchist spirit" is possible only under a rigid socialist organization because the economic anarchism of capitalism produces multiple tyrannies ("The Impossibilities of Anarchism" 23). Not only does the way to communism lie through individualism, but genuine individualism is possible only after "the most resolute and uncompromising" communism. What is most fearful about the principle of equality is its pitiless exposure of natural inequality. Here as elsewhere, idealist illusions that seem benign are really pernicious.

THE IDEAL OF JUSTICE

The illusion that the world can be divided into the deserving and the undeserving is the foundation of the most sacred of ideals: the ideal of justice. But there is no such thing as economic justice because there is no such thing as justice. There are only various more or less arbitrary and conventional ways of dealing with conflicts between individuals in a given community. Since there are no independent scales—apart from each person's own preference—for weighing one individual's "worth" or "deserts" against another's, it is sensible to treat all equally, to grant moral as well as social and economic equality. This is precisely Shaw's position, most thoroughly described in the preface to *Major Barbara*, where he imagines a society stripped of the illusion of justice, in the moral as well as economic spheres. Such a society cannot justify either the economic punishment of poverty or any of the other tortures our penal ingenuity has devised. The punishment of poverty makes its victims worse, not better, and so, believed Shaw, does every other kind of punishment. Again, the victims of the system are not united in opposition to it. The illusion of justice—the fantasy that one can pay for misdeeds through punishment—serves the guilty in a manner similar to the way inequality serves the "idiots" of society: it protects them from having to face themselves. As the worthless of society shun the honest image of their own worth, so do the guilty seek refuge from the glare of their own consciences. They can be saved as Major Barbara saves Bill Walker, by bringing them inexorably face to face with their own souls, but like Todger Fairmile, they will struggle against their salvation with a strength born of terror. Again the irony that the "natural" solution—in this case the regulation of ethical behavior by the conscience of each individual—is possible only under the most controlled and disciplined of circumstances.

These natural solutions to human problems never happen naturally. The abolition of decency laws will not have everyone going around naked. The purpose of clothing is to hide not our beauty but our ugliness. Modesty has nothing to do with it. The natural growth of the individual soul as well as of society depends on the acceptance of the naked truth about our souls; the ideal of justice is precious to us *because* it is a lie.

IMPRACTICABLE PEOPLE

Responsibility to oneself, provided it is honest and the subject has not been degraded into inhumanity by poverty and brutality, is a powerful moral restraint. The trick is to prevent evasion of this terrifying responsibility. Realism means responsibility: the responsibility to face moral truths. But if Shaw's vision of a responsible society makes fearful demands of its citizens, it requires even more of its governors, for they must eventually confront the existence of souls so atrophied that they are irredeemable: those Shaw refers to as "impracticable people." Like his Major Barbara, Shaw does not accept that these are "scoundrels" (which is not a description but a license to inflict injury with an air of piety), he merely observes, as he did of actual inmates he had seen, "that as it was evidently impossible to reform such men, it was useless to torture them, and dangerous to release them" ("Imprisonment" 857). Shaw's answer to the inevitable question, What, then, do you do with them? is simply: Kill them. No issue more starkly illustrates the difference between Shaw and the sensitive humanitarians with whom he was normally allied. He cannot be said to support capital punishment, for he did not accept any form of punishment. He rejected the three conventional objectives of criminal imprisonment: retribution, deterrence, and rehabilitation. The first is a barbaric superstition, the second—because it depends on certainty, not severity—would be possible only at the cost of ignoring the rights of the innocent, and the third is inconsistent with the first two. The only thing left, for Shaw, was to abolish prisons altogether, rehabilitate those who are capable of rehabilitation, and then acknowledge your failures as failures. If they cannot be either reformed or tolerated in free society as they are, they should be killed, humanely and anesthetically, as are rabid dogs. One thing that unites persons on both sides of the capital punishment controversy is the belief that the worst thing you can do to a person is to kill him. Shaw did not share that conviction.

Many of Shaw's admirers, who generally oppose the killing of convicted criminals, are apt to pass over his view on this subject as a forgivable if disturbing eccentricity. It is not; it is an essentially Shavian position, one very close to the core of his ethical faith. There is more to his lifelong advocacy of the euthanasia of the criminally unfit than a simple conviction that death is more humane than life imprisonment.

A realist preference for death over imprisonment can be better understood after looking at some of the arguments presented in the current American controversy by the opponents of the lethal chamber: capital punishment is racist; it discriminates against the poor; it discriminates against the powerless and ignorant generally; innocent people will almost certainly be executed; death costs more than life imprisonment. All of these arguments are fallacious. Of course, the arguments *for* the death penalty are just as faulty, and there is one sound and unanswerable argument against capital sanctions: the profession of a conviction beyond reason that killing is so terrible we should never do it for any reason. That is just the sort of nonrational argument Shaw used against vivisectors and sportsmen.

There is no other genuine reason; the rest are just rationalizations. The real reason for Shaw's unusual position may be his reaction against a disturbing implication of the fallacy that underlies all four arguments. If there is racism, discrimination, and unequal treatment generally in the application of the death penalty, then it is inequity that is the problem, not the death penalty. It is childish or worse to pretend that a racist system of justice will cease to be racist when the death sentence is eliminated. As for poverty and powerlessness, the rich and powerful will never be treated by any social system the same as the poor and weak; that is what being rich and powerful is all about. Abolish the lethal chamber and nothing significant will change. To assert that the possibility of executing innocent persons is a reason to ban the death penalty is nonsense. Or rather, it is nonsense unless you honestly believe that the imprisonment of innocent persons is an acceptable alternative to their execution. If innocent persons are being condemned, whether to prison or the electric chair, the problem lies in the process by which guilt is determined, not in the nature of the sentence. Shaw responded to this argument with strained patience: "But really you cannot handle criminals on the assumption that they may be innocent. You are not supposed to handle them at all until you have convinced yourself by an elaborate trial that they are guilty" ("Imprisonment" 883). The final argument of the abolitionists is similar. Capital cases, they point out, cost more because of the lengthy appeals process. But the purpose of the appeals is to ensure that the progress of justice has been scrupulously fair. It either performs that function or it is a waste of time and money. If it is not needed, it should be eliminated; if it is needed, then it is appropriate whether or not the prisoner is under sentence of death. Indeed, if that is the case, then the existence of the death penalty assures the scrupulous examination of criminal charges that should be the right of all accused.

These arguments are not forgivable rationalizations for an admirable humanitarian impulse; they are dangerously irresponsible evasions. That is the philosophical reason why Shaw preferred the horror of killing to the horror of imprisonment. The former forces the judges to be honest, to face the fact that they cannot avoid inflicting an injury on fellow human beings. It is not the sadists or the self-righteous moralists but the squeamish reformers who have made the modern prison such a diabolical instrument of torture (861). They are seeking their "own salvation, not that of the lawbreaker" (864). They do not seek it honestly. The trouble with the arguments against capital punishment is that they convict their presenters of indifference to very real evils, the solid evidence for which they have themselves painstakingly researched. If you are to fight social ills effectively, you must be willing to be honest about their true nature. The last rationalization—that a capital sentence costs the taxpayers more than a life sentence—is the most damning. If the extra cost of appeals reflects nothing more than foot-dragging and cowardice, then the hardhearted death advocates are right: the process should be speeded up and the expensive delays eliminated. If they are really needed to ensure that justice is done, then the humanitarians are arguing, in effect, that we could economize on crime by skimping on the protection of the innocent.

This is virtually Shaw's last word on the subject:

Then there are people like Ibsen's Peer Gynt, who funk doing anything irrevocable, and will commit the horrible atrocity of imprisoning a human creature for life rather than mercifully kill him anesthetically, and if possible, without his knowing it. We can dispose of this phobia by pointing out to the abolitionists that a day's imprisonment is just as irrevocable as decapitation. If that does not silence them nothing will. (*Everybody's Political What's What?* 282)

They have not been silenced, for most are really concerned not with irrevocability but with what politicians, in cynically frank avowal of their dishonesty, call deniability. It is an old story. When Sophocles' Creon learned that his terrible decree had been violated, he declared that the culprit must be stoned to death. Then, faced with the prospect of inflicting this horror on his own niece, he chose the more cowardly course of having her entombed alive. This, he proclaimed, absolved the state of her death, on the theory, one supposes, that if she was foolish enough to starve to death, it was her affair. Such ruses fool only those who desperately want to be fooled.

Realism is hard, not because the mask it must pierce is so dense or opaque but because we find the face beneath unbearably hideous.

It is the face of responsibility.

II

A Guide to Art and Life

4

A Playwright's Progress

DRAMATIC REALISM

In April 1894 London critics had exuberant praise for a new play by a fledgling playwright; they were delighted by a hilarious, "fantastic, psychological extravaganza" (Archer, *Theatrical World* 109) and enormously amused by a "droll, fantastic farce" (Walkley 67). The ungrateful author attacked them for not realizing that he was a "realist playwright" and that play, *Arms and the Man*, an example of the strictest dramatic realism. His self-assessment was not taken seriously. Much has changed in the one hundred plus years since, but Shaw's claim to be a "realist playwright" is still not taken seriously. We grant him a better understanding of human nature and social conditions than did his contemporaries, and we recognize him as the greatest English language dramatist in several centuries, but "realist"? Yes, Shaw, we say, we now understand the point that you were making, that you understood the truth better than your critics and had a vastly better comprehension of character psychology, but we will not make the mistake of taking you literally. You may have come close occasionally, and you often used realism for your own ends, but you were never a thoroughgoing realist.

It is difficult to assess Shaw's claim to dramatic realism. Few literary terms prove more elusive when we attempt to trap them in neat, objective definitions. Most important for many people, Shaw shamelessly sprinkled his plays with incidents and actions that defy our commonsense notions of realism. Shaw loved to twit his critics, and there is a distinct bantering tone in "A Dramatic Realist to His Critics," his defense of the "strict realism" of *Arms and the Man*. Shaw's irrepressible clowning always allows us to take seriously that which we approve and dismiss the rest as an exaggeration or a joke. Still, he always insisted that his way of joking was to tell the absolute truth, and there are instances when he asserted his realism as a playwright without a perceptible twinkle in his eye.

When Shaw called himself a dramatic realist, he was using the term in a unique and unconventional way. It was a Shavian joke: for the truth is that Shaw's notion of what constitutes realistic drama is worthier of the term than its accepted meaning. It may be argued that Shaw's use of the term—no matter how sensible, appropriate, or logical—was idiosyncratic and thus invalid; language is necessarily conventional, as Saussure made clear, and even genius is not privileged. Humpty Dumpty was wrong: no individual can make a word mean whatever he wants it to mean. There is no answer to this argument; if you insist on the conventional (and thus legitimate) meaning of "realism," Shaw's dramatic works do not qualify; or rather, they meet the accepted standards up to a point and then fall short. Even the critics who think that some of Shaw's works are realistic do not agree about which plays those are. An idiosyncratic meaning can gain acceptance when three conditions are met: first, that it is a significant meaning that is presently unfitted with an accepted word; second, that it is reasonably close to an established usage; and third, that its variant use is made explicit in the context—that the "term" is "defined." As to the first condition, Shaw's version of realism not only lies at the heart of his dramatic method (although it is by no means the whole of it) but also was a lifelong way of seeing the world that pervaded his political, economic, religious, and philosophical ideas. "Realism," however it might be embellished with fantasy, imagination, or merely the unfamiliar, is the very core of everything that can be called Shavian. The second condition is also met, for as improbable as it may seem, Shavian realism has in practice much in common with the traditional literary theories, if not the practice, of Emile Zola and his like. Shaw keeps to the essentials and merely discards that which is untenable. Shaw failed the final condition; he did not make his meaning clear, but if we look closely and take Shaw seriously we can clarify the nature of Shavian dramatic realism.

This book is about Shaw's view of the world and the way that view dictated how he conducted his life, not an examination of his dramatic work. But his view was different from that of others, and consequently he had to develop his own style, his own form of dramatic art. That journey toward a distinctly Shavian dramaturgy illuminates the philosophy which guided it. What follows is intended to examine only the way the Shavian style developed, not to examine it in its entirety.

Illusionism Is Not Realism

Many impediments lie in the path of understanding the nature of literary realism, but one—the distinction between realism and naturalism—can be dispensed with quickly. Following the example of George Becker, I will treat "realism" and "naturalism" as essentially interchangeable terms. While in certain realms of discourse useful distinctions can be made between the two, they are essentially parts of a single movement. But the greatest obstacle to understanding genuine realism is the commonsense, or everyday, usage of the term. The word has acquired associations in its casual usage that produce contradiction and confusion in discussions of critical realism. When we use the term casually or impressionistically we compare what we see with the template of our biases. Commonsense realism is mere illusionism. The purpose of illusionism in art is not to direct our attention away from the work of art *as art* and focus it entirely on that which is being represented, as is often thought. When we marvel at a lifelike work of art we are delighted that our perception—normally so trustworthy—has been tricked. The aesthetic principle is the same as that of a magic show. We delight in the skill with which we are deceived.

A little reflection shows that this aesthetic conflicts with the aims of critical realism. Illusionistic techniques are appropriately applied to such things as settings and costumes when the aim is to show the physical determinants of human behavior. The mischief is created in the representation of morals, social institutions, and human motivation, which are the real concern of the critical realist, who wants to present unfamiliar, even shocking, truths about them. The illusionist presents the familiar and the expected: an image we will recognize. Thus he is apt to pander to prejudices and conventional stereotypes. That is essentially why a play like *The Second Mrs. Tanqueray* seemed a masterpiece of realism to most of its author's contemporaries. It does not seem so to many modern critics, but that is not because they are more clever or perceptive; they merely have different prejudices and cherish different stereotypes. The illusionist aesthetic necessarily flatters our preconceptions and is thus a barrier to the aims of the genuine realist. The illusionist does not show us something new, something we had not seen before; he shows us the familiar and the known in an unexpected setting.

When either Shaw or Ibsen is criticized for his lapses from realism, it is usually for a failure to provide a convincing illusion. Shaw was quite brazen about introducing the most amazing coincidences into his plays, but

Ibsen is also called to task for his use of the "contrivances" of the well-made play. Such objections are utterly irrelevant. Ibsen was no more interested than Shaw in creating superficial photographic illusions of life— *Candid Camera* realism. He was exploring consciences, desires, and the conflict of human wills. The revisionist criticism that seeks out the "contrivances" of the "well-made play" in the work of turn-of-the-century realists is fallacious as well as irrelevant because it is based on two dangerously erroneous assumptions. In the first place, all plays, like all other works of fiction, are contrived. They are consciously put together to create an effect or to convey a message or both. This is true even of the most extreme "slice-of-life" naturalists, who are often so intent on creating the illusion of reality that they sacrifice honest observation to popular prejudice—such as the assumption that the nastier and dirtier something appears the more real it must be. Second, well-made plays were not contrived to appear contrived: they were crafted to create the illusion of reality, an illusion fabricated from the expectations of the audience. They appear "contrived" to us because we do not share those expectations, but we should not imagine that whenever something in a play by Ibsen or Shaw reminds us that we are indeed in a theater, that we have discovered a flaw in their realism. If it is a flaw, it is a lapse in illusionism, something often incompatible with critical realism.

We need to suppress the temptation to apply the rule of commonsense realism to the plays of the realists, including Shaw, and to seek a more rigorous, as well as more appropriate, standard. The difficulty is that commonsense realism pervades our thinking about realism, and for good reasons. It is easy to slip from talking about the purposes of realism into discussions of its style, and when we think about a naturalistic style we are all too apt to think in illusionistic terms. So the confusion arises inevitably, in no small part out of the efforts of the most rigorously scientific realists themselves. Realism is first of all a way of viewing the world; it declares, like all serious artistic movements, that the function of art is to tell the truth, and it has definite ideas about the nature of that truth. So the heart of literary realism is a philosophy, but that philosophy must generate new artistic forms or styles. Unfortunately, the new illusionist style favored by the realists actually obscured the ends to which it was presumably only a means.

CONTRADICTIONS IN SCIENTIFIC REALISM

The source of the difficulty lies in two contradictions at the heart of the realist's artistic program. Emile Zola and other writers in the realistic movement rightly claimed kinship to earlier artists who had defied convention in an effort to expose the truth, but their program also offered something entirely new. Their innovations, as George Becker outlines them, were in three basic areas: philosophical premises, choice of subject matter, and technique. The second two were outgrowths of the first. Their premises were scientific, and their new paradigm for the proper function of art was the scientific experiment—or more precisely scientific methodology, for science developed similar techniques for study in the "field" where genuine experiment is not possible. The first contradiction arises from the attempt to apply techniques that have proved spectacularly productive in one field of endeavor to another in which they are irrelevant. Art is not science; specifically it is not the study and accumulation exclusively of facts, either "controlled" in the laboratory or methodically documented in the field. Art is not theory rigorously tested by fact but observation distilled through the intelligence and imagination of an artist. The paradigm breaks down in practice. Zola, who was not as extreme as he appears in his more emphatic remarks, conceded as much when he observed that "a work will never be more than a corner of nature seen through a temperament" (198).

The scientific paradigm was compelling to Zola and his followers because they were convinced that science was the only genuine path to the truth, and if art was not to condemn itself to oblivion or triviality it must capture the spirit and nature of science. Their mistake was not to limit themselves to presenting the *artistic interpretation* of truths discovered scientifically. But because they wanted to present the world revealed in case studies, they gave in to the temptation to make their works *look* like case studies and thus became purveyors of illusion. They then could be justly accused of presenting falsehoods as facts and violating their own principles.

Shaw did not make this mistake, but he sympathized with those who did. He declared that he, like Zola, sought a "really scientific natural history" as the basis of plays and novels (Pref. *Three Plays by Brieux* 1192). But even in his first, "unpleasant" plays, Shaw's method was distinctly different from that of Zola and his followers. When he dealt with slums and prostitution he showed us not the squalid life in the tenements and the degradation of the brothel but the comfortable life of those who profit by them. But he understood what Zola was doing and why he did it. Zola did not want to tell pretty stories:

> He wanted to tell the world the scientific truth about itself. His view was that if you were going to legislate for agricultural laborers, or deal with them or their business in any way, you had better know what they are really like; and in supplying you with the necessary information he did not tell you what you already knew, which included pretty nearly all that could be decorously mentioned, but what you did not know, which was that part of the truth that was tabooed. For the same reason, when he found a generation whose literary notions of Parisian cocotterie were founded on Marguerite Gauthier, he felt it to be a duty to show them Nana. And it was a very necessary thing to do. (Pref. *Three Plays by Brieux* 1192)

So Shaw had no sympathy with those who objected to the "nasty" concerns of the naturalists; the unpleasant truths are precisely those that must be exposed and proclaimed because their concealment only protects them. Evil cannot be fought unless it is faced. But the preoccupation with filth, he believed, became itself a convention or a fashion. "Their [Zola's and Ibsen's] imitators assumed that unmentionability was an end in itself— that to be decent was to be out of the movement" (1193). Shaw also had limited faith in the usefulness of looking exclusively at the putrid underside of society. Although necessary as an antidote to ignorance and illusion, it could also distort.

> The Real has always been a hard bird to catch. Plato did not succeed in getting it under his hat until he had divested it of everything that is real to the realists of noveldom to-day: these gentlemen are not Platonic realists. They do not seem to have got much further than an opinion that the romance of the drawing-room is less real than the romance of the kitchen, the romance of the kitchen than that of the slum, that of the slum than that of the sewer, and, generally, that reality is always in inverse proportion to self-control, education, health, and decency. ("Realism, Real and Unreal" 110)

Shaw was convinced that what often passed for realism was merely a romantic treatment of a sordid subject. One can see the difference between what is conventionally thought of as realistic and what Shaw imagined realism to be about when one compares *Mrs Warren's Profession* to Maupassant's novella *Yvette*. Realism should stimulate the mind, in Shaw's view, not stir the passions with a pungent mixture of sensuality, cynicism, and romantic sympathy: the romance of the tawdry brothel.

There is a further unfortunate tendency to make attractive the evils one should portray as repellent, for if a writer "takes a culpable prostitute for his heroine, he makes a heroine of a culpable prostitute; and no mechanical heaping of infamy and disease upon her in the third volume will quite despoil her of that glamour" (111). This is clearly not what the sincere naturalist (as opposed to the merely fashionable one) aims for; he professes to expose evils that they might be eliminated. Shaw differed from even the sincere naturalists in his skepticism that needed reform could ever really be effected in this way.

> The corruption of society to-day is caused by evils which can be remedied only by the aspiration of the masses toward better things and not by the shrinking of the classes from horror known to them only by clever descriptions. . . . When, on any definite issue, the apathy or selfishness of the classes stands in the way of needed reform, then have at their consciences by all means, without the very slightest regard for their "delicacy." But to persist in showing the classes repulsive pictures of evils which they are powerless to abolish, without ever striving to show the masses the better conditions which they have the power to make real as soon as they have the will, is shallow policy put forward as an excuse for coarse art. (111)

Here we approach the heart of Shaw's philosophical differences with more conventional realists. The realists' faith in heredity and environment led them to portray human beings as creations of circumstances, even to thinking of the most degraded specimens as somehow closer to nature and the ultimate truth about humanity (Becker 24). Reform was to be effected by changing their circumstances. For Shaw, any form of progress or evolution was dependent on the growth of human will. To the extent that that could be produced by sensitizing the consciences of the privileged, well and good, but a more urgent task is to awaken the souls of the exploited to desire better things. Shaw diverged from the naturalists at the same juncture where he parts with traditional socialists. Marx believed that the proletariat already burned with higher aspirations and the determination to achieve them. Shaw knew better, which is the point of Undershaft's message to his daughter. One cannot expect high aspirations and the courage to achieve them from people who have been systematically degraded. Shaw insisted that "the working-man can alter the present system if he chooses, whereas the capitalist cannot because the working-man will not let him" ("Illusions of Socialism" 418). So his message to millionaire philanthropists was that they should "create new needs: the old ones will take care of themselves" ("Socialism for Millionaires" 403). New needs are created by awakening human aspiration.

Perhaps this is why Shaw felt impotent in his chosen profession. The theater is not a particularly good tool for doing what he believed most needed doing: stirring the souls of people who were insensitive to the finer things of civilization—including its art. Poverty will end when those who suffer most from it determine to end it, but poverty has degraded their souls and destroyed their will. The only thing to be done about the poor is to relieve them of poverty, and that cannot be achieved with art. One may awaken the souls only of those whose bodies are not half-starved and brutalized: the comfortable classes who profit from exploitation of the poor. One way to do that is to shock their consciences with that terrible truth: the way of the "unpleasant plays." The method Shaw eventually chose attempted to awaken a respect for reality and the courage to face the truth without having it shoved violently in one's face. He was following the Chinese proverb that one can feed a man for a day by giving him a fish or feed him for life by teaching him how to fish. How well he succeeded is another matter; the task was formidable.

His biggest obstacles were those faced by Zola or anyone else attempting to promote unwelcome truths: to make the audience listen and think about what he had to say and to make them believe that it is indeed the truth. Shaw knew why Zola "wanted, not works of literary art, but stories he could believe in as records of things that really happen" (Pref. *Three Plays by Brieux* 1192). Prosaic as they may seem, they were necessary for his audience.

> If Zola had had a sense of humor, or a great artist's delight in playing with his ideas, his materials, and his readers, he would have become either as unreadable to the very people he came to wake up as Anatole France is, or as incredible as Victor Hugo was. He would also have incurred the mistrust and hatred of the majority of Frenchmen, who, like the majority of men of all nations, are not merely incapable of fine art, but resent it furiously. . . . What they like to read is the police intelligence, especially the murder cases and divorce cases. The invented murders and divorces of the novelists and playwrights do not satisfy them, because they cannot believe in them; and belief that the

horror or scandal actually occurred, that real people are shedding real blood and real tears, is indispensable to their enjoyment. (1190)

So Zola indulged in a particular kind of illusionism in order to reach his audience, but it meant that he had to add extraneous sensational elements to his fiction, even though such abnormalities were not part of his real business, which was to convey general, and genuinely scientific, truths. Shaw sought to reach a different audience, one whose views of the world were shaped by the playhouse. He naturally chose, as Martin Meisel abundantly demonstrated, to adapt the familiar forms and conventions of the contemporary theater. He still had to give his audiences the truth as he saw it and convince them it was indeed true. His first attempts were not fully satisfactory. Strindberg observed that whenever what Shaw called scientific natural history was simply poured into the old dramatic forms, "the new wine has burst the old bottles" (395). The development of a new form, sufficiently familiar to be recognized and enjoyed but robust enough to convey the strong new potion, meant the evolution of a distinctive Shavian style.

Shaw was thus sympathetic to the first of the contradictions that ensnared naturalism because he recognized that it arose from the need to make unpalatable truths pleasant or interesting enough to be swallowed. That Zola sought to achieve that end through a kind of illusionism that Shaw rather conspicuously avoided is important only if one makes the mistake of believing that illusions are the essence and purpose of realism. Zola's "police intelligence" illusionism and Shaw's theatricalism have the same purpose: to engage the audience. They are different sugarcoatings for the pill of realism.

The second contradiction concerns the true heart of realism as both Shaw and Zola understood it. George Becker points out that

the basic ideal of the movement was and is rigorous objectivity; in spite of this it was almost impossible not to take a position, at least implicitly, about man and his fate, particularly since the whole climate of thought in which realism flourished was one of scientism. As Arthur McDowall says, "Realism in art undoubtedly refers us back to a physical, existing reality," which is anterior to and independent of the individual mind. It is sceptical of . . . the events which escape the otherwise ineluctable laws of causality. It is this last term which is the key to the realist position: the universe is observably subject to physical causality; man as a part of the physical continuum is also subject to its laws, and any theory which asserts otherwise is wishful thinking. (34)

As Becker suggests, it is not possible to avoid this difficulty. Science itself is never completely objective, no matter how conscientiously it may strive toward that end. The business of science is not a matter of merely collecting facts but must be a constant interplay of fact and theory. Scientists and philosophers of science have increasingly acknowledged the importance of preconceived notions and unconscious assumptions in determining the direction of science. Preconceptions are even more unavoidable in the case of the artist, who must filter reality through imagination. Shaw's position avoids that weakness of the traditional realists because he acknowledged his subjective biases—his "will-to-believe"—while the realists imagined themselves as objective and utterly impartial observers. The most important difference between Shaw and Zola, however, is in their metaphysical assumptions. If one attempts to evaluate Zola and Shaw by their own criteria—as purveyors of truth, not creators of art—one cannot avoid the question, Which of the two metaphysical systems is most nearly true? Our immediate concern, however, is that different views of the truth produce different styles of artistic work.

Shavian Realism Is Super-Scientific Realism

Where Zola and his followers accepted the mechanistic determinism of scientism which insisted that every event in the universe—including human behavior—was produced by mechanical, physical law, Shaw saw will as an independent causal agent that also has the power to influence physical events. Mechanical causation is insufficient to explain everything that happens; where the living will comes into play, it is necessary to use teleological explanations to describe the universe adequately. Shaw the artist thus regarded human motivation and its consequences as his primary subject matter, while Zola chose to examine the environmental conditions he assumed were the ultimate causes of human behavior. This may be part of the reason why Shaw succeeded as a dramatist and Zola as a novelist: those forms may just be better suited to their respective visions of truth.

Shaw still had much in common with the traditional realists, despite their essential philosophical difference and the divergence in style it produced. Objecting to critics who saw the characters in *Candida* as simple embodiments of ideas, he told Augustin Hamon:

My plays are studies in the natural history of mankind: I am simply a dramatic Buffon or St Hilaire. When you read Buffon's description of the Horse you do not begin to ask whether Buffon regarded the Horse as a triumph of speed, or a triumph of traction power, or a triumph of fidelity; you understand that he is simply trying to shew you what sort of animal a horse is. Well, in Candida I am simply trying to shew you the sort of animal the people in Candida are. I take a great interest in animals of that sort, just as Buffon did in animals in general; and I write for the gratification of people who share my interest. (*Collected Letters* 2:668)

This passage shows his differences as well as his similarities, for while he presents himself as a "naturalist," his first concern is with human "animals" in and of themselves, while a Zola would be at least as interested in the environmental forces that (presumably) made them what they are. The assumptions that an artist brings to his work must affect his perceptions of the objects of his study. As Zola said, "A work of art will never be more than a corner of life seen through a temperament" (198). When Shaw looked at the sort of "animal the people in Candida are," he saw not puppets helplessly shaped by a relentlessly mechanistic universe but agents of something mysterious called a "will," which obeys its own rules and shapes its surroundings at least as much as the environment shapes will. He saw manifestations of the Life Force, imperfect but divine.

Slice-of-Life

Shaw even praised the technique of the "slice-of-life," by which he meant the absence of neat, satisfying endings, and not the sort of fiction that pretends to exhibit to the public a kind of arbitrary "core sample" of life as it is lived. For Shaw, "slice-of-life" meant plays without either "catastrophes" or endings. By "catastrophe" he meant the sort of sensational abnormality familiar to fans of crime stories. The "endings" were the traditional weddings and slaughters: "The moment the dramatist gives up accidents and catastrophes, and takes 'slices of life' as his material, he finds himself committed to plays that have no endings. The curtain no longer comes down on a hero slain or married: it comes down when the audience has seen enough of the life presented to it to draw the moral, and must either leave the theatre or miss its last train" (Pref. *Three Plays by Brieux* 1194). On more than one occasion Shaw took Ibsen to task for concluding his plays with corpses. "The tragedy of Hedda in real life is not that she com-

mits suicide but that she continues to live" (1193). Much of Shaw's admiration for Chekhov was prompted by the Russian's ability to depict this
sort of ridiculously pathetic tragedy. When Shaw said that "the tragedy of
modern life is that nothing happens, and that the resultant dulness does
not kill" he might well have been describing Chekhov, although at the time
he was not acquainted with the Russian master (1194). Later, Shaw declared that "everything we write in England seems sawdust after Tchekov
and the rest of them [the Russians]" (Collected Letters 3:439). Shaw objected to the conventional happy ending as much as to the tragic one, and
his own comic endings, even when they might appear conventional, leave
something unresolved.

One reason for this objection to "endings" again shows his differences
with conventional realists. The curtain came down, he said, when the audience had seen enough "to draw the moral"—or in other words, when they
had heard the conclusion of the argument. An "interpreter of life," as he
insisted a dramatist must be, is someone who presents a case, even if the
argument is in the form of an imaginative recreation of living people in
real situations. "There is only one way of dramatizing an idea; and that is
by putting on the stage a human being possessed by that idea, yet none the
less a human being with all the human impulses which make him akin and
therefore interesting to us" (Perfect Wagnerite 28). The ideas that Shaw
wished to dramatize, however optimistic they might be, invariably contained the urgent message that things are not acceptable as they are and
must be changed; the point of the traditional ending, whether tragic or
comic, was to leave the audience satisfied with the way things are. He was
opposed to "endings," in the traditional sense, because they would deny
the truth of his message. In practice he often came close to a conventional
comic ending but only rarely approached the expectations the audience
had of tragedy, not merely because of his personal inclination to comedy
but as an expression of his philosophical outlook as well. He despaired of
the cynical pessimism which insisted that clear vision necessarily saw the
world as an irredeemable cesspool, always maintaining that "I see plenty
of good in the world working itself out as fast as the idealists will allow it"
(Pref. Pleasant Plays 1:385). He urged only that honest optimism replace
idealistic romantic conventions. Nowhere is the difference between the
Shavian view and the conventional view clearer than in the battle between
Shaw and the traditionalists over the ending of Pygmalion. To a realist, the
ending provided by Shaw is a happy ending—the only one possible—and
that engineered for Gabriel Pascal's film version of the play is a recipe for

disaster and an utter defeat for Eliza as a human being. In Shaw's ending Eliza becomes a strong, self-respecting, and admirable person; in Pascal's she is reduced to choosing perpetual slavery to a bad-tempered man who will always treat her poorly, not because he is mean or cruel but only because he is thoughtless and self-absorbed. To see this is to understand what Shaw meant by "learning to respect reality" (Pref. *Pleasant Plays* 1:385).

The Tragic Fallacy

There are, however, sound philosophical reasons for Shaw to shun the *tragic* ending. There are two principal views of the "meaning" of the tragic ending (apart from the "meaning" of tragedy as a whole, which is rather more complex). One is that it encapsulates a "tragic view" of life, a view both pessimistic and resigned. Shaw's discussion of tragedy generally reflects this view. The other, and older, conception of the tragic denouement is that it represents the expiation of a moral flaw in an otherwise good character. This notion naturally, if illogically, gets mixed up with the concept of a saint's martyrdom. It is as if we in the audience felt that if one can balance one's moral ledger by discharging debts with pain, a surplus of suffering will give us a positive balance, even to earning sainthood when the agony is great enough. Two notions to which Shaw's philosophy is most opposed are hopeless despair and retributive justice. Most people think that despair and expiation are concepts shunned by the weak and embraced by the tough-minded; Shaw saw them as debilitating and intoxicating drugs that shield weak consciences from responsibility. To despair is to declare that there is nothing to be done and the spurious quality of a conscience redeemed by pain rather than good works is obvious. Shaw's comic endings are conclusive in that they finish up the action of the play; they are happy (usually) in that they show hope for the future; and they are open-ended in insisting on the responsibility of the characters to realize that hope. Every such ending, in other words, is a beginning. "Happily ever after" is an opium dream, a coward's way of obtaining the escape of death without its terror.

DRAMATIC REALISM AND MORAL EQUALITY

Shaw agreed with the techniques of traditional realists insofar as he agreed with their view of reality. The core of his dramatic realism, however, seems strange at first to anyone used to thinking of Zola and Maupassant as representing the epitome of realism. Shaw's realism is rooted in his belief in moral equality, the logical result of seeing that moral epithets are only distorting lenses with which we obscure our vision of real human beings. He equated the "inevitable return to nature" of all good literary art with the elimination of heroes and villains (*Quintessence* 214). He summed up the defense of his realism in *Arms and the Man* by declaring that "the whole novelty" of the play "lies in the fact that it is void of malice to my fellow creatures, and laboriously exact as to all essential facts" ("Dramatic Realist" 339). In the same vein, he insisted in a letter to Archer that his "whole secret is that I have got clean through the old categories of good & evil, and no longer use them even for dramatic effect." He implies that this makes him more a realist than Ibsen, who, he says, "is by old habit a pessimist" (*Collected Letters* 1:427). This notion is most eloquently expressed when he lectures audiences on how to understand the characters of the new drama: "When you have called Mrs Alving an emancipated woman or an unprincipled one, Alving a debauchee or a victim of society, Nora a fearless and noble-hearted woman or a shocking little liar and an unnatural mother, Helmer a selfish hound or a model husband and father, according to your bias, you have said something which is at once true and false, and in both cases perfectly idle" (*Quintessence* 198). For Shaw, this is the core and essence of dramatic realism. A painter with astigmatism will produce distorted works of art, and a playwright who sees people as "selfish hounds" or "model husbands" will produce distorted characters and thus unrealistic plays. The dramatist—and the actor—must create the part "from its own point of view" (*Drama Observed* 2:488). When you start out with judgments you set a dark glass of moralism between you and your subject which will prevent an honest depiction. Shaw was right to believe that the fact that "with reasonably sound specimens, the more intimately I know people the better I like them" is what allowed him to be a realistic dramatist because the opposite inclination is what leads one to prefer "stage monsters—walking catalogues of the systematised virtues— to his own species" ("Dramatic Realist" 326). Such monsters might as well be catalogs of vices, which is the point of Shaw's criticism of Sir Arthur Wing Pinero in his oft-quoted observation about *The Second Mrs. Tanqueray:* "The moment the point is reached at which the comparatively common gift of 'an eye for character' has to be supplemented by the higher dramatic gift of sympathy with character—of the power of seeing the world from the point of view of others instead of merely describing or judging them from one's own point of view in terms of the conventional systems of morals, Mr Pinero breaks down" (*Drama Observed* 1:271).

Shaw is not accusing Pinero, who was unquestionably talented at painting what he saw, of being an unskilled observer, and the fact that his audiences generally wore lenses of the same moral tint as his meant that his reputation for faithful portrayal was—as far as it went—perfectly justified. Shaw admits this: "Mr. Pinero . . . is . . . simply an adroit describer of people as the ordinary man sees and judges them" (272). The reason Shaw's characters still seem vivid and alive after nearly one hundred years and Pinero's (by and large) do not is simply because we have changed the color of our lenses (not, alas, that we have dispensed with them). The advantage of portraying characters from their own point of view is not that you prevent the audience from seeing them through spectacles of conventional ideas, for you cannot stop them. You might provide details that will be difficult to fit into preconceived notions and even provoke some change in attitudes. You can certainly avoid flattering conventional prejudices. Ultimately people will observe your characters through the same moral eyeglasses as they do real people but only if you have presented them as real people. If you have designed them for a particular style of lens, they will appear false when the style changes, even though for the moment the average person will declare them to be more accurate depictions than those painted without distortions at all.

To portray a character from her own point of view is not the same as to show her in the kind of flattering setting and dressed in the self-justifying moral garments she might herself have chosen for a formal portrait. You must observe her carefully and paint what you see rather than how you feel about what you see. You must also ask *why* she does what she does but must never couch the answer in moralistic terms. The answer to "Why did she leave her husband?" cannot be "Because she is a faithless wretch" (or, for that matter, "fearless idealist"). The scientific realist objects that to delve into personal motivation is to go beyond what can actually be observed onto the subjective grounds of interpretation; Shaw answers that no artist can avoid interpreting according to his understanding and assumptions and that it cannot be helped in any case, for the spring of human action lies in human motivation.

Realism and the Higher Type

Shaw's concern with motivation explains another difference between him and the realists of Zola's school. Becker claims that realism "seems to contain a kind of implicit Benthamite assumption that the life lived by the greatest number is somehow the most real" and quotes Maupassant as asserting a writer's obligation to "always incline to the mean, to the general rule" (25). The naturalists gravitated to the lowest common human denominator because that brought them, they thought, "nearer to nature and the savage state" (24). Shaw sought his subjects among the more intelligent, witty, articulate, and creative specimens of humankind. One of his reasons was a sound naturalistic one: he was painting the people he knew. His portraits were drawn from nature, and he had the good fortune to know intimately many fascinating and exceptional people (*Collected Letters* 2:34). But the more profound reason is that Shaw saw the higher type, not the lower, as closer to the heart of nature. Healthy, fully nourished souls are closer to the truth about the human spirit than are brutalized and degraded specimens. Also, since Shaw was concerned with the springs of human behavior, *seen from the point of view of the subject,* it helped to choose subjects who were particularly articulate.

We thus come to another point of divergence from conventional realism. In his early years as a playwright, Shaw proclaimed his realism because his audiences were bewildered by the attempt to "substitute natural history for conventional ethics and romantic logic," but he knew that by the time they became familiar with the novelty of real characters, they would also see his "stage tricks" and "stage puppets" for what they were (Pref. *Plays for Puritans* 2:47). Two years after his defense of the realism of *Arms and the Man,* he made a distinction between the first three "unpleasant" plays, which "were what people call realistic," and the following four "pleasant" plays, which "are not 'realistic' plays" (*Collected Letters* 1:632). The phrasing and the quotation marks around the second "realistic" suggest that his own view of realism was different from the conventional one. In later years he was more forthright, confessing that he had never "been what you call a representationalist or realist. I was always in the classic tradition, recognizing that stage characters must be endowed by the author with a conscious self-knowledge and power of expression, and . . . a freedom from inhibitions, which in real life would make them monsters of genius. It is the power to do this that differentiates me (or Shakespear) from a gramophone and a camera" (*Shaw on Theatre* 185). In the same vein he claimed that "it is the business of the stage to make its figures more intelligible to themselves than they would be in real life; for by no other means can they be made intelligible to the audience" (Pref. *Saint Joan* 6:73). He once referred to his "practice of making my characters say not what in real life they could never bring themselves to say, even if they understood themselves clearly enough, but the naked soul truth, quite ob-

jectively and scientifically presented, thus combining the extreme of un-
naturalness with the deepest attainable naturalness" (Nicoll 202–3). For
Shaw, the truth, "objectively and scientifically presented," is not the superficial image captured by a camera but something deeper.

Realistic Ends and Realistic Means

It is hardly surprising that Shaw was not doctrinaire about realism, for
doctrinaire attitudes are a form of idealism. Like other self-styled realists,
he rejected the illusions of romanticism, proposing, like them, to substitute the "objectively and scientifically presented" truth. The truth, for
Shaw and for them, was determined by observation unobscured by judgment. The facts must be faced before they can be acted upon. The *means*
used to convey that truth to an audience are an entirely different thing.
While Shaw recognized that Zola's attempts to create a documentary illusion, a sense of observing an actual slice of life, could be useful to certain
realists, he never lost sight of the real goal. He never made the mistake,
common even among those who should know better, of confusing illusionistic style with realistic substance. The serious writer is always an interpreter of life who often must sacrifice surface verisimilitude to deeper
truths. This is particularly true of the theater, which places severe constraints on those who wish to probe deeply but which is by nature tolerant
of improbabilities. For Shaw, "absurdity is the one thing that does not matter on the stage, provided it is not psychological absurdity" (*Drama Observed* 2:753). Shaw made no attempts to disguise his breaches of verisimilitude. His job was to expose truths that might ordinarily remain buried.
The coincidence that has the holder of a mortgage on slum property propose to the daughter of the slumlord, all the while ignorant of the nature of
the real estate from which his income is derived, would be too fantastic to
be tolerated if the purpose were to produce an illusion of life as most
people live it. Shaw is obviously after a more profound reality, and the
contrivances he uses to expose it are nakedly revealed. The real mark of the
well-made play was not coincidence but the tricks playwrights used to seduce the audience into believing that such contrivances were natural and
inevitable. Shaw thought such sleight of hand not only dishonest but unnecessary: "Half the explanations and contrivances with which [melo-
dramatists] burden their pieces are superfluous attempts to persuade the
audience to accept as reasonably brought about, situations which it is perfectly ready to accept without any bringing about whatever" (*Drama Observed* 2:560).

Dramatic Techniques

It is not enough just to dismiss conventional, or traditional, techniques. A new artistic vision requires a new method of presentation—new techniques. Shaw experimented considerably before arriving at a distinctly Shavian mode, a style optimally suited to his particular perspective: an aesthetic of Shavian realism to match the realism of Shavian vision. His difficulty was in large part that his picture of the world was so unusual, so foreign to anything his audience expected, that he could not merely present it as he saw it, for they would insist on trying to twist it into something familiar, something they could understand. Failing to do this, they were merely shocked or annoyed. The evolution of Shaw's distinct style was driven by his various attempts, first to reach his public—to have his plays produced or published—and second truly to communicate with them once he had their attention.

At least three distinct yarns are woven into the fabric of Shaw's particular dramatic technique, from the beginning of its evolution to it most mature form. First is his use of traditional theatrical forms and conventions, second his insistence that his characters be "real" people shown from their own point of view, and third the belief that a dramatist must be an "interpreter of life," not merely a recording machine. The second two are the pillars of his dramatic realism and grow directly out of his view of the world. The first is not our major concern, but a few words are necessary to clarify its relation to the essentials of the Shavian dramatic method. A serious artist conveys a vision of the truth. The style of such an artist is not an aesthetic end in itself but a means to a philosophical end. Methods are always shaped by purposes. When Shaw used popular theatrical conventions, he did so exactly as far as it suited his purposes. Whenever the popular forms conveyed a vision different from his, he either abandoned or subverted them. That is why he cheerfully admitted using the old-fashioned tricks of comedy and melodrama but strenuously objected to any suggestion that he allied himself to the well-made play.

The Well-Made Play

The well-made play is not defined by the various tricks it uses, for most of these go back at least to Plautus and have been brazenly exploited by such certified dramatic geniuses as Shakespeare and Molière. The well-made play represents something foreign to genius: a particular aesthetic, the expression of a petty worldview that posits economy and respectability as supreme if not sole virtues. The well-made play is defined by an aesthetic of obsessive tidiness.[1] The well-made play is always about keeping the lid on things, about keeping drawers closed and doors locked. Its most notorious feature was the substitution of the logic of economy for that of natural probability and human psychology. Nothing must be introduced that is not used. If a gun is exhibited, Chekhov said, it must be fired (Magarshack 45). There is nothing whatever wrong with a dramatist's introducing a gun early which is used later; the fault lies with an aesthetic that accepts such a sequence as logical causation *in lieu of* real psychology and natural probability. If there were no better reason for Hedda Gabler's suicide than the fact that one of the two dueling pistols introduced in the first act had not yet been fired, no one would have heard of Ibsen's play today. As it is, the assertion that Ibsen's handling of the dueling pistols was a trick borrowed from the well-made play is nearly as insignificant as true.

The aesthetic of the well-made play is introduced in the plays of both Ibsen and Shaw only to be subverted. Shaw strongly objected to plays that were "constructed." His preference for an organic development based on human psychology was not just a function of his superior aesthetic sense; the artificial, fabricated quality of the well-made play was essential to its viewpoint, a view of the world directly counter to the one Shaw wished to present. The point of the well-made play is not that it is without human psychology and passion but that the passion is controlled, wrapped up, and contained. It was deliberately dishonest. The well-made play is the perfect expression of the repressed psychology of bourgeois respectability. It titillates the audience by first exposing its secret lusts and repressed terrors and then tightly locking them up again. The scaffolding of dramatic construction was always visible, not because the playwrights were inept (as it seems to us) but to reassure the audience: the bottle is always there so that the genie of lust and disorder may be made to return to it. The well-made play is like a magician's box with many doors and sliding panels; what it contains is titillating and terrifying. The magician-playwright shows glimpses of the seductive monster within, even letting it appear to escape from time to time, but always locks it up tightly in the end. This is why dramatists like Ibsen and Shaw were so furiously opposed to the well-made play: it satisfied its audience exactly to the degree that it evaded those problems which Shaw and Ibsen wished honestly to confront.

Ibsen uses the well-made play more distinctively than Shaw. He shows us the box and all of its doors and reveals the monster within, but instead of locking it up, he finally opens it all up and lets the ogre out. The dramatic mechanism, which had been virtually an end in itself, becomes in Ibsen's hands a metaphor for the "whited sepulcher," the facade of artificial respectability hiding a diseased society. In other words, well-made construction in its traditional manifestation represented the successful repression of disorder by the restraints of bourgeois respectability, while Ibsen's subversion of it exposed it as a middle-class mask of respectability covering a foul disease.

In the running dispute between Archer and Shaw about the value of "construction" in drama, Archer seems most annoyed by Shaw's insistence that Ibsen (to say nothing of Shakespeare, Sophocles, and Molière) was in the Shavian camp rather than that of the constructors. For Archer the difference between "good" (that is, "crafted") drama and the "amorphous" kind Shaw produced was the difference between a cat and a jellyfish; Shaw responded that the difference was that between a dead cat and a live one (*Collected Letters* 3:836–37). Shaw fully recognized Ibsen's craft (*Collected Letters* 3:833); he merely insisted that what is important in Ibsen resembles Shaw more than Sardou. "Ibsen's method was the vital method, not the mechanical one" (*Collected Letters* 3:837). The portrayal of real people coming to grips with real problems, not the cleverness of plot assemblage, makes Ibsen's plays live. The structure that matters is that produced by the natural unfolding of the action.

Uncertain Dramatic Beginnings: *Widowers' Houses*

Shaw's technique differs from Ibsen's to the extent that his point of view is different. Where Ibsen, the "pessimist" by "old habit" (*Collected Letters* 1:427), contrasts the painted mask with the decayed face, Shaw's more positive view is that the mask is unnecessary if only we can learn to respect reality: expose the pallid face to fresh air and sunshine and it will become robust and healthy. Shaw's initial efforts as a playwright were in the vein of Ibsen and Zola to the extent that he wished to expose social evils so that they might be corrected. The difference in his way of seeing those evils necessitated a different way of presenting them, a new dramatic technique that was not easy to develop. On the one hand, it was simple for Shaw, with his realist's vision, to see that illusionism is irrelevant to naturalism and that Zolaism could become a superstition when it came to believe that ugliness is more real than beauty and police reporting more natural than drawing-room conversation. On the other hand, it was more difficult to find the aesthetic means to embody his own version of the truth. From a certain point of view, Shaw's first four plays were failures. I do not mean they are bad plays; on the contrary, their virtues are manifest and many. The characterization is vivid and honest (as it is in his novels), the action develops honestly from the interplay of character and circumstance, and considerable wit is displayed in playing off honest situations and real people against the conventions and stereotypical expectations of contemporary theater. The plays failed from *Shaw's* point of view because they were unable to shatter the idealist eyeglasses of their audiences sufficiently to let them actually see the real people in real situations that he had offered. Shaw's attempts to get past the blinding idealism of his audience became the search for a definitive Shavian style (always only a means to an end) that emerged finally with *Candida*.

His first play, *Widowers' Houses,* is the most artless in this respect (although I maintain that it is a better play than most critics imagine). The dialogue provoked by its production between Shaw and his critics is revealing. Shaw merely dismissed attacks on his "craftsmanship" or his "artistry." From our perspective they certainly seem as silly and beside the point as Shaw must have thought them, but the assaults on his characterization may have been more important to him. At least he took considerable effort to answer these attacks.[2] Archer's comments are especially illuminating, first because his reactions are fairly typical, and second because he is both lucid in expounding them and adroit in anticipating Shaw's rebuttals. Much of the criticism assumes that the point of the piece is a satirical attack on the viciousness and inhuman cupidity of the middle class. One critic (quoted by Shaw) gives the tenor of the rest: "The mere word 'mortgage' suffices to turn hero into rascal. Mr Shaw will say that is his point—scratch a middle-class hero and you find a rascal" ("Author to Dramatic Critics" 214). That is not Shaw's point, and Archer knew it. He too thought the characters to be uniformly vicious, but he understood that it was not in Shaw's interest to make them so: "Mr Shaw would only laugh if I called it bad art; so let me say, what is equally true, that it is exceedingly bad argument. You cannot effectively satirise a class by holding up to odium a grotesquely exceptional case" (Evans 51–52). Shaw agreed entirely with that last statement: "I certainly had no intention of spoiling the moral of my play by making the characters at all singular" ("Author to Dramatic Critics" 215). He clearly did not think they *were* singular, for he had drawn them from life. But as an artist who wished to reach the public, he had to address the fact that his audience generally found them not merely singular but singularly unpleasant. Worse, this was as true of his

supporters as of his detractors. His opponents were "unconscious pessimists" who sought refuge in the pleasant lies of the stage because they
could not bear to face reality. His supporters cheered him on, urging him to

> "tear the mask of respectability from the smug bourgeois, and show
> the liar, the thief, the coward, the libertine beneath."
>
> Now to me, as a realist playwright, the applause of the conscious
> hardy pessimist is more exasperating than the abuse of the uncon-
> scious, fearful one. I am not a pessimist at all. ("Dramatic Realist"
> 325)

As Shaw saw it, his job "as a realist playwright" was to make people face
the truth and *know that they have both the power and the responsibility
to change it if they find it distasteful;* it was not to throw stones at the
middle class and urge his public to join in. If we keep this in mind, we see
that the criticism of *Widowers' Houses* may have struck deeper than Shaw
was willing to admit. If the public could see nothing but the depiction of
egregious scoundrelism, they missed the essential point. A focal point of
the discussion, both in the attack of the critics and Shaw's response to
them, was the character of Blanche. Her undisciplined ill temper, Archer
realized, was not the product of ineptitude in an inexperienced dramatist;
Shaw clearly intended to make her what she is. But Archer could see no
reason for it. Why, he asked, "should he have made Blanche a vixen at all?
It is all very well to steer clear of the ordinary sympathetic heroine, but
why rush to the opposite extreme?" (Evans 51). If we ignore the tone of
offended idealism, this is a valid question. Shaw's rejoinder was simply
that he "confesses to having jilted *the* ideal lady for *a* real one" (Shaw's
emphasis) (Pref. *Widowers' Houses* 680). That explanation is insufficient
because it does not say why this *particular* real lady was chosen to be a
part of this particular dramatic composition. A conventional realist might
reply that he had seen such people in such a setting and chose to depict the
truth as he actually saw it. We get a sense of this when Shaw defends
his portrait of Blanche by saying that we "want a theatre for people . . .
who have some real sense that women are human beings just like men,
only worse brought up, and consequently worse behaved" (681), but Shaw
never uses the standard defense of the traditional realist: that "I paint only
what I see before me, without comment or interpretation." He always contended that the dramatist should be an interpreter of life. Shortly before he
had admitted to having "recklessly sacrificed realism to dramatic effect in
the machinery of the play" (679).

In calling the first three plays "unpleasant" he was describing his own feeling about them as much as that of the public, confessing that "the mere perusal of [them] induces loathing in every person, including myself, in whom the theatrical instinct flourishes in its integrity" (*Drama Observed* 2:694). Even in his vigorous defense of *Widowers' Houses* he makes this "reservation":

> It is saturated with the vulgarity of the life it represents: the people do not speak nobly, live gracefully, or sincerely face their own position: the author is not giving expression in pleasant fancies to the underlying beauty and romance of happy life, but dragging up to the smooth surface of "respectability" a handful of the slime and foulness of its polluted bed. . . . I offer it as my own criticism of the author of Widowers' Houses that the disillusion which makes all great dramatic poets tragic has here made him only derisive. (670–71)

The key to Shaw's characterization in his first play lies in the phrase "the people do not . . . sincerely face their own position." There is something intrinsically ugly about seeing people evade responsibility, people engaged in what we would now call "denial." The traits that so annoy critics about the persons of this drama are different ways of evading reality. Blanche's sharp temper as well as Trench's passive resignation are, in some sense, both symptom and cause of their denial. Blanche, brought up to be a "lady," reacts with ladylike revulsion to the filth of poverty and explodes with anger at any suggestion that it might have anything to do with her. Trench merely sulks. He is too honest and too conscientious to take refuge in the facile hypocrisy of his friend Cokane and too unimaginative to see a way out. Shaw's point (as valid today as then) is that this is the way perfectly ordinary people do behave.

Shaw's difficulty, then, was to reconcile this kind of unflinching realism with his desire to make his public understand "that my attacks are directed against themselves, not against my stage figures" (Pref. *Unpleasant Plays* 1:34). Unfortunately, even the expressions he used here ("handful of the slime and foulness of its polluted bed") help confirm the interpretation of the "hardy pessimists" that Shaw was to find so exasperating later. He did not want to abuse or assault his audience, for he knew that you do not make people better by verbal attacks any more than by physical ones; you make them worse. He wanted to open their eyes and awaken their consciences. You do that only if you assume that they have consciences to rouse.

Shaw made only two more stabs at the kind of realism that is intent on exposing ugly truths. Perhaps he found the task to have been too much, for he wanted to show intolerable situations while insisting to the audience that the characters who do tolerate them are no different from themselves. He did not want to tint his characters with an artificial stage glamour, nor did he wish to vilify them. He wanted to show them accepting the unacceptable, yet he wished members of the public to see themselves on the stage and identify with these ordinary people: ordinary people acquiescing in (and thus collaborating with) infamous activity. Above all, he wanted the public to see that the infamy need not be accepted. This is clearly not a simple task.

Successfully Unpleasant Realism: *Mrs. Warren's Profession*

He came closest to actually achieving this stupendous goal in *Mrs. Warren's Profession*. The last of Shaw's unpleasantly realistic plays, it best shows how Shaw differed from the traditional realists when he was working their vein. The play was inspired in some part by *Yvette*, a novella by Maupassant. Whether or not Shaw actually read the book, it provides an interesting comparison; the similarities are so strong that they make the contrasts striking. Shaw admitted only that Janet Achurch had told him the story, which he dismissed as "ultra-romantic," and that he said he would "work out the real truth about that mother some day" ("Mr. Shaw's Method and Secret" 440). His characterization of the work as "ultra-romantic" suggests to some that he either did not in fact read it or that he misunderstood its tone (Bullough 344). In the conventional sense, the story as Maupassant tells it is realistic, but there are reasons, I believe, to think that Shaw would see it as highly romantic even if he did read it.

The tone is entirely different from anything Shaw would ever write. Yvette is a young woman who has been raised in a brothel run by her mother, yet she has somehow avoided being contaminated with knowledge either of her mother's profession or of the nature of the house. She attracts the attention of a man-about-town who finds her irresistible. He is intrigued by the way she combines a reckless, brazen manner with what at times seems extreme innocence or naïveté. He pursues her and she teases him. Finally, when he believes he is about to make his conquest, it appears that she expected a proposal of marriage. His amazed reaction is the turning point that leads her to discover the truth. She then discovers her mother with a lover and later confronts her with the discovery. The mother defends herself much as Mrs. Warren does, although more snappishly than thoroughly. Yvette then tries but fails to commit suicide, reviving in the arms of her suitor and begging him to love her. He discreetly destroys the note she had left explaining that she wished to die rather than become a courtesan.

The "realism" of the piece is produced by a counterpoint between the allure of a charged erotic atmosphere and the cynical revelation of its tawdry nature. Until the pivotal point in the story, the viewpoint is strictly masculine: the women are described entirely as objects of desire. The mother is careless and luxurious:

> She was one of those women who were created to love and to be loved. From the lowest of origins, she had risen through love, making it a profession almost without knowing it; acting on instinct, with an inborn talent, she accepted money as she did kisses, naturally, indiscriminately, using her remarkable instinct in a simple and unreasoning manner as do beasts, made clever by the exigencies of their existence. (73)[3]

There is little here, objectively speaking, that might not be said of Mrs. Warren, but Shaw tries to show us the woman from her own point of view whereas Yvette's mother is seen entirely from without. Shaw's brothel keeper is amiable and vulgar: "She may be a good sort; but she's a bad lot, a very bad lot," as Frank so brightly puts it. Yvette's mother (who goes under the name of the Marquise Obardi) is demeaned and glamorized at the same time. She is a sensual animal, soiled but exciting. Yvette, in the first part of the story is an entrancing enigma, a tantalizing and elusive prey, brightly, pertly, and suggestively leading her pursuer on. Only when he emphatically rejects the possibility of marriage between them are we suddenly made privy to her own thoughts. Subsequently she appears as a naive child whose mind has been shaped by romantic novels and whose manners were picked up thoughtlessly from her surroundings. She is a bewildered, pathetic victim. Her attempted suicide by chloroform draws her into a confused and desperate dream from which she emerges in a passive and total acceptance of the life that fate has given her. We know that her lover, to whom she has now submitted utterly, will leave her just as he would any whore.

Maupassant's technique is to offer a sensual and glamorously unrestrained world which he continuously undercuts by revealing its nasty, repellent, and cynical side. Shaw avoids either extreme. The world he presents is distinctly prosaic and ordinary except that a number of the characters happen to be involved, in one way or another, in the business of prostitution. Unlike Maupassant's Obardi, who makes money and love by instinct, like an animal, Mrs. Warren treats her business as if it were a shoe shop. Yvette wants marriage and is denied it; Vivie is offered marriage and rejects it in disgust. Maupassant's story ends with a woman helplessly submissive in the arms of a worthless man; Shaw's play concludes with the young woman coolly dispensing with a worthless man together with love, romance, and filial obligation as she starts out on her independent way. Shaw avoids making "a heroine of a culpable prostitute" by presenting the prostitute as frowsy and distinctly unseductive. He carefully makes it clear that her vulgarity is not a diagnostic trait of her profession, for Mrs. Warren has a sister, also a former prostitute, whose ladylike ways have won respect for her in a cathedral town.

The Hypocrite in Spite of Herself

Archer had complained of the character drawing in Shaw's first play that it is not realistic to place naked souls onstage. People in real life, he objected, take as much trouble to hide their souls as their bodies (Evans 52). To show the whole truth, he felt, one must display the raiment of hypocrisy while also revealing the contours of the body beneath. Presumably Archer believed that Pinero had achieved such a portrait of transparency in Paula Tanqueray, but simply to show the contrast between the profession of conventional ideals and their actual violation implies acceptance of the ideals, and Shaw wanted to transcend the moralist point of view entirely. He did not want to expose how people fail to live up to conventional ideals; he was trying to paint people "from their own point of view," which is to say from the point of view of their own genuine motivations. But the sort of people he was portraying in the unpleasant plays are self-deceiving, rather than cynical, hypocrites; they do not themselves acknowledge "their own point of view" in the sense that Shaw meant the phrase. How, then, can one portray them honestly without falling into the trap of accepting the moralistic judgments of an idealistic society? Can one paint them honestly from their own perspective when they themselves accept the falsifying judgments of society?

Shaw avoids the trap in *Mrs. Warren's Profession* by *telling* us about the successful hypocrisy of sister Liz in her cathedral town and *showing* us the apparently frank Mrs. Warren, who blurts out the truth, not because she is honest but because her hypocrisy lacks art. In the end we see that she too "lived one life and believed in another" (1:355). That is the point of the final scene between Vivie and her mother. In their first confrontation Mrs. Warren plays the conventional mother, then, under her daughter's cool and implacable onslaught, she breaks down to reveal her true self. Of course, when she attempts to resume her hypocritical pose her daughter sees through it.

We see Shaw's progress toward his own form of realism most clearly in the character of Vivie. She is markedly different, not only from Maupassant's Yvette but from Blanche in *Widowers' Houses*. Vivie and Blanche were both raised as "ladies" and protected from the sordid circumstances that shaped their parents lives, but Vivie has a self-awareness of her advantages of which Blanche is incapable. She is superior in Shaw's eyes, both to Blanche and to her mother, because she condemns her mother only for living one life and believing in another. Where Blanche repudiates the poverty from which her father sprang in a fit of ill-tempered denial, Vivie coolly accepts her mother for what she is, without judgment, and without becoming sentimentally blinded to the fact that she has indeed been raised to be too good for her mother's life.

That the personalities of Shaw's two young women differ is obvious; what is significant is that the character of Vivie better serves Shaw's dramatic and philosophical purposes than that of Blanche. When Archer asked: "Why make Blanche a vixen at all?," Shaw could only reply that he had supplied a particular real young lady in place of the expected universal "ideal" one and that Blanche's temper and attitudes were not uncommon among women of her circumstances. That might be enough for the conventional realist, but Shaw was striving, first, to be an interpreter of life, and second (but most important), to penetrate and if possible eradicate those artificial categories of good and evil that prevent us from seeing people as they really are. In Blanche and Trench he showed us two very ordinary people faced with their own involvement with something abhorrent to their consciences; lacking the imagination to see a way out, they react by becoming irritable. Trench retreats into sullenness and cynicism while Blanche has a blazing fit of temper if anyone is so inconsiderate as to touch that sore spot in her psyche. Shaw could plausibly argue that this is a perfectly truthful portrait. It is not, unfortunately, what most of his audience saw. They perceived an attack on the entire bourgeoisie, a picture of a class of moral monsters, utterly vicious and corrupt. The Sartoriuses in the audience, knowing themselves to be kindly but realistically practical humanitarians, could dismiss Shaw as a vitriolic liar; the enemies of the bourgeoisie could shift all the blame for the evils depicted on the likes of Sartorius, Blanche, and Trench, thus allowing themselves to wallow in self-righteousness. Both would miss the point. Ordinary characters might do for the ordinary realist but not for the Shavian realist, simply because when they were portrayed honestly, without the filtering lenses of conventional morality, they were not perceived as ordinary. Something more was needed.

Extraordinary Characters in *The Philanderer*

We get a taste of that something in *The Philanderer*. The technique may have been borrowed in part from Ibsen. When Shaw told Archer that he no longer used the categories of good and evil even "for dramatic effect" he probably had in mind a device of the new school of drama he had described in the *Quintessence*. Modern writers, he said, "will trick the spectator into forming a meanly false judgment, and then convict him of it in the next act, often to his grievous mortification. When you despise something you ought to take off your hat to, or admire and imitate something you ought to loathe, you cannot resist the dramatist who knows how to touch these morbid spots in you and make you see that they are morbid" (219). As Carpenter shows, this technique is used in the *Unpleasant Plays*, but it evolves in a decidedly Shavian fashion. Its use is relatively crude, possibly even accidental, in *Widowers' Houses*. True, we are led to view Sartorius as a conventionally villainous slumlord (after first hinting that he has a conventionally disgraceful secret), and then we listen to his thoroughly reasonable defense of himself. Blanche and Trench are presented as more or less conventional young lovers but turn out to be something quite different. But it is hard to say that we are really challenged to question our own values, particularly our self-righteous tendency to blame others for the ills of the world. Sartorius's rationalization, however valid as to the facts, does not really make him an empathetic character, and the young lovers probably engage our curiosity (at least that of those of us intrigued by the vagaries of the human psyche when it is negotiating the stormy waters of romantic love) more than our sympathy. *Widowers' Houses* provided a superficially conventional romantic comedy with a strong dose of something sharply acrid and bitter. It is like picking up a chocolate to discover it tastes of aloes. The conventional marriage in Shaw's second play is certainly tinged with bitterness, but it is also complicated with contrasting qualities. We are not merely to see white as black and black as white. Our sympathies are confused, not merely inverted. Julia, the "womanly woman," is at least as bad-tempered as Blanche, but Shaw allows us finally to see that she is a victim as well. Her sister Sylvia, although a relatively minor character, provides an important counterpoint. Her mannishness is obviously contrasted to Julia's undisciplined femininity and links her to Charteris, for they are both rebels on principle. He is a principled philanderer and she a principled transvestite. Both are grotesque responses to a grotesque social code that seeks to force men and women into becoming "ideal" husbands and wives in "ideal" marriages, yet they are probably the two most astute and observant characters in the play. Julia and Grace are also coerced into unhappy choices by the same tyrannical code. While Grace's self-possession is highlighted by Julia's hysteria, they are similar in that both are forced into self-denying choices by their circumstances. Both are denied a loving marriage on honorable terms; the difference is that Julia does not have the strength of mind to abstain from marriage altogether and Grace does. We cannot admire Julia, but in the end we pity her, and our admiration for Grace is tempered by distaste for the choice that is forced on her. In Grace we get a foretaste of Vivie.

Vivie

Vivie, most unlike Blanche, is not ordinary. She may well be, as Shaw claimed, "a real modern lady of the governing class," but she is certainly not an average specimen of middle-class English females ("Method and Secret" 440). Like Grace, she is unusual because she needs to be, both for her own salvation and for Shaw's dramatic conception. An ordinary girl might well react like Yvette, although Shaw would reject both the attempted suicide and the conclusion that a girl in her situation was doomed to either the convent or the brothel. Yvette's despair was that she wanted marriage but was destined to become a courtesan; Shaw makes it clear through Mrs. Warren that the alternative Yvette thought of as a paradise closed to her was just another form of sexual slavery. "What is any respectable girl brought up to do but to catch some rich man's fancy and get the benefit of his money by marrying him?—as if a marriage ceremony could make any difference in the right or wrong of the thing?" (1:313). Vivie firmly and decisively rejects marriage. In a superficial sense she is a combination of both Grace and Sylvia. She has Grace's strength of mind, but her mannishness seems natural to her, whereas that of Sylvia appears rather affected, a symptom of fashionable "Ibsenism." She also, surprisingly, has something in common with Blanche. They both had parents who knew at first hand the choices forced on the poor, and both benefited from their parents' desire to give their children what was denied to themselves. The result in both cases is an unbridgeable chasm between parent and child. Both parents have succeeded in raising their children above themselves. Blanche, however, has become a lady only in the conventional sense: a useless creature whose claim to superiority is the habit of idle and pampered living and a strong distaste for vulgar realities. Vivie has taken a step to becoming a lady in Shaw's sense: "she who, generously overearnsing her income, leaves the nation in her debt and the world a better world than she found it" (*Intelligent Woman's Guide* 500). She is genuinely better than her mother, partly because she is realist enough, first, to appreciate her parent on her own terms and know that she owes her advantages to the unpleasant choices her mother made, and second, to know that the chasm between them is real and permanent, not something that can be bridged by mere sentimental appreciation. The final scene, in which she calmly and cheerfully, but emphatically, rejects love, romance, and art, is the natural result of Vivie's personality, but it strikes precisely the right dramatic and philosophical chord. The ending is unpleasant but not without hope. Her cool masculine manner is an appropriate contrast to a world in which feminine sexuality and sentiment have been degraded into commodities in the possession of male slave masters, although it is hardly the answer for all women. Her economic independence is a token of the solution necessary if the problem is to be answered for all women, yet it is achieved here at the cost of social isolation. We can sympathize with her utter rejection of art and romance when we have seen how thoroughly corrupt they have become, but most of us feel the loss far more keenly than does Vivie. There are no heroes; all (with the possible exception of Crofts) are given sympathetic traits or scenes, but in the end all are indicted as accessories or principals in prostitution. So are we in the audience. Vivie's ambiguous character ends the play: her financial independence represents the only cure possible, but she, like the others, turns her back on the disease and firmly shuts the door. In short, although the play ends on a note of hope, not despair, it never lets us take our eyes away from the brutal realities that, with our acquiescence, are allowed to continue.

Shaw demonstrated in *Mrs Warren's Profession* that he could produce an effective dramatic picture of unpleasant social realities, presented from the perspective of his own hopeful realism, but he never repeated the experiment. Perhaps he simply became convinced that it was pointless to show the privileged class "repulsive pictures of evils they are powerless to abolish" ("Realism, Real and Unreal" 111). In any event, he henceforth focused his dramatic energies on teaching his audiences to respect reality rather than forcing them to view aspects of reality that few could respect. Both techniques are reflections of his philosophy, but the latter reaches more nearly to the core of it. Idealism is pernicious because it is a wall erected between a sensitive conscience and reality. It protects the sensitivity of the idealist from unbearable horrors, but it also protects the evil from which the idealist is hiding. Only by facing evils can we combat them, and social evils cannot be conquered by individuals but only by society. Thus as members of society we must learn to face reality, to do without the blinders of idealism, and to respect the truth as well as ourselves.

RESPECTING REALITY: MORE UNCERTAIN BEGINNINGS

His first attempt in that direction—*Arms and the Man*—was, like his first "realistic" play, enormously successful in drawing attention to the author and a failure from the author's point of view. Shaw was disappointed with the first production of his premier "pleasant" play in part because of misunderstanding on the part of the performers, but the difficulty is inherent in the play itself. The point of Shaw's endeavor was to inculcate a respect for reality, not to deride idealists. He was not trying to present Sergius and Raina as a pair of hollow pretenders but as people who are sincerely trying to live up to artificial standards. The difference between them is that Sergius is a thorough idealist whose self-respect depends on the attainment of impossible and unnecessary standards, while Raina has sufficient self-confidence to accept reality when it is plainly laid out for her. For Shaw, this meant that Sergius is at least as tragic as he is ludicrous (*Collected Letters* 1:429). Today, when the heroic ideals he took so seriously are dead and forgotten, it is extremely difficult to find an actor who can play Sergius as anything but a pompous fool. Even at the time he wrote the part, Shaw himself considered it to be "unsafe in second rate hands" (*Collected Letters* 1:442). Shaw was not trying to set up embodiments of popular ideals and then punch them full of holes, although that is typically the effect of the play, even today. Mockery is the attitude of the disillusioned idealist, not of the realist.

Shavian Realism in *Candida*

The fully realized Shavian dramatic method emerges only with *Candida*. This is the first play that decisively breaks with the technique of tricking the spectators' judgments, the juggling of the categories of good and evil for "dramatic effect" that Shaw first described in connection with Ibsen. *Arms and the Man* would also seem to provide good examples of this kind of dramatic sleight of hand. The audience's judgments of Raina, Sergius, and Bluntschli are bound to change during the course of the play. There is a difference, however. Shaw's insistence that he no longer used the categories of good and evil "even for dramatic effect" occurred in a letter attacking Archer's criticism of *Arms and the Man*. That Shaw would wish to abandon such judgments is not surprising because the very essence of Shaw's moral position is that all such categories falsify reality and obscure the truth. This is really the difference between Ibsen and Shaw, at least as Shaw saw it: Ibsen is always seeking to replace outworn ideals with new and better ones, while Shaw saw no need for ideals at all. His point in *Arms and the Man* is not that Bluntschli is the true hero and Sergius a hollow sham; it is not a question of showing that those we had admired are contemptible and those we despised are commendable. It is folly to declare, like Sergius, that life is a farce because we have discovered it is not a fairy tale. Reality is more interesting and more worthy of respect than any such childish fancies.

Shaw's next play makes this distinction between himself and Ibsen explicit. Shaw called his play a "counterblast to Ibsen's *A Doll's House,* showing that in the real typical doll's house it is the man who is the doll" ("Shaw Reveals Who Was Candida" 603). Morell, he said, "is really nothing but Helmer getting fair play" (*Collected Letters* 1:612). The plot of *Candida* has little in common with that of *A Doll's House*. In that respect, the play is similar to *The Lady from the Sea*, but plot was not Shaw's concern in contrasting the plays. He was calling attention to differences in the depiction of character. In no play by Ibsen is the technique of tricking the spectator into a meanly false judgment used more obviously than in *A Doll's House*. Here Ibsen is clearly using the categories of good and evil to produce a dramatic effect. Nora, Helmer, and Krogstad are all portrayed in the beginning of the play in ways calculated to elicit conventional responses, but by the conclusion the judgments on all three will have been reversed. The villainous Krogstad becomes a sympathetic victim; the upright Helmer is transformed into a shallow and selfish tyrant; and Nora, who seemed so charmingly frivolous, is seen to be resourceful and heroic. Nora discovers that the ideal on which she had based her life was false, a mask for a cheap and tawdry reality; she leaves to seek an ideal worth living for. She still believes in the miracle of a "true" marriage but knows that she must first seek it elsewhere.

Candida is also about disillusionment, but the effect is distinctly differ-ent. Both Morell and Marchbanks idealize Candida, and both ideals are shattered, but the point is not to make us despise the reality. Morell's ideal marriage is shattered so that he might learn to appreciate and respect the real one. For his part, Marchbanks emphatically rejects that same reality, but it is made clear that his choice has only relative validity. He must seek his own way. Here is the essential difference between *A Doll's House* and *Candida:* one rejects the old ideal as something soiled and fraudulent and offers a tentative hope for a shining new ideal, while the other substitutes two realities for the discarded ideal, one a prosaic but admirable present, the other a hope for an advance in the future. Marchbanks may represent, for Shaw, a vision superior to that of Morell, but he saw them as merely adjacent rungs of a ladder rather than opposites. Shaw's discussion of this play in the preface to the *Pleasant Plays* revolves about the question of how to derive conflict from a fundamental unity. "There is only one reli-gion, though there are a hundred versions of it." Drama, however, requires conflict; Shaw's task was to portray the conflict without betraying the un-derlying unity: "To distil the quintessential drama from pre-Raphaelitism, medieval or modern, it must be shewn at its best in conflict with the first broken, nervous, stumbling attempts to formulate its own revolt against itself as it develops into something higher." In all of this enigmatic dis-cussion of the play, Shaw never alludes to the title role. The play is not about Candida but about the conflict between Morell and Marchbanks, a struggle of "pre-Raphaelitism . . . *in revolt against itself.*"

"Here, then, was the higher but vaguer and timider vision, the incoher-ent, mischievous, and even ridiculous unpracticalness, which offered me a dramatic antagonist for the clear, bold, sure, sensible, benevolent, salu-tarily shortsighted Christian Socialist idealism" (Pref. *Pleasant Plays* 1:374–75). Shaw makes every effort to place Morell in a sympathetic light, both first and last. His humble acceptance of Candida's loving but lightly mocking judgment at the end of the play is, at least in the hands of a capable actor, invariably moving. True, Shaw once referred to him as the "butt" of the play and said that Marchbanks represents a higher, if less coherent, vision of the truth, but in a sense Morell's more mature person-ality expresses better the unity essential to Shaw's message. He may be, as his name suggests, a "moral" idealist, but he does not moralize, in the sense of dispensing damning judgments on those who differ with him. He tells Burgess, despite his loathing for the older man's economic activities, that "God made you what I call a scoundrel as He made me what you call a fool. . . . It was not for me to quarrel with His handiwork in the one case more than in the other" (*Candida* 1:530). Indeed, Morell provides us with one of our most important insights into Shaw's view of the world. When Prossy makes disparaging remarks about a certain group of people, Morell startles her by protesting that they are his "near relatives." She is relieved to realize that he means "only" that they have the same Father in Heaven. Morell sighs: "Ah, you dont believe it. Everybody says it: nobody believes it: nobody" (1:519). The key to understanding Shaw is to know that he did believe it, with a complete and unfailing faith.

"A perfect dramatic command," Shaw told Archer in a letter about *Candida*, "either of character or situation, can only be obtained from some point of view that transcends both" (*Collected Letters* 2:33). The dramatist does not takes sides, at least in the sense of attacking one side and defending the other. Dramatic conflict, for Shaw, was the conflict of human nature with itself in its struggle to become more than itself. It is not a conflict between good people and bad, between the false and the true. It is like the snake's struggle to shed its old skin. Old aspirations, which began as manifestations of the will and thus of divine purpose, become leathery corsets that must strangle the growing will unless they are destroyed and discarded. Shaw's sympathies were always with the new, but truth must acknowledge that the old skin once served the same purpose as the new and even sheltered and protected its infancy.

Every artist with an unfamiliar vision requires unprecedented techniques. New wine demands new bottles. The "interpreter of life" must do more than argue a case if, like Shaw, his interpretation of life involves assumptions so unfamiliar that the average spectator literally cannot see them. For Shaw, that meant a rejection of the Manichean worldview in which Right and Wrong are irreconcilable opposites, and Right must vanquish Wrong for good to triumph. Shaw's view assumes moral equality but evolutionary inequality. We are all children of one father (in Barbara Undershaft's words), all trying to move in the same direction (albeit often fiercely divided about the road to take), yet some of us are clearly further along the way. Whatever Shaw had to say, whether on marriage and divorce, parents and children, language and class, or doctors and patients, it was imperative to say it in that context. The difficulty arises because Shaw insists that there is indeed both evil and good in the world but that the triumph of good is never brought about by blame and punishment. The distinction is difficult to make, especially when dealing with the kinds of social evils that are the subject of the "unpleasant plays." It is difficult, as

Shaw seems to have realized, to paint an evil without appearing to invite your public to throw stones, either at individuals or at humanity in general. After *Candida* Shaw generally took particular care to dwell not on the evil but on the attempts to strive for the good. This is not an easy task; it is a little like trying to show a conflict while portraying only one side. The techniques he developed to do this became the mature Shavian style.

NEW BOTTLES FOR SHAW'S NEW WINE

Although Shaw's plays came less and less to resemble the conventional drama of his youth and became increasingly "amorphous" or "organic," depending on one's view, it should not be thought that his use of the conventional dramatic forms of his times was a compromise or "selling out" of his larger aims. He was quite at home with the absurdities and outrageous coincidences of farce and with the heroics and high moral passion of melodrama. It is true that his use of farcical devices confuses some serious critics. They are accustomed to absurdity used satirically, but when it is not clearly attacking something, as is the case in *You Never Can Tell*, it is dismissed as frivolity. Shaw was both serious and (in his own terms) a realist, but he was not interested in realistic plots. He was not a materialistic determinist, out to demonstrate the pervasive influence of environment on the psyche, nor was he a concocter of well-made confections, intent on giving an air of naturalness to elaborately artificial constructions. He was concerned with the human will, its manifestations, its misunderstandings, its triumphs, and its defeats. If the confrontations and conundrums his human subjects meet with are brought about by outrageous contrivances of the plot, so much the better. The fantastic air of farce is one in which unchallenged social assumptions can be safely questioned and sacred moral verities can be assaulted without sending the audience into panic. Plays like *Man of Destiny* and *You Never Can Tell*, although far from being major works, have much more to say than the popular fare on which they are based, but their "frivolous" plot structures lead critics to dismiss them. And although Shaw *was* deeply committed to honest character psychology, his characters were never clinical studies but always elements in an artistic composition, chosen and shaped to meet his aesthetic and didactic aims. One can see this by examining the patterns of character portrayal in his first ten plays, those that most obviously show the influence of popular models. Each of those works is built around one of two themes that are perennial audience favorites: romantic love and heroism in the face of physical danger. For Shaw both of these represent healthy manifestations of the Life Force, so he does not cynically debunk them, but he does challenge conventional expectations about them. The nature of the challenge corresponds to the nature of the theme. There is some overlap, but romance is the nucleus of the "pleasant" and "unpleasant plays" (except *Man of Destiny* and possibly *Arms and the Man*) and heroism is the core of the *Three Plays for Puritans*. This is true even of *Mrs Warren's Profession*, although the romance of Vivie and Frank is overwhelmed, in more than one sense, by the general corruption of the sexual instinct that is the theme of that play. The most common device in those plays is the overturning of gender stereotypes. Frank is a quasi-masculine parody of the stereotypical worthless woman: his ambition is to become a kept man, but he wants to do it in style. Vivie's masculinity hardly needs comment, but in breaking off from her mother and Frank she is cutting herself off from not one, but two, whores. *The Philanderer* plays blatantly with gender stereotypes; *Widowers' Houses* pits a violently aggressive female against a passive, reluctant male; and Valentine in *You Never Can Tell* flaunts his effeminate lightness and frivolity and even uses them as weapons against Gloria's awesome strength. Morrell and Candida *appear* at first relatively conventional, but Marchbanks provides a source of X rays that pierce their facades. He of course is an explosive compound of almost hysterical cowardly effeminacy and terrifying strength and determination. We should not conclude from such character portrayals that Shaw believed that we are all really androgynous (or that men are really effeminate and women masculine), for if we look at the plays with a military theme (*Man of Destiny* and *Arms and the Man* together with the *Plays for Puritans*) we find that we are firmly back in the land of manly men and womanly women. Judith Anderson, Cleopatra, and Lady Cicely are as feminine while Richard, Dick Dudgeon, Caesar, and Captain Brassbound are as masculine as the most stalwart of traditionalists could want. The plays of sexual negotiation overturn gender roles, but the plays of military action and physical danger challenge received notions of valor and courage. *Arms and the Man* and *Man of Destiny*, which deal with both themes, occupy a middle ground.

The challenge to expectations of the audience corresponds to the challenges that the characters experience themselves, for all of these early plays depict journeys of discovery in which characters more or less painfully learn who they themselves really are, either with respect to society, to each other, or to their own self-image. The drama emerges from the struggle of the will to realize itself, and conflict comes from false notions—ideals—either in others or in the hero's own soul, that stand in the way. Evil certainly exists, but it is pushed into the background, and Shaw developed various techniques to dramatize his view that evil is not a unitary force in its own right (Evil with a capital "E") but a consequence of the failure of will—the Will of which our individual wills are all a part—fully to realize itself and achieve its ends.

THE STRUGGLE OF THE WILL IN A THEATRICAL WORLD

All of the plays are permeated by the Shavian philosophy, but they also take up specific issues, often the same issues that Shaw was addressing in his expository prose at the time. Charles Berst finds the seed for the portrayal of Napoleon in *The Man of Destiny* in a casual remark Shaw makes in his witty essay "How to Become a Man of Genius" (90). Berst does not go far enough; the entire play could be seen as a dramatic realization of the ideas expounded in the article. There is even an undoubtedly unconscious echo: in the essay he says that he "invented" a "fictitious" person called Bernard Shaw, insisting that "there is no such person," and the Strange Lady says of the twin brother she invented, "Theres no such person" ("Man of Genius" 344; *Man of Destiny* 1:645). Essay and play hinge on solving problems by creating fictitious persons. The theme is the human need for ideals—false and artificial though they be—and its implication that those who wish to accomplish anything in the sphere of public action must learn to embody them. They must embody these ideals without necessarily believing in them, which may in fact be a liability. They must, in other words, be actors in order to achieve their serious ends. The play, as Berst thoroughly demonstrates, is an acting contest. The outcome of the contest is ambiguous; at the end both Napoleon and the Strange Lady concede defeat, but of course one or both could still be acting. In a certain sense both win as both achieve their objectives. The overt action of the play is as close to the thematic heart of the well-made play as Shaw ever got: the struggle to keep secret the contents of a sexually incriminating letter, but the outcome violates well-made decorum, for Napoleon learns the contents of the letter by surreptitiously reading it but essentially agrees to go on acting as if he had not. In Victorien Sardou's *Madame San-Gêne*, a play with marked similarities but disputed relation to Shaw's play, a jealous Napoleon insists on testing his wife (in that case the later wife, Marie Louise of Austria; in Shaw's play Napoleon has just won the battle of Lodi and is merely the incipient emperor, while the wife under suspicion is Josephine). He obtains a letter, reads it, and it turns out to be perfectly innocent: the evil genie of sexual impropriety is returned to the lamp. Shaw's Strange Lady, like Sardou's Madame San-Gêne, is trying to protect a friend whose reputation and honor are endangered by the revelation of an indiscretion. Both women "lose" in that Napoleon gets the information he demands and they wished to keep from him, but whereas Sardou plays a theatrical trick on the audience, Shaw's ending provokes subtle questioning of the idols of honor and respectability—indeed, of morality itself. The issue in Shaw's play is the function of ideals—specifically those of morality and respectability—in the world of public action: do they help or hinder in getting things done? Both the Strange Lady and Napoleon disparage moral idealism, and each accuses the other of being enthralled by them, although at the very end the Strange Lady claims to pay "homage" to him because she "adore[s] a man who is not afraid to be mean and selfish" (1:656). Napoleon thereupon accuses her of being "English," explaining that she shares with the English the ability to use ideals to achieve one's own ends:

> Every Englishman is born with a certain miraculous power that makes him master of the world. When he wants a thing, he never tells himself that he wants it. He waits patiently until there comes into his mind, no one knows how, a burning conviction that it is his moral and religious duty to conquer those who possess the thing he wants. Then he becomes irresistible. . . . There is nothing so bad or so good that you will not find Englishmen doing it; but you will never find an Englishman in the wrong. He does everything on principle. He fights you on patriotic principles; he robs you on business principles; he enslaves you on imperial principles; he bullies you on manly principles. (1:658–59)

The Englishman, in other words, is the master of the technique, discussed in chapter 2, of using ideals "as excuses for doing what we like" (*Quintessence* 177). We can safely accept Napoleon's speech as accurately presenting Shaw's view of the English, but there is some question whether his assessment of the character of the Strange Lady is to be trusted. Tied to the question of which of the two "wins" their little game is the deeper question about which of the two is more free of slavery to ideals. In the initial stage direction Shaw describes Napoleon as *imaginative without illusions, and creative without religion, loyalty, patriotism, or any of the common ideals.*

Not that he is incapable of these ideals: on the contrary, he has swallowed
them all in his boyhood, and now, having a keen dramatic faculty, is ex-
tremely clever at playing upon them by the arts of the actor and stage
manager" (1:608). Despite this characterization, the action suggests that
part of him at least is enthralled by ideals. In his back and forth game with
the Strange Lady, he has all the advantages: his superior physical strength,
his position of command, and the fact that the letters in dispute belong to
him by law and custom. Yet the Strange Lady generally manages to preserve the upper hand. She does so partly by using "common ideals," notably by playing the role of the weak female rapturously adoring a masculine conquering hero, but when he proves insusceptible to the more
obvious ploys of feminine helplessness, she plays on his own ideal of himself as a man above ideals, telling him, "You are not afraid of your own
destiny. . . . And . . . that is why we all begin to worship you" (1:633). Yet he
is not quite ready to accept the image of himself as utterly above morality
and similar ideals; at several points he checks himself and lapses into conventional oratory about "self-sacrifice" and service to the French republic.

The lady contrasts herself to Napoleon by insisting that she *is* a slave:
"My courage is mere slavishness: it is of no use to me for my own purposes. It is only through love, through pity, through the instinct to save
and protect someone else, that I can do the things that terrify me" (1:631).
Note that she does not say she is a slave to morality, respectability, duty, or
anything of the sort. She is the abject subject of "love," "pity," and "the
instinct to save and protect someone else." But in the pursuit of the goals
demanded by those tyrants she is utterly unscrupulous. She is also more
resourceful and observant than her opponent. Both she and the general
turn what they learn from the other into weapons. At one point she incau-
tiously uses a phrase she had employed earlier in her deception of the lieutenant and thus tips her hand to Napoleon, but while he learns from the
exposure of her acting, she learns from his exposure of his true self. She
learns from his contempt for her "feminine weakness" ploy his pride in
being above such ideals and promptly uses that against him. When he obtains the letters by convincing her that he would not hesitate to rip them
from her bosom, she tells him as much of the truth as she dares but is
naturally speechless when he asks: "Then why not send it [the incriminating letter] to her husband instead of to me?" (1:637). Concluding that she
is lying, but lying ineptly, he instructs her how to answer such a question:
say that the husband would not read it because it would result in public
humiliation, a checked career, and a possible duel. Her attitude and ap-

proach change immediately. She clearly, if indirectly, lets him know that the letter reveals his wife's involvement with the Director Barras and even challenges him to read it. He regards her with suspicion:

NAPOLEON. You seem to have forgotten your solicitude for the honor of your old friend.
LADY. I do not think she runs any risk now. She does not quite understand her husband. (1:641)

She realizes that she can get what she wants—to protect Josephine from scandal and humiliation—because Napoleon cannot harm her without harming himself, and he is too pragmatic, too free of ideals, to be willing to do that.

Their contest is not yet over. To avoid scandal Napoleon needs to establish evidence that he never received the letter; he thus implements a scheme that will destroy the unfortunate lieutenant's career. The Strange Lady finds she cannot permit that. The same generous impulse that led her to risk death to protect a faithless, lying, selfishly manipulative woman impels her to further risk to save the career of a foolish and incompetent officer.

In his second play built around a "great" man of history, *Caesar and Cleopatra*, Shaw shows us two intensely willful persons, where one more advanced in natural ethics than the other acts as mentor to the less advanced person. Cleopatra has learned much from Caesar but will never be a Caesar because her nature is bound by its bloodthirsty and vengeful lusts. It is hard to avoid the conclusion that Shaw anticipated that relationship in *Man of Destiny*, with the Strange Lady as the evolutionary superior of Napoleon. Napoleon misjudges her at the end as at the beginning: she is not comparable to the English idealist he describes. She does not cloak her own selfish ends with a glorifying "principle"; she does what she does, regardless of danger to herself, because she is driven by something within her that is larger than herself. She admires his freedom from principle because her own freedom from such artificial restraints is even more thorough, although she may not recognize it. She admires his selfishness, partly no doubt because it is the expression of a magnificent will quite like her own, but also because, much different from her own, it is not constrained by something larger that she *may* (her sincerity can be questioned whenever she praises him) regard as a "womanish" failing. Napoleon may be the "man of destiny," but the Strange Lady is a clearer expression of the world-will.

Amiable Incompetents and Clever Clowns

Like *Candida*, then, but in a different way, *Man of Destiny* presents a conflict, not of good and evil but of different stages of the same force, different manifestations of the world-will. It demonstrates the developing Shavian approach in its presentation of minor characters as well. Napoleon and the Strange Lady are extraordinary characters; Giuseppe the innkeeper and the nameless lieutenant are marked mediocrities, but they are not quite ordinary. Shaw discovered in the unpleasant plays that audiences dislike ordinary characters honestly portrayed, perhaps in the same way that we all find mirrors unpleasant when the light is too harsh. Giuseppe and the lieutenant are creatures defined by their limitations, but they are highly theatricalized. They are, in a strictly technical sense, fools. That is, they are theatrical embodiments of certain common human failings or limitations whose very shortcomings are endearing to us because, as creatures of the theater, they turn their liabilities into assets. They can do this, paradoxically, precisely because of certain essentially human qualities that they lack such as shame or self-awareness. The fool's defining quality and supreme weapon is his imperviousness to pain. The crudest and most obvious examples are the denizens of the world of children's cartoons who endure all sorts of physical assaults that would be lethal in real life but are to them mere inconveniences. The two minor characters of *Man of Destiny* are more complex, but their secret is the same. The pain in this case is moral and psychological rather than physical. They are distinctly different personalities and are given correspondingly different moral anaesthetics. They represent in a certain fashion two poles defined by the themes of the play: role-acting and freedom from ideals. The lieutenant is the play's sole idealist; Giuseppe is a pragmatist untroubled by ideals or much else. The lieutenant is stupid and dense but eager and energetic; Giuseppe is clever and observant yet phlegmatic and devoid of ambition. It is no wonder that Napoleon admires Giuseppe and despises the lieutenant: the lieutenant is both an incompetent soldier and a deluded idealist, while Giuseppe, curiously, seems to personify the traits Napoleon assigns to those he calls "the high people." The high are like the low in that "they have no scruples, no morality," but the "low are unscrupulous without knowledge, . . . whilst the high are unscrupulous without purpose" (1:657). Napoleon is doubtless not thinking of people like Giuseppe but of materialist intellectuals to whom morality is superstition contrived to keep fools in check (in this speech Napoleon reveals a point of view quite different from Shaw's own), yet the description objectively fits Giuseppe well. The innkeeper treats life as a game and its participants, like himself, as performers. He is without shame because he is indifferent to honor and similar idols. The lieutenant, in contrast, is without shame because he is stone blind to his own failings and inadequacies. Both are unfailingly cheerful and pleased with who they are. We might find their real-life counterparts trying: an innkeeper without scruples is not an invariable joy to his guests, and an incompetent military officer is hated by both superiors and subordinates, but on the stage we cannot dislike such cheerfully amusing creatures.

Henceforward, in his efforts to present his own view of the human drama, one with often intense conflict but without villains or saints, he relied heavily on the types of characters we encounter in *Man of Destiny*. There are the major characters: strong-willed people like Napoleon and the Strange Lady who are either satisfied with pursuing their wills and are possessed by larger purposes like the lady, or are devoted to more or less egoistic ends, or are in conflict to some degree with their own wills, like the general. The minor characters are largely fools (in the aforesaid technical sense) who can transform limitations we might despise in our neighbors into delights on the stage. They might be witty and will-less like Giuseppe or obtuse and oblivious like the lieutenant, but they manage to avoid making us hate them while also reminding us of the pervasiveness of human foibles.

Some of Shaw's major characters are fortunate souls whose expansive wills are whole and free from internal conflict, such as Caesar or Joan, but more interesting are those who find their strong wills in conflict with high-minded ideals, such as Gloria in *You Never Can Tell*. If *The Man of Destiny* dramatizes "How to Become a Man of Genius," *You Never Can Tell* is the dramatic expression of the first chapter of *The Quintessence of Ibsenism* (with a glance at the third). Gloria was raised as a rationalist by a mother who was a champion not merely of women's rights but of all the ideas represented by J. S. Mill, Tyndall, Huxley, and George Eliot. She has learned to repudiate such ideals as obedience and womanliness. She is an individual, free from superstition; she declares, "I obey nothing but my sense of what is right. I respect nothing that is not noble" (1:730–31). Her mother is justly proud of the "sound training" she has provided for "Gloria's mind" (1:749). Yet she finds herself in love with Valentine, a charming but lighthearted and lightheaded young man for whom the "Higher Education of Women" is nothing but a ploy in the eternal duel of the sexes. To her horror and shame she is drawn to someone she cannot find noble and thus sees as her "duty" not to respect. They fence with each other, he delighted both with the joy of being in love and his imagined skill as a duelist of sex, she struggling with her unconscious determination not to lose him in conflict with her humiliation at finding herself no longer mistress of her will. When her inner battle appears on the point of breaking her and it seems she must either abandon Valentine or be defeated by him, she saves herself and dramatically reverses the situation. Suddenly, she instinctively resolves to put her reason and her strength in the service of her will: she firmly grasps Valentine with both hands and kisses him. He instantly realizes that she is now totally in command and that while Valentine the lover has gained his beloved, Valentine the duelist of sex has been ignominiously defeated. She promptly orders him, to the dumbstruck amazement of all, "Tell my mother that we have agreed to marry one another" (1:791). The struggle, the conflict of the play, is over when Gloria learns how to bring harmony to her soul.

Of the minor characters of this play the most interesting from the point of view of a distinctly Shavian dramaturgy are the delightful twins, Dolly and Phil. They share Gloria's "modern" education but Valentine's frivolous and carefree attitude. Like Giuseppe (albeit in a far, far different way), they are witty and observant without purpose or passion. Like him, too, they are brilliant and self-conscious performers. Their lack of engagement or commitment only enhances their extraordinary powers of observation, and their remarkable cleverness and brilliant sense of self-presentation almost totally conceal their callowness and lack of heart. In them good breeding and a thoughtful, rational upbringing have produced a peculiar variety of "lady" and "gentleman" stripped of the old-fashioned restraints of Victorian respectability. The result is Harlequin and Columbine, roles they most effectively play whether in traditional costumes or their modern, fashionable equivalent. They provide the tone of brilliant gaiety that resonates throughout the play, providing both the charm of youthful wit to season the irrationality of sexual passion and the metallic hollowness to accent the fatal gap in Gloria's "scientific" education.

Of course, Shaw does not always people the backgrounds of his plays with theatrical but shallow wits and amiable incompetents, figures like Johnny in *Misalliance* who can be dismissed as, in Lina's words, "what is called a chump; but . . . not a bad sort of chump" (4:250). At times the needs of the dramatic situation demand something else. Shaw usually avoids portraying angry, bitter, and hateful people, but in *The Devil's Disciple*, for example, he required an exemplar of ugly, hateful "goodness" to act as foil to Dick Dudgeon's attractive, compassionate "badness," so he created Mrs. Dudgeon, but he was careful to get rid of her as soon as she was no longer needed by abruptly and unceremoniously killing her off. Often he goes out of his way to show us a sympathetic side to unsympathetic characters. Crampton is a thoroughly disagreeable man, but through the eloquence of M'Comas we are made to see his side of things. Indeed, M'Comas himself appears generally as a ridiculous old fogy when he is confronted by Dolly's outrageousness, yet here he is shown as a sympathetic and effective solicitor (as Dolly points out). Sometimes this balanced presentation of character can be quite dramatic, as in the case of De Stogumber in *Saint Joan,* who is driven mad when he witnesses the consequences of his fanatical hatred. Shaw understood that hateful people who commit dreadful acts do exist, but as "an interpreter of life" from his own philosophical vantage, he felt bound to find dramatic ways to say that despite the undoubted presence of both good and evil, there are no real saints or villains.

He used other techniques besides the sympathetic portrayal of character to check the tendency of the audience to judge his portraits. The atmosphere of playfulness and paradox that pervades many of the plays keeps the audience off balance and uncertain just what to take seriously. His overt embracing of theatricality and, especially in his later plays, figments of fantasy and echoes of myth serve the same purpose. He may have been more successful with the latter technique, for his use of theatricality and especially his undisguised flaunting of the theatrical conventions of his time have confused some readers and spectators, or at least some critics. They have been led by the echoes of Sardou in *The Man of Destiny* and the farcical improbabilities of *You Never Can Tell* to dismiss these pieces as frivolous products of Shaw's unfortunate tendency to play the clown, or worse, as irresponsible attempts to pander to popular taste. But Shaw always was true to his own vision, even though in many ways he was perfectly at home with "popular taste" and actually rather fond of it.

Melodrama and Farce

It is important here to make clear distinctions. Shaw was quite at home with the improbabilities, absurdities, and high spirits that we associate with farce, and he was even capable of using certain elements characteristic of the well-made play: the struggle over an incriminating letter and the threat of sexual scandal that impel the action of *The Man of Destiny*, but he strenu-ously objected to the philosophy of the well-made play and intensely dis-liked the specific form known at the time as "farcical comedy," which epito-mized the values exploited by the well-made play. This is clear if one compares the uses he made of melodrama with the way he exploited the technique and form of farcical comedy. His use of melodrama in *The Devil's Disciple* and *Captain Brassbound's Conversion* is relatively straight-forward. He had written in 1895 that a "really good Adelphi melodrama is of first-rate literary importance, because it only needs elaboration to be-come a masterpiece" (*Drama Observed* 1:312–13). Shaw unashamedly ex-ploits the heroics, the narrow escapes, the threats of violence, and the high moral passion of melodrama. He merely substitutes genuine character psy-chology for conventional stereotypes and a realist morality for the simple black and white schema of traditional melodrama. From Shaw's didactic point of view, the *Plays for Puritans* succeed where *Arms and the Man* had failed. Like *Candida*, they present moral conflict in such a way as not to deny the underlying unity; they do not just reverse our perceptions of who is the villain and who the hero, they undermine those concepts. Much modern drama does this; Shaw's distinction is that instead of implying that we are all villains, he tries to show that we are all capable of heroism.

  Caesar and Cleopatra and *The Devil's Disciple* are elaborations of stan-dard melodrama; to a lesser degree *The Philanderer* is an elaboration of farcical comedy. Shaw exploits the techniques of farcical comedy, but where *The Devil's Disciple* is true to the spirit of melodrama, *The Philan-derer* is at odds with the spirit of farcical comedy. It plays with the form and comments on it, subverting its traditional ends. A farcical comedy such as Feydeau's *A Flea in Her Ear* depends on the acceptance of a rigid stan-dard of sexual morality in which appearances are of the highest value. It is the ultimate expression of the well-made play. In it, the playwright and audience play a game of peek-a-boo with sexual scandal. Its object is like that of a roller-coaster ride: to provide the maximum thrill of danger in an environment of total safety. *The Philanderer* certainly has a superficial re-semblance to farcical comedy. The theme of sexual impropriety is not lack-ing, and there is a fair amount of lying and evasion—another staple of farcical comedy. The most distinctive feature of the form is the second act setting in some notorious den of iniquity, a place where the characters may experience the maximum temptation to sin together with the maximum threat of exposure. For the usual trysting place, Shaw substitutes the Ibsen

Club, a den of iniquitous ideas, where sexual propriety is systematically challenged, but in the realm of fashionable avant-garde ideology rather than extramarital flings. The joke is amusing, but it is only a joke; the thrill of threatened exposure and the satisfaction of its evasion are absent. Shaw is showing that the real scandal is the stupidity of marriage laws that force people into unnecessary evasions and unhealthy relationships. He attacks the very premises on which farcical comedy is built. The new wine naturally bursts the old bottle; that is its purpose. Another way to look at it is to observe that while *The Devil's Disciple* works as a melodrama, *The Philanderer* does not work as farcical comedy. It is instead a clever attack on both the form and the social institutions that made it possible, although it is dated because the targets of its satire are deceased: marriage laws and their enforcing ideals have changed, farcical comedy has become quaint and tiresome, and Ibsenism is hardly the current essence of political correctness among progressive intellectuals.

The process of demolition is most clearly seen in Shaw's treatment of that essential premise of farcical comedy: the absolute necessity of suppressing all evidence that deviates in the slightest from conventional propriety. To get the full benefit of what farcical comedy has to offer, you must accept the idea that the world will come to an end if the truth comes to light. The exposure of the least impropriety must be regarded as the equivalent, to continue the previous metaphor, of falling out of the roller coaster. Such a notion is useful to a realist only as a target, and that is how Shaw uses it. *The Philanderer* begins with the moral tangles that are the meat of ordinary farcical comedy. People are brought together who want desperately to stay apart, and the usual lies, flights, and evasions ensue, but at the curtain of the first act, when exposure seems imminent and the situation is normally "saved" by yet another evasion, Shaw simply blurts out the truth. And of course, nothing happens. There is a similar trick in *Arms and the Man*. The device of the photograph which Raina imprudently and romantically autographed and slipped into her father's coat in the expectation that Bluntschli would find it is classic material for well-made farcical comedy. There are the usual—and most amusing—juggling tricks performed to keep the young lady's father from discovering the incriminating photo, but in the end, when we would expect the successful destruction of the damning evidence, it is brought baldly into the open. The jig is up. And again, nothing happens. Nothing, that is, except that the characters are brought a little closer to a real, rather than artificial, solution to their difficulties. On that level *The Philanderer* is as successful as *Arms and the Man;* it is vital and amusing because it shows us real people with real passions in an intensely farcical situation. The mechanism collapses to reveal human souls; a similar collapse in a conventional farcical comedy would leave nothing, for the characters are only gears and levers of the machine.

Organic Structure

So Shaw's use of traditional forms never compromised his larger purposes; he used them precisely to the extent that they served him. Whenever they threatened to conflict with his primary aims, he abandoned them, so the first of the three threads mentioned earlier is unnecessary. The other two threads of his dramatic fabric are a different matter. Both were essential, yet there is a potential conflict between Shaw's method of letting the characters dictate the story to him and his insistence that the artist be an interpreter of life. The former was his natural bent. Shaw is at his most carelessly charming when he is chatting to us about the stories his characters press on him. We are not used to seeing this side of Shaw in its pure form. It prevails in the early novels and the late extravaganzas, but in his best-known work it emerges only occasionally, as in the epilogue to *Pygmalion,* which Shaw admits at the outset ought to be irrelevant. But the plays after *Saint Joan,* however didactic, all have an air of inviting us to enter into an intellectual looking-glass world, following wherever these more or less fantastic characters choose to lead us. We see Shaw following his characters without regard for his ostensible mission at the beginning of his novella *The Adventures of the Black Girl,* where Shaw precedes his parable and morality tale with a delightful but largely irrelevant story about the spiritual odyssey of a well-meaning missionary. After the *Plays for Puritans*—successful attempts, like *Candida,* to integrate Shavian purpose into traditional forms—we begin to see a more relaxed style, a Bernard Shaw who has become confident as a playwright and is more completely following his own bent.

The next two plays, *Man and Superman* and *John Bull's Other Island,* abundantly show the qualities Archer called amorphousness and Shaw thought of as vitality and natural growth. Archer was looking for balance and symmetry, virtues natural to a building, where a wall on one side of the roof must be countered by a wall on the other if the building is to stand. The builder rightly plans his entire structure before he lays a brick or hammers a nail, but Shaw, at his most Shavian, allowed his dramatic inspiration (which was always also a philosophical one) to grow while he followed where it led. The result is not formless, as Archer thought, but the form is that of a tree rather than a table. This is clear in *John Bull's Other Island,* a play in which the most sympathetic characters are largely passive, watching helplessly as the idiotic (in Shaw's sense) Englishman takes control almost as a rolling snowball grows. It ends in an oddly inconclusive way, with the three main characters looking out on the Irish landscape and into a future only the Philistine can find satisfactory. *Man and Superman,* in contrast, seems at first like a conventional comedy with an awkward and cumbersome philosophical debate improbably grafted onto it, like a large if benign tumor that must be amputated to make the patient presentable in public.

The two plays are strangely complementary, for though they take very different routes, their destinations are sadly alike. The prevailing mood of *John Bull's Other Island* is one of frustration and stagnation, impossible dreams in a deadlock with intolerable realities; that of *Man and Superman* is bustle and movement and action and vitality. Yet in both we are left with only dreams and hopes, not clear plans for reaching them. The revolutionist's rhetoric is as useless, practically, as the mad priest's dream. *Man and Superman* is like the Irish play in that it is actually an organic growth, not the careless patching together of two unrelated forms that some see in it. Even without the Don Juan sequence, *Man and Superman* does not have the expected architectural shape. The flight to Grenada does not satisfy a taste for architectural symmetry, but it is a perfect expression of the action of the play. The dream sequence is also a natural growth, for as Tanner's flight through the Sierra Nevada is a flight from responsibility and social integration in the form of marriage, the dream is the transition that makes his final capitulation fully intelligible. The dream is not reallly about Don Juan in Hell (the title given by others to the sequence) but about how Don Juan, having furiously sought Hell, found it not to his taste and leaves for Heaven. Hell is the home of the idiots (that is, the individualists), of the seekers after pleasure and freedom from responsibility. The segment would more accurately be called "Don Juan Renounces Hell," which means that he embraces hope. Freedom from hope, as the Statue tells us, is one of Hell's greatest attractions because it is freedom from responsibility (2:642). Consequently, hope (not boredom) is Heaven's supreme terror. Hope means embarking into unknown waters without illusion about either the dangers to be faced or your own limitations in facing them, knowing that your failure, although fearfully probable, will necessarily be laid to no charge but your own. The difference between the marriage of Violet and Hector and that of Ann and Tanner is the difference between those who see marriage as the font of happiness and those for whom it is a yoke of responsibility. For Violet and Hector, with their unconventionally conventional hearthside dreams, marriage is the wonderful Hell of happiness; for Tanner and Ann it is the terrifying Heaven of responsibility and reality. That is why Tanner flees while Hector seeks it out. As Bernard Dukore points out, the dream sequence contains several stark contrasts to the frame play, the most notable of which is that in the frame John Tanner loses, and in the dream Juan wins (*Bernard Shaw, Playwright* 170). Tanner is a victim who loses freedom; Juan is a visionary who chooses responsibility.[4] The dream in the dry open air of the Sierra Nevada provides the counterpoint necessary fully to understand the play. Cut that, and, despite the abundance of wittily philosophical dialogue, the story is just one of a successfully predatory female and her silly-clever prey. It is a pleasant tale that works well in the playhouse, but it is not the whole story.

The difference in the tones that conclude *John Bull* and *Man and Superman* belies the similarity of their viewpoints. The melancholy of the first is a chord produced by three sad notes: the shallow triumph of the practical Englishman, Broadbent, the coldhearted cynicism of the anglicized Irishman, Larry, and the hollow dream of the mad visionary, Keegan. But it is Keegan's vision we are left with: the dream of unity for a world so gapingly divided. Although the conclusion of *Man and Superman* reverberates with comedy's traditional promise of fecundity and new life, the final note is the hollow sound of Tanner's impotent rhetoric: "Go on talking," says Ann, confident of the harmlessness of his words. Both plays point hopefully to the future without providing a map to take us there. The madman's dream of material and spiritual unity that ends *John Bull's Other Island* is like the apotheosis of the Life Force in *Man and Superman:* both must be taken on faith, like Divine Providence. The call for the Superman has the ring of crying for the moon, like the madman's dream. In any case, to submit to Providence is to eschew responsibility and bow to a higher power. That is clearly not enough for the Shavian religion, in which "the priest is the worshipper and the worshipper the worshipped" (*John Bull* 2:1021). The Life Force is not a transcendent deity, an all-controlling Father who envelopes us in His protecting embrace. It is an immanent and imperfect force, a Becoming rather than a Being.

Shaw was a dramatic realist whose subject was the living human will:

the objective, scientific examination of human aspiration in conflict with itself. His plays were a manifestation of his philosophy, an attempt to show how the conflict, diversity, and chaos that seem to pervade our lives is in actuality rooted in a fundamental unity. There is no battle between good and evil, or right and wrong; there is only the eternal struggle toward apotheosis, only life striving to become Godhead. *John Bull's Other Island* and *Man and Superman*, although close to the heart of Shaw's philosophy, are incomplete because they fail not only to provide a map but even to show us the first step on the journey. Without that we may as well submit to Providence, for we know not whither to turn.

5

Major Barbara

THE ORGANIC AND THE DIDACTIC

Major Barbara provides the first step of Shaw's journey out of hell into heaven, out of the despair of impotency to the triumph of Godhead. We should not expect it to supply a map, for the region is uncharted. It does show us how we must start, which is task enough, for the first step is as difficult and terrifying as the exit from the womb. *Major Barbara* is the single most complete statement of Shaw's philosophy and the epitome of the dramatic method he developed to express that philosophy. It is the most Shavian of Shaw's plays. By now he had mastered the technique, first successfully used in *Candida,* of presenting a reality both difficult to contemplate and worthy of respect. His chosen role as "interpreter of life" is no longer disguised in popular theatrical confectionery but is brought into the foreground, while the action moves simply where his dramatic imagination takes him. And for the first time we see evidence of internal conflict in his dramatic method: a clash between the free narrative of real people struggling with their circumstances and the need to provide an "interpretation" of something far below the surface of life as it is consciously lived. To serve the parable, Shaw put constraints on his characters that we do not see in any previous play. There are awkward moments when one character is clearly feeding a line to another, such as the following exchange in the second act:

CUSINS. . . . Barbara is quite original in her religion.
UNDERSHAFT [*triumphantly*] Aha! Barbara Undershaft would be. Her inspiration comes from within herself.
CUSINS. How do you suppose it got there?

UNDERSHAFT [*in towering excitement*] It is the Undershaft inheritance. (3:120)

"How do you suppose it got there?" is not a question worthy of Cusins,
but it allows Undershaft to makes his paradoxical point.

This conflict of purpose may be the reason Shaw found it necessary to
do the must extensive revision he had yet undertaken of any play since
The Philanderer. The changes were of a different nature from those applied
to the early play. The revisions of *The Philanderer* tended to cut out Shaw's
penchant for letting the characters dictate to their author where to take
the play and to bring it more into the familiar, structured pattern of farcical comedy, that is, to make it less "organic" and more conventional; the
changes made to *Major Barbara* help resolve potential conflicts between
Shaw's "organic" and didactic tendencies and so help make it even more
Shavian, rather than more conventional. The most sweeping changes were
to the second scene of the third act, which was entirely rewritten. Shaw
was right in his dissatisfaction with the original, for the first draft was
dramatically inferior to the final product, but missteps can be illuminating.[1] One of the most interesting changes is an alteration in the moral and
intellectual debate between Cusins and Undershaft. In the original draft
(called the "Derry" manuscript), Undershaft is unambiguously the winner
and Cusins is clearly brought around to Undershaft's point of view. In the
final version, Cusins is changed but remains his own man at the end. The
resulting intellectual ambiguity is interesting, and the exact nature of its
significance is an important question in determining the play's meaning.

ANOMALIES IN THE ACTION

The dramatic structure of the play is especially unusual. In all of the pre-
ceding plays the action is a clear development of the desires of the characters in conflict with each other and their circumstances: classic examples
for a teacher of play analysis. *Caesar and Cleopatra* may appear an exception, but its episodic nature is merely a shell for the true action: the partly
successful education of Cleopatra. When Shaw uses a conventional "com-
plication" to change the course of the action, it helps complete the picture,
showing us more fully how the characters behave by altering their circumstances. The change in the status of the slums proposed by Lickcheese in
Widowers' Houses and the arrival of the American navy in *Captain Brassbound's Conversion* both change the action in order to illuminate it. The

fundamental conflict remains clear and consistent. Despite the intense philosophical concerns of both *Man and Superman* and *John Bull's Other Island*, Shaw lets the unfolding of the story take precedence over any attempt to contrive the morality of the piece. The result is a pair of organic if unconventional works that are more successful as art than as complete statements of Shaw's beliefs. *Major Barbara* is a different case.

An overview of the play's action will make its oddness clear. The first scene ends with a reversal that sets the tone for numerous shifts the action will take as the play progresses. We are led to believe that Lady Britomart is (apparently for the first time) asking her eldest child to make an important decision regarding the family finances, then we suddenly learn that the decision has been made and that Stephen was being asked only to take responsibility for it. This might be just an amusing way to provide exposition, but it is characteristic of the entire play, which is a mosaic of altered and overturned expectations. Indeed, the scene between Lady Britomart and Stephen introduces an action that is dropped toward the end of the first act, ignored entirely in the second, and picked up again in the third only to be resolved in a casual anticlimax. The problem presented by the first act, like that of *Widowers' Houses,* is the need for money and the moral difficulty of obtaining it from a "tainted" source—in this case the profits from the death and destruction factory of Stephen's father, Andrew Undershaft. We are made to suspect that Stephen's sister Barbara, a recent convert to the Salvation Army, will have moral objections to both the money and her father's character. As soon as the father makes his entrance, this expected conflict melts away and is forgotten. The money is not mentioned, the daughter shows herself to be surprisingly free of moralizing priggishness, and the father becomes unaccountably fascinated with both the daughter he has just met and her religion of poverty. A new question arises from the meeting of father and daughter. It is a kind of battle of missionaries; each will try to convert the other and both agree to submit to the attempt. Undershaft will visit the Salvation Army shelter, and Barbara will come to the munitions works. This action, which involves two distinct steps, is also interrupted by the resumption of the question raised in the first act. The question of obtaining additional income for the two sisters, which is treated with awkwardly indelicate delicacy in the first act, is settled with casual abruptness in the first scene of the third act. When Andrew, obviously ignorant of the purpose of his invitation, asks after his first entrance, "What can I do for you all?," Lady Brit tells him that he need not do anything but sit and enjoy himself, a remark that puts everyone out of countenance and successfully evades the issue. Andrew's entrance in the third act is very different; he barely has time to draw a breath before Lady Brit peremptorily and emphatically demands more money for the girls. Undershaft agrees without a murmur. Strife occurs when she demands the inheritance of the factory for Stephen, but as Undershaft is resolute that it will go to a foundling as the tradition demands, and Stephen immediately renounces his claim, that conflict, too, disappears. Then the only difficulty—obviously not the central conflict of the play—is for Undershaft to find a suitable profession for Stephen, whose priggishly aristocratic upbringing has made him unfit for almost all gainful employment. But just as Stephen's inheritance of the factory is put entirely out of question, we casually learn that Undershaft has yet to find a foundling to inherit the munitions works. In the middle of the last act a new "action" is introduced. Then that is forgotten for the moment, as they gather together to accompany Barbara on her promised visit to the factory of death. It turns out to be a model of cleanliness and respectability rather than the pit of Hell, and Cusins, the neurasthenic and bespectacled professor of Greek, claims by a quibble to be an eligible foundling, offering himself as a candidate for the inheritance. His proposal is accepted virtually without hesitation. The conflict is not Cusins's trying to persuade Undershaft to accept a weak, inexperienced academic as his apprentice; it is not about his struggle to become the master of an arms empire that dominates Europe. No, it is Cusins's inner struggle with his conscience over the moral propriety of acceptance. The battle between Undershaft and Cusins at the end of the play is about the arms manufacturer's attempt to persuade the professor to abandon his moral standards. So many strange things have happened by now that we are not surprised when he accepts, or even when Barbara tells him that if he turned it down she would jilt him for the man who accepted. The "big" question at the end of the play is whether the young idealists will take on the factory; Cusins is the only one who asks the eminently sensible question: Why would Undershaft take on Cusins?

There is a sense in which we are being overly scrupulous here; it is a little like looking at the complexion of a beautiful woman with a powerful magnifying glass so as to "prove" how grotesque she really looks. The play is not incoherent, for the overall action is limpid: the mutual challenge of father and daughter and its conclusion in the father's favor. But there are many digressions and extraneous details whose purpose is not immediately apparent. We might expect that in a historical epic like *Caesar and Cleopatra*, where the busy pattern of historic fact is apt to clutter up the picture, but *Major Barbara* is presented frankly as a parable.[2] One expects a parable to be simple and—at least relatively—uncluttered. Part of the problem is that Shaw is using "real people I have met and talked to" as a means of telling his tale (*Collected Screenplays* 485). That makes the play much more interesting, but it complicates the task. Even more important is that the moral of this parable is not simple; Shaw crams a great deal into an evening's traffic on the stage. Even the action that emerges when one steps back far enough from the play is not without its peculiarities. The mutual attempts at conversion do not even proceed in a direct and straightforward manner but are indirect and oblique. When Undershaft visits the Salvation Army shelter, Barbara does not spend any time trying to convert her father; she gives her entire attention to the conversion of Bill Walker. When Barbara comes to the munitions factory, her father spends only a few minutes talking to her; he devotes most of his time to converting Cusins, despite the remarkable, even obsessive, interest he had shown in Barbara during the two previous acts.

We have barely touched on the difficult *philosophical* issues of the play. It is not surprising that readers are confused by it, but at a good performance audiences are unaware of these difficulties. The play has a remarkable coherence in spite of all of these apparent irrelevancies and discontinuities. All of the complexities are resolved in the throughline of the play, which is ultimately simple, consistent, and unambiguous. A careful look at both the overall action and the details shows how they come together in an almost perfect whole.

An Illusory Conflict

The parable opposes two sets of seemingly irreconcilable principles, polar opposites that must be eternally at war: spirit against matter, religion against atheism, altruism versus egoism, heroic idealism opposed to cynical pragmatism. The triumph of Undershaft—or at least the triumph of Undershaft and Lazarus, Ltd., over the Salvation Army—can be interpreted as Chesterton saw it: "*Major Barbara* . . . contains a strong religious element; but when all is said, the whole point of the play is that the religious element is defeated" (190). A more popular view, at least among Shaw's fans, is that the play represents a Hegelian dialectic with the succession of Barbara and Cusins to the Undershaft throne as the final synthesis of spirit and power, idealism and pragmatism, growth and destruction (for example, Whitman 223–30). Although some, like Wisenthal, feel that Shaw successfully presents Cusins as an advance on Undershaft (and perhaps even Barbara), others are not convinced (*Marriage* 75–79). Turco, for example, believes that the play ultimately fails because Shaw does not succeed in presenting Cusins as a clear advance over his predecessor. Most critics now would reject Chesterton's view that religion, represented by Barbara, is defeated by materialism in the person of her father. Turco, in particular, has noted the many similarities between father and daughter. The difficulty is that critics are inclined to seek salvation in Cusins. Many find this view appealing, and there is evidence in the play to support it, but it is wrong. The play can be interpreted in a Hegelian manner, but Cusins does not represent the synthesis that emerges from the play as a whole. The real enemy is idealism, which is the refusal to look hard truths in the eye. Like *Candida,* but on a much deeper level, *Major Barbara* develops a conflict from an underlying unity, and the point is that the conflict is illusory or unnecessary. Many of the complexities and apparent contradictions are the result of the fact that the moral conflict, which first appears to Cusins so unavoidable, is artificial. The play does not deny the existence of evil, insisting emphatically that it cannot be avoided; it only denies the possibility of isolating and destroying it. Evil is not something that can be cut out like a cancer; it can only be transformed. It is part of us and we are part of it. We can try to repudiate it as alien to us, and we will find that we can do so only by choosing death over life, declaring a victory while accepting annihilation. But the play does represent the defeat of idealism, and if, like Chesterton, you are unable to see religion as other than a form of idealism, you must perforce agree with him about the moral of the play.

From such a point of view the play must be unbearably pessimistic. More important, much would appear irrelevant or incomprehensible, so complete understanding demands a realistic point of view. The play's purpose is to show us the path to heaven, a path forever invisible to idealist eyes. Only from the realist's point of view do all of the pieces of the dramatic picture—a map of the world and the spirit—fit meaningfully together.

RESPONSIBILITIES AND CHOICES

In *Major Barbara,* as in Shaw's other plays, the issues develop through the relationships of different sets of characters. One of Shaw's favorite devices is a triad of characters representing a range of approaches to a particular ethical or social problem. They might be presented in the abstract, like the Philistine, idealist, and realist of the *Quintessence,* or as three major characters in a play, such as Broadbent, Larry, and Keegan in *John Bull's Other Island.* The use of three points of view permits greater complexity and avoids a simple dichotomy that would tempt us to see the issues as opposites of right and wrong. Here, the obvious trio is Undershaft, his daughter Barbara, and her fiancé Cusins, but nearly all of the characters are set off against each other in revealing ways. Sometimes the characters are paired and then bracketed with another person or set of characters. Lady Brit and Stephen are contrasted to Undershaft and Barbara. Mrs. Baines and Barbara represent different views of the mission of the Salvation Army. The four proletarians of the second act—Snobby, Rummy, Peter Shirley, and Bill Walker—serve as foils for and mirrors to each other.

Stephen and his mother, who open the play, are the representatives of the aristocracy, the traditional ruling classes. The scene between the two of them is not merely exposition; it begins, with a single note, the theme that will resonate in many complex chords later in the play. The issue is money, and the question is where to get it. Or so it seems, for we quickly learn, with Stephen, that the money must come from Undershaft's factory of death because there is no other possible source. Lady Brit's true objective in consulting with her son is not to ask for advice but to avoid responsibility for a moral decision that, although necessary, appears distasteful. She has made her decision and acted on it; she merely wants Stephen to take responsibility for it. In this scene, Lady Brit is the schoolmistress and Stephen her pupil. She instructs him, in word and deed, how the aristocracy approaches difficult moral questions. Stephen's horror of mentioning such "frightful" things as his father and his money produces this admonition from his mother: "It is only in the middle classes, Stephen, that people get into a state of dumb helpless horror when they find that there are wicked people in the world. In our class, we have to decide what is to be done with wicked people; and nothing should disturb our self-possession" (3:73). Thus we have the ruling-class solution: boldly face the facts, confidently take the money, and deftly shift the responsibility onto someone else.

This approach is not without its price. Lady Britomart steams into view as a classical dowager dreadnought, a moving mountain of indomitable will, but we later see that it is all bluff. She has no genuine power apart from her (very considerable) strength of character. When her husband, who has real power and knows it, opposes her, she is helpless. Even her son, who seemed so firmly under her thumb in the first scene, has only to declare his independence to achieve it. The strength that comes from position and the appearance of power is not inconsiderable, at least not until it is challenged by real power. In that way Stephen and his mother are alike. Had the business passed on to him, Stephen, like "all the other sons of the big business houses," would have had to hire a manager to run it. Even then the enterprise would run primarily on its own momentum, as Undershaft wisely notes (3:145). When that possibility is rejected by both Stephen and his father, the discussion moves to finding an alternative career. Stephen's aristocratic disdain for any ordinary profession eliminates all but one avenue: "He knows nothing and he thinks he knows everything. That points clearly to a political career," Undershaft sarcastically reminds them. Andrew may have had something of that sort in mind all along, as the other career choices were suggested merely as stepping-stones on the way to becoming prime minister. Even in the unlikely event that Stephen ever did make it to such a pinnacle of political eminence, his power would be circumscribed in much the same way that his mother's is, for in his next speech Undershaft declares, "*I* am the government of your country: I, and Lazarus." The moral choices of Andrew and his mother isolate them from real power in ways that may not be readily obvious but are debilitating nonetheless. They are the "butts" of the piece, but Barbara and Cusins are equally weakened by their attempt to take the moral high road. The differences between the aristocratic position of Stephen and Lady Britomart and that taken by Cusins are obvious, but the similarities, which are crucial, are overlooked. Stephen is sincere in his simplistic morality, but he is immature and naive. His mother's hypocrisy grows from an unwillingness to give up either the moralism she shares with Stephen or the money and power she gets from Undershaft. Cusins, as we shall see, suffers from a more subtle form of the same disease.

The relationship of mother to son parallels in many ways that of Undershaft with Barbara and Cusins—both taken together and separately. Stephen is his mother's protégé as Cusins and Barbara are Undershaft's. Stephen has his position by virtue of birth and upbringing; Cusins and Barbara are both, in a very real sense, adopted, for Undershaft has not previously known his daughter. Seen from another viewpoint: Barbara and Cusins must both qualify for their inheritance, while Stephen simply has the mantle laid across his shoulders. More interesting, both heirs try to defy and even repudiate the bequests, yet there is a real question how effective their claims to independence will be. Stephen declares his autonomy, but on the central questions of morality and power how different will he be—how different *can* he be—from Lady Britomart? Even as he goes his own way, showing a healthy ability to learn from his mistakes by apologizing to his father about his prejudices regarding Perivale St. Andrews, he reveals his naïveté afresh. Like the educated gentleman he is, he caps his admiration for the wonderfully organized town with a quotation from Milton: "Peace hath her victories no less renowned than War" (3:160). This is a stark contrast to Cusins, whose "it's all horribly, frightfully, immorally, unanswerably perfect" shows him to be as painfully sensitive to irony as Stephen is unconscious of it (3:158). Stephen's hypocrisy is only slightly obscured by his confusion about the inconsistencies in his position. These particular victories of peace are, of course, made possible only by war. And why does he applaud the operation now that he has found it to be clean and respectable? His objection was to the exploitation of war and destruction; that has not changed. Did he imagine, like his sister, that just because Perivale St. Andrews is engaged in the manufacture of weapons it must have been "a sort of pit where lost creatures with blackened faces stirred up smoky fires and were driven and tormented by [Unershaft]" (3:154)? Yet he cannot escape his moralistic conviction that pain is good for the soul. The pampered son of wealth and breeding worries that too much luxury will destroy the workers' independence and sense of responsibility. Unlike Barbara, he has no comprehension that responsibility means having something to do and knowing that if you do not do it it will not be done, not from having experienced egregious suffering. This superstition of the English upper classes allowed them to believe that having run a gauntlet of floggings at the hands of sadistic schoolmasters qualified them to govern an empire.

Parents and Children

If Stephen's independence of his mother is questionable, the same question can be raised about the succession of the Undershaft inheritance by Barbara and Adolphus. The closing line of the play—"Six o'clock tomorrow morning, Euripides"—underscores the unsettled nature of that question by reminding us that Cusins had not even agreed to the working hours Undershaft demanded.[3] How much will the next Andrew Undershaft be like or different from the present one? How much will the necessities imposed by the world and the realities of manufacturing and selling arms change the ideals of the saver of souls and the humanitarian professor of Greek? This is what the play is about: the spiritual and moral contest between father and daughter—solemnly agreed upon like a medieval joust.

The overturned expectations are nowhere more complex and enigmatic than in the relationship of the father, his daughter, and her suitor. All three are more than we might expect them to be, both in themselves and in their relations to the other two. Undershaft is the most obviously inscrutable. He is discussed as if he were a towering monster of evil; his first entrance reveals him as kindly, considerate, thoughtful, and somewhat embarrassed by being surrounded by a family he does not know. Money was the sole item on this meeting's agenda, but that is evaded—by the person who called the meeting—and the conversation is turned to religion—by Undershaft. He begins to question Barbara about the Salvation Army, and when his wife attempts to change this (to her) unpleasant subject by asking that Charles play something on his concertina "at once," he stops them by saying: "One moment, Mr Lomax. I am rather interested in the Salvation Army. Its motto might be my own: Blood and Fire" (3:88).

The reactions to this announcement are characteristic: Lomax is shocked, but Barbara, with perfect calm and unperturbed good nature, invites her father to come down to the shelter and "see what we're doing." She even has the audacity to ask the millionaire profiteer in mutilation and murder, the man who has all of Europe under his thumb, if he can play anything in their planned march. To Lomax's unspeakable amazement, he accepts as naturally and calmly as Barbara had asked. Father and daughter hit it off splendidly, and their common ground is religion. The opposition, for the moment, is represented by Lomax, who takes up the cause of moral purity championed earlier by Stephen and his mother. He succeeds in making the contradictions in that position even more obvious than had Lady Brit: "The cannon business may be necessary and all that: we cant get on without cannons; but it isnt right, you know." Lest anyone miss the point, Undershaft explains that he is not "one of those men who keep their morals and their business in watertight compartments." He is speaking for himself, as a munitions manufacturer, but his observation is valid for anyone who, like Lomax, regards the cannon business as necessary. This, as we shall see, includes just about everyone—and especially anyone who wishes to make the world a better place rather than just to deplore its wickedness.

Father is more firmly drawn to daughter in the exchange that follows his observation that there "is only one true morality for every man; but every man has not the same true morality." Stephen's contemptuous dismissal, that "some men are honest and some are scoundrels," is met by Barbara's "Bosh! There are no scoundrels." Immediately interested, Undershaft asks if there are any good men. When she assures him that there are neither good men nor scoundrels, he offers his challenge: "May I ask have you ever saved a maker of cannons?" Undershaft has clearly recognized something in his daughter that impels him to claim her, for if the audience suspects at this point that *he* is considering becoming one of *Barbara's* converts, they will be disabused in the next act.

The coda that resolves this scene is a counterpoint of religious attitudes. Barbara asks for "Onward, Christian Soldiers," Lomax volunteers "Thou'rt Passing Hence, My Brother," and Lady Britomart calls for prayers. The lines are drawn. Forced to choose, both Undershaft and Cusins declare their allegiance to Barbara's position rather than those of Lomax and Lady Brit, but there are differences. As usual, Undershaft is not explicit; he merely says that he has "conscientious scruples," but Cusins is diplomatically honest: he objects to the ritual confession of sin as unjust and untrue. He has worked for his moral rectitude, he has earned it and is proud of it, and he will not have it denied. His position is different from that of Lomax, Stephen, and Lady Britomart, or of Barbara and her father. He avoids the hypocrisy and confusion of the one by courage and honesty but lacks Barbara's cheerful rejection of moral stereotypes. Cusins does believe in scoundrels, or he would not work so hard to avoid becoming one.

Undershaft is, if anything, even more puzzling when we see him at the Salvation Army shelter. He is astonished that Barbara would suggest that he is a secularist, protesting that he is a "confirmed mystic," but pressed to identify his religion more specifically, he declares merely that he is a millionaire (3:110–11). When Cusins asks the same question, he explains that he believes that there are two things necessary to salvation: money and gunpowder. He does not explain the "mystical" nature of money, gunpowder, or his millions. Nor does he provide a metaphysical or spiritual basis for this "religion," other than to imply that it is the foundation on which ethical and spiritual values must necessarily rest (3:116). But his attraction to Barbara emerges more powerfully than ever. If there is doubt about the nature of his religion, there is none about his purpose here at the shelter: it is to win his daughter away from the Salvation Army to become apostle and missionary of the Undershaft religion. This is the exchange between Undershaft and Cusins:

> UNDERSHAFT. . . . We have to win her; and we are neither of us Methodists.
> CUSINS. That doesnt matter. The power Barbara wields here—the power that wields Barbara herself—is not Calvinism, not Presbyterianism, not Methodism—

UNDERSHAFT. Not Greek Paganism either, eh?

CUSINS. I admit that. Barbara is quite original in her religion.

UNDERSHAFT. Aha! Barbara Undershaft would be. Her inspiration comes from within herself.

CUSINS. How do you suppose it got there?

UNDERSHAFT [in towering excitement] It is the Undershaft inheritance. I shall hand on my torch to my daughter. She shall make my converts and preach my gospel—

CUSINS. What? Money and gunpowder!

UNDERSHAFT. Yes, money and gunpowder. Freedom and power. Command of life and command of death. (3:119–20)

This is a notable bit of dialogue. Undershaft sees more in Barbara than an intelligent and determined young woman deluded by religion. He is not like Peter Shirley, who thinks she would have been a "very taking lecturer on Secularism" if she had only learned to use her reason (3:111). Barbara's religion is her own; it is not something she has taken from the Salvation Army but something she has given it. Her father thinks it is his bequest. The unavoidable but amazing conclusion is that he sees his own religion in his daughter. He insists that the gospel she must preach is salvation by money and gunpowder.

The Undershaft Inheritance

What is the nature of Barbara's religion? Cusins sees that the power she uses is a power that uses her, just as later Undershaft speaks of being driven by a "will of which I am a part" (3:169). Is there a deeper reason for Undershaft to see himself in Barbara, or is he, as Cusins believes, simply mad? We see Barbara's religion at work in her treatment of Bill Walker. To understand Barbara—and her relation to her father—we must look carefully at the way she handles Bill, but there is another clue to Barbara's spiritual power that is often overlooked.

In many ways Barbara's unique and individual religion is in harmony with that of the Salvation Army; this is why she could so easily find a home there. Cusins describes the Salvation Army as "the army of joy, of love, of courage," and we have many opportunities to see those qualities in Barbara personally (3:116). There is certainly no striking difference between Barbara and the Salvation Army with respect to what Shaw sees as the two opposing camps of Christianity: what he calls "Crosstianity" and (confusingly) Christianity. Crosstianity preaches salvation through the gibbet, while Christianity teaches the vanity of punishment and revenge. Logically, the two points of view are hopelessly irreconcilable, so that you would think that the division between them would form a major split dividing the followers of Jesus of Nazareth. Not so. It is a tribute to the powers of hypocrisy and muddled thinking that one can easily find members of the two camps sitting side by side in the same pew, listening to a sermon in which both of these contradictory notions are wholeheartedly endorsed. The reason the two are inconsistent is transparent. Salvation through the cross is the theory that two wrongs make a right carried to its most extravagant extreme. Evil must be balanced by evil, and the evil represented by the sins of humanity is so great that it can be wiped out only by the greatest imaginable wickedness: the torture and murder of God. The doctrine of atonement is thus deprived even of its only reasonable excuse: deterrence. God becomes humanity's whipping boy, but since the atonement was paid ere our own sins were possible, we need not even worry lest our sin bring pain to another; the sin has been paid for in advance and in full. It could be cynically argued that since God made man to sin, it is only right that God should be punished for it, but this is not what the Crosstians have in mind. The Christian doctrine of the Sermon on the Mount, in contrast, is (at least as Shaw understands it) a flat rejection of expiation as an attempt to cancel wickedness with more wickedness. The one belief is founded on the endorsement of atonement as solidly as the other is on its rejection. Barbara and the Salvation Army are in agreement here: they accept the injunction to judge not; they return good for evil, kindness for cruelty, and a helping hand for battering blows. They celebrate the life and teachings of Christ rather than His torment and execution.

There is a difference between Barbara and the others on this question, but it is subtle and largely latent—latent, that is, until Undershaft adds the catalyst that makes it manifest. On one level Undershaft's actions are plain: he wants to win Barbara over to Perivale St. Andrews, and the first step is to win her *away* from the Salvation Army. But how did he know his method would be effective? This question is not often asked. Most assume that he shows his daughter that the Salvation Army, because it is financially dependent on the likes of Bodger and Undershaft, is inescapably corrupt, but Shaw explicitly rejects this interpretation in his preface. Authors can be wrong about their own works, of course, but they at least deserve a hearing, and Shaw is emphatic on this point: he repudiates the notion that the Salvation Army "reduced itself to absurdity or hypocrisy" by accepting the donation of a distiller and a cannon founder. He condemns as idolatrous superstition the notion that certain coins are tainted by the hands through which they have passed. He notes with approval the assertion of an actual officer of the Salvation Army that "they would take money from the devil himself and be only too glad to get it out of his hands and into God's" (Pref. 3:35). An understanding of how Barbara's religion differs from that of the Salvation Army must begin at the most obvious and striking point of departure: the fact that Mrs. Baines accepts the money and Barbara does not. If the reason for Barbara's rejection is an unwillingness to accept tainted money, then Mrs. Baines is closer to Shaw's own position than is Barbara. That is unlikely. It would also mean that Mrs. Baines, in her open-eyed pragmatism, is closer to Undershaft than is his daughter. But if Barbara is *less* enlightened than the Salvation Army—from the *Undershaft* point of view—it is difficult to see why he should think her so special.

Religion and Responsibility

Barbara's disillusionment at the end of the second act illuminates the distinctive nature of her faith. It *is* special, for Barbara understands a fundamental truth missed by Mrs. Baines: the truth about the admonition to abstain from judgment. In the preface Shaw points out that "you can no more have forgiveness without vindictiveness than you can have a cure without a disease" (3: 43). The essence of vindictiveness is the concept that a misdeed is something to be repaid. Forgiveness is the cancellation of a debt, and sin (to use Barbara's terminology) is not a debt. It cannot be erased; it can only be stopped. This, Shaw says, is a profound point of his disagreement with the Salvation Army, and Barbara is on his side, not the Army's. Barbara demonstrates the practical wisdom of the Sermon on the Mount in fighting brutality and cruelty. She treats Bill Walker as an equal, a fellow sinner and child of God. She talks about his assaults on Jenny and Rummy as casually as she might his clothing or his trade: she actually suggests it *is* his trade. She does not bully, threaten, or condemn him. In fact, she does nothing to save his soul, as that is generally understood. She merely encourages Bill's soul to save *him*. Rummy's violent vindictiveness justifies his brutality, and so, in a real sense, he is comfortable with her. Together they inhabit a world in which anger begets anger and violence excuses more violence. When Barbara tells Bill that he cannot buy his salvation, either in coin or in kind, what she really means is that she will not let him buy off his soul, she will not permit him to bribe his conscience.

Moral responsibility, the theme raised and evaded in the first act, is the core of Barbara's morality and the expression of her religion. Her enemy is its evasion. In Barbara's religion, salvation is achieved not through works, not faith, and certainly not pain or atonement, but by responsibility to one's own soul. Anything that erects a wall between a man's conscience and his consciousness is her foe.

The wall closes like an iron gate when her father signs his check. Barbara treats her father and Bill Walker alike; as she sees it, they "are the same sort of sinner, and theres the same salvation ready for them" both (3: 89). Curiously, Undershaft invites the comparison. He first offers twopence to round out the meager collection from their meeting, then proposes to add ninety-nine pounds to the one Bill bids for the purchase of his soul. He appears to be testing his daughter, testing her devotion to the religion of responsibility. She does not waver: "You cant buy your salvation here for twopence: you must work it out" (3: 123). Jenny Hill, an orthodox Salvationist, argues for taking the money. Barbara's refusal shows precisely where she differs from the Army. She understands, where Jenny does not, that the acceptance of conscience money, however desperately needed, defeats the work of saving souls—at least as Barbara conceives that work. Undershaft's action highlights the difference and reveals the strategic weakness in Barbara's position: she cannot do without conscience money because that is all the money available. Bill is not convinced that consciences cannot be bought here; he contends that he is not allowed to buy off his soul only because he cannot come up with the price.

All this leads to the scene of hushed awe in which Undershaft signs his check. The charged pause is broken by Bill's "Wot prawce selvytion nah?" Barbara's silence, maintained after her initial brief expression of dismay at the news of Bodger's offer, is over as well. Her father's check confirmed Bill's cynicism and justified his contempt. His conscience has been bribed by proxy. She must protest now, as keenly as she feels the Army's need for the money, because *her* vision of the Salvation Army is on the edge of annihilation. She cannot demand moral responsibility only from those who cannot afford the price of irresponsibility. Even if she could accept such inconsistency and discrimination, she knows that as long as the Bill Walkers of the world understand that consciences are for sale, her sword must turn to straw. After a valiant last stand, she accepts the inevitability of defeat. Like a soldier yielding his sword, she submits her badge of Salvation to her father. It is unconditional surrender.

Undershaft has helped to illuminate Barbara, but he himself remains a mystery. If anything, he has become more enigmatic: Why, short of maliciousness, has he done this? He robs her of her faith, but what does he offer in return but cynicism and pessimism? Undershaft challenges his daughter to seek a new and better faith when she sees that the old one has failed. Like Barbara, we would be glad for a better one, but can see only a worse. Does he want to break her spirit? To destroy the very qualities that had drawn him to her? Everything he has said suggests that he believes her particular religious inspiration allies her naturally with him, and not the Salvation Army; he wants Barbara *because* of her unique religion. The faiths of daughter and father become one in the final scene.

Father and Daughter

Barbara's attention is directed toward Bill Walker rather than her father in the second act, and Undershaft does battle with Cusins rather than his daughter in the third. This curious indirectness is the consequence of the point that Shaw makes: that there is no real conflict between father and daughter, that they are two sides of one coin, two manifestations of the same spirit. The apparent conflict between the two is a misunderstanding, the result of Barbara's youth and inexperience. In this parable, Barbara stands for religion, spirit, and morality; her father for matter, wealth, and destructive power. The third act brings them together by showing that the barrier between them is only a wall of lies erected to protect weak and sensitive consciences from reality. There is a genuine conflict in the play, however: a conflict between ideas. Barbara and Undershaft are on the same side. Theirs is the camp that views the world as one, not divided into good and evil. Their world has no scoundrels or good men, only children of the same Father: or in Shavian terms, different expressions of the Life Force. We see one side of that unity in the second act and another in the third. The reason that Shaw needs Bill Walker to provide a subject for Barbara's soul-saving skills is that, while they are effective and greatly needed in this soul-destroying world of ours, they would be useless against her father. They are not too weak; they are simply redundant. Retribution, atonement and repayment are the bricks and mortar with which Bill Walker, like most of us, builds walls of evasion around his soul; Barbara saves it by tearing down the walls. Bill is not allowed to escape from his conscience with money or pain. Andrew Undershaft does not attempt to avoid his soul; he takes pride in standing up and facing it. He refuses to spend money on "hospitals, cathedrals, and other receptacles for conscience money," and puts his spare cash instead into research on bombs and bullets (3: 89). His motto is "Unashamed." Since he refuses to hide from his conscience, he can remain unashamed only by doing nothing shameful. His soul does not need salvation because it is already strong and free.

Undershaft's clear conscience is not enough to demonstrate an affinity between father and daughter if all it means is that her conscience is strong and healthy while his is dead or dying—if Barbara is a saint and Undershaft a scoundrel.[4] If that is so then Barbara's defeat does mean cynicism and despair. Dramatically, the question is whether Barbara can accept the cannon foundry and what it represents without compromising all that she represents. The answer to this question lies in Undershaft's "true faith of an Armorer" and the mottoes of the seven successive Undershafts. Barbara declares that there are no saints or scoundrels; she practices what Shaw calls moral equality, and she espouses, by her actions, the Christian precept to "judge not." The Armorer's faith is the logical extension of that rule. The second Undershaft was explicit on this point: "ALL HAVE THE RIGHT TO FIGHT: NONE HAVE THE RIGHT TO JUDGE" (3: 168). The Armorer's faith still shocks and puzzles critics, although Shaw takes pains to explain it in his preface. It is not a glorification of machismo and combat for its own sake; it is the ultimate test of Barbara's principles of moral equality, an affirmation that you cannot divide the world into good people and bad. Undershaft, like his daughter, is an ethical anarchist. He is not necessarily a social anarchist, as we see both in his speech on social organization to Stephen and, more significantly, the experiments in social cooperation and community welfare he has created in Perivale St. Andrew. Undershaft understands the need for social organization, but he also understands that socialism must be founded on what Shaw called the "Anarchist Spirit" (*Impossibilities of Anarchism* 23). The organization of civilization must not outrage the consciences of its individual members. Whenever it does, it will justify the "morality of militarism" and individualist defiance that Undershaft represents. As Shaw observes, "the justification of militarism is that circumstances may at any time make it the true morality of the moment" (Preface 3: 50). The one true morality for each man or woman, Undershaft maintains, is dependent on circumstances. His own circumstances include a financial dependence on the manufacture of arms, but all who find their consciences outraged by a social system that methodically degrades and brutalizes large numbers of its citizens will find that militarism must become their own true morality—if they have the courage to face reality. "The consent of the governed" has been the accepted foundation of our political theory for centuries, yet Undershaft's bald statement of its implications still shocks the very people who regard themselves as the champions of liberal democracy.

Foundations are not pretty, and Undershaft represents the foundation of the same principles of which Barbara embodies the superstructure. He makes this clear in the brief exchange he has with her in the final scene. He saved her soul from the crime of poverty and allowed her to become Major Barbara, to become a champion of spirit and saver of souls. Foundations, however hard to look at, are essential. You cannot free the soul without first freeing the body; you cannot serve others without first serving yourself; you cannot give to others if you have impoverished yourself. And you can only choose from the alternatives which are presented to you. Undershaft says:

> I had rather be a thief than a pauper. I had rather be a murderer than a slave. I dont want to be either; but if you force the alternative on me, then by Heaven, I'll chose the braver and more moral one. I hate poverty and slavery worse than any other crimes whatsoever. (3: 174)

Make no mistake, when Undershaft says that poverty and slavery are crimes, he means that the pauper and slave are criminals. By accepting the degradation society has imposed on them they are guilty of unspeakable sins against the Life Force that can be redeemed only by the courage to rebel against it. Undershaft offers them the means. When bloodshed is the only alternative to degradation of oneself, "Thou shalt starve ere I starve" becomes the foundation of all ethics.[5] What is wanted is "courage enough to embrace this truth" (3: 173).

That is why Andrew Undershaft needs Barbara. Undershaft points out that he "can make cannons: [he] cannot make courage and conviction" (3: 169). That is what is wanted. He can provide the means for those who are willing to risk their lives in order to save their souls, but he cannot give them the will to do it. That is the truth about his own well-fed, comfortably housed, and self-satisfied workers. He has not only saved them, like his daughter, from the crime of poverty; he has saved them from the need to fight their way out of it. There is no reason to believe that they would have had the necessary courage and conviction if he had not. If the conviction needed is faith in their own equality, they would fail the test; Undershaft is the only one who thinks of the workers as equals: they want nothing to do with such radical notions. Andrew comments that the mosaic in the William Morris Labor Church, "No Man Is Good Enough to Be Another Man's Master," shocked his men. Obviously, the motto was his idea (this is explicit in the original manuscript) (3: 162–63). There is plenty of hierarchy and inequality at Perivale St. Andrew, but none of it originates from Undershaft, save that which is a spontaneous reaction to his personality. It is created and enforced by the workers themselves, although the inequality in income that justifies the hierarchy and is justified by it merely augments the profits of the owner, as Undershaft wryly notes. Shaw is making the same point Gunnar Myrdal made the foundation of his 1944 study of American race relations:

> Our hypothesis is that in a society where there are broad social classes and, in addition, more minute distinctions and splits in the lower strata, *the lower class groups will, to a great extent, take care of keeping each other subdued,* thus relieving, to that extent, the higher classes of this otherwise painful task necessary to the monopolization of the power and the advantages. (68) (Emphasis in original)

Cusins, like most of the critics, sees nothing but cynicism in Undershaft's recognition of this truth, but Shaw's point is that this attitude among the exploited perpetuates their exploitation regardless of the wishes of the upper-classes. Most liberals and socialists come from the comfortable classes. The irony is not, as Cusins believes, that the workers are Undershaft's willing accomplices in his gulling of them; it is that no one can be forced to accept the responsibility of freedom who prefers the comfort and safety of slavery. If men are docile and acquiescent when forced into brutal and degrading circumstances, should we expect them to accept painful responsibility when they are well-fed and self-satisfied? Shaw believed that one of the worst effects of poverty was to maim souls beyond redemption, but nourished bodies do not necessarily produce flourishing souls. In the Derry manuscript, Undershaft tells Barbara that she is proof of the "principle that if you take care of people's bodies their souls will take care of themselves," but he also accepts Cusins's description of his workers as slaves: "To those who are worth their salt as slaves, I give the means of life. But to those who will not or cannot sell their manhood . . . I give the means of death" (200–06). In the revised version, he merely challenges Barbara to "Try your hand on my men: their souls are hungry because their bodies are full" (3: 173). Some hearty souls, like Barbara's, will thrive untended if they have good soil, but most others require more careful attention. That is Barbara's job.

The unity that binds Undershaft and his daughter together is the unity in which they both believe. Neither is afraid of evil because neither believes in its existence as a separate entity, a formidable Other. Each has utter confidence in the basic goodness of other human beings: Barbara in Bill Walker, and Undershaft in the varieties of human beings to whom he sells his arms. Many otherwise perceptive critics go astray when confronted with Undershaft; they cannot comprehend how such a unity is possible because they imagine that Undershaft advocates indiscriminate murder, but that is not in the least what he is saying. Like his daughter, the sire of Major Barbara has faith in the consciences of his brothers and sisters—fellow children of God. Barbara trusts Bill's conscience to persuade him not to assault women, and Andrew appeals to the consciences of the poor to demand their freedom and dignity—and to be willing to kill if it is not granted. For Shaw, as for Undershaft, poverty and slavery are forms of living death; to accept them is to acquiesce in your own murder. If killing is the only alternative offered to you, to choose the sword is to choose life. The issue is whether to passively accept a large evil rather than actively choose a lesser one. Most tolerate the greater evil rather than allow themselves to feel contaminated by active participation in the lesser. Undershaft does not, and that is the source of his contempt for the lust after "personal righteousness."

Some critics imagine that Shaw is offering Undershaft as a kind of Savior of Mankind, an idea he vehemently repudiated (*Collected Letters* 3: 629). The search for a savior is quixotic folly because saviors are an idealist delusion. If Shaw often depicted strong, positive and dynamic characters like Undershaft it was not because he was dotty about Great Men, as some imagine; it is because he believed in the future and wished to point us toward what we might become rather than rub our noses in our present follies. Caesar, Undershaft, Joan, and Lady Cicely are not supermen and superwomen, because the superman does not yet exist. They are only hints as to what he might become. Barbara and her father are both such beacons of the future because they have unified souls, they have faith in their own wills, and they have each dedicated themselves to a cause beyond themselves. They are both doing God's work because they have given themselves over to the Will of which they are a part, the piece of deity in each of them. They look at the world with open eyes and know the only way to combat the copious evil they see is to face and transform it. To flee only grants it possession of the field. They are realists. Barbara's vision was at first obscured by her youth and ignorance, but she has her father's eyes. The real conflict is not between father and daughter, but between realism and idealism. Idealism, not surprisingly, has many champions. Nearly everyone else in the play expresses some idealist notion, but the most important advocates of the idealist viewpoint are Stephen, his mother, and especially Cusins.

Cusins

Yes, Cusins is an idealist. He is the best example of that superior variety of the human species to be found in all of Shaw's plays. He is highly intelligent, strong in will, conscientious to the point of self-destruction, and remarkably perceptive. He illustrates in an extreme degree both the admirable and the pernicious traits Shaw saw as the marks of an idealist. The principle difference between his idealism and that of Lady Britomart or Stephen is that he is far more perceptive and clear-headed, so that idealism leads him to bitter irony and cynicism rather than hypocrisy and self-deception. Cusins is set apart ethically from Lady Brit and Stephen by the fact that they are moralists while he is conscientious. Undershaft makes the difference clear when he says to his wife: "My dear: you are the incarnation of morality. Your conscience is clear and your duty done when you have called everybody names." Morality tells us to condemn those whose behavior we find disagreeable; conscience tells us how we ourselves should or should not behave. Stephen's concern that too much pampering will be bad for the souls of workers is a more subtle form of morality because it is unconscious of any similar deleterious effect his own privileges might have on his character. Stephen regards a clear conscience as his birthright; Cusins knows he has to work for his. Stephen worries about maintaining the character of others (especially those in the lower orders); Cusins worries about his own. Undershaft, however, classes Cusins as a moralist along with his wife. Cusins's lust for a clear conscience he calls "patronizing people who are not so lucky as yourself" (3: 177). This is an interesting statement of the principle of moral equality, implying that a person born with a flawed character is unlucky in the same way as one born with a club foot. Bill Walker is a ruffian largely as a result of his circumstances, according to Undershaft, for he ventures that he could save his soul more effectively than Barbara just by giving him a job and a decent income. Environment is not the only culprit: there are congenital character defects as well as physical ones, but a person born with a murderous temper is quite as unfortunate as one born with a withered arm. A moral disability is as worthy of compassion as a physical one. That is why Undershaft equates the lust for personal righteousness with "patronizing people not so lucky as yourself." It is Undershaft's equivalent of the Christian "There but for the grace of God, go I." The very fact that Cusins wants to avoid being a rascal means that he too divides the world into rascals and heroes. He would distribute the black and white hats differently from Stephen or Lady Britomart, but the principle is the same.

This is how Undershaft greets Cusins's claim to believe in love:

> UNDERSHAFT. I know. You love the needy and the outcast: you love the oppressed races, the negro, the Indian ryot, the underdog everywhere. Do you love the Japanese? Do you love the French? Do you love the English?
>
> CUSINS. No. Every true Englishman detests the English. We are the wickedest nation on earth; and our success is a moral horror.
>
> UNDERSHAFT. That is what comes of your gospel of love, is it? (3: 177)

This passage is an assault on liberal idealism that has puzzled even the best of Shaw's critics. When Shaw says that we are all expressions of the Life Force, imperfect manifestations of God's attempts to become perfect, Shavians nod in assent, but when he insists that is as true of the thief as the saint, or the capitalist as the worker, many cannot take him seriously. But the gospel of love falls apart when love is denied to those you have condemned as wicked: those less fortunate than yourself. So Cusins is a moralist as well, but rather than directing his moral scorn safely outward like Stephen and his mother, he directs it toward himself and those groups of which he is a member. If Barbara and her father are alike in possessing unified souls, Cusins's soul is marked by division and conflict. Shaw describes him as a man whose health is being destroyed by a perpetual struggle between his conscience and impulses of which he does not approve. To judge from the passages he quotes, his favorite Greek tragedy is *The Bacchae*, and like Pentheus, he is being torn apart. Pentheus is both drawn to and repelled by Dionysus; Cusins is drawn to both Barbara and Andrew Undershaft in spite of his conscience, and he casts both of them in the role of Dionysus.[6] Yet he calls Barbara his "guardian angel" and turns to her father to exclaim "Avaunt!" (3: 156). He describes himself as a "poor professor of Greek, the most artificial and self-suppressed of human creatures" (3: 117). His answer to bigotry, intolerance, and class snobbery is to reverse the roles of the condemned and the privileged. Instead of damning others, he damns himself. He identifies himself with the English when he calls England the wickedest nation on earth. After accepting the role of apprentice to Undershaft, he justifies himself by saying that he loves the common people and wants to arm them against the intellectuals, a group to which he himself conspicuously belongs. His love of the poor is only pity, which Undershaft contemptuously dismisses as the "scavenger of misery." His condemnation of the English and the intellectuals is self-hatred inspired by guilty consciousness of his own privileges and comforts. His attempt to achieve moral purity by avoiding contact with wickedness is doomed. It is not only ruining his health, but when the strain is brought to crisis at the conclusion of the second act, he suffers what amounts to a moral nervous collapse and wallows hysterically in what he is convinced is evil, even to the point of getting drunk with the man he calls the Prince of Darkness (who stays characteristically sober). Unlike Barbara and Undershaft, he views transgressions as debts to be repaid. He approves, to Barbara's dismay, of Bill's attempt to pay for his misdeed, and rejects forgiveness, not (like Shaw and Barbara) because the concept is fraudulent, but because "we must pay our debts" (3: 114, 178). Many critics, themselves liberal intellectuals, believe that Cusins will be an improvement on the old Andrew Undershaft because of his commitment to arm the oppressed rather than the establishment. This is a desperate hope at best. The new Undershaft, like the old, will have to sell to whom he can in order to thrive, and can no more make courage and conviction than his predecessor. Barbara is the real hope, because the job at hand is to awaken dormant souls.

REVISIONS

There were two significant trends in the many changes Shaw made to the final scene of the play: one was to make Cusins a strong and more steadfast advocate of the idealist viewpoint. The other was to pull Barbara more into the background. The portrayal of Cusins in the Derry manuscript is dramatically unfocused; in the final version he is a stronger opponent to Undershaft. Speeches are added to set him apart from Undershaft and others deleted that had shown him coming over to the older man's position. The original ending was less ambiguous with respect to the struggle between Cusins and Undershaft. Barbara, on the other hand, has considerably less to say in the final version of the last scene. Some of her dialogue, like her reproach to her father about robbing from her a human soul, is moved to earlier in the play. Some minor lines are given to other characters, and others are cut. Curiously, the effect of this is to give her greater strength, as the men are engaged in a struggle for her—more specifically, for the spiritual power and moral authority she represents. The parable is also better served since some of her almost peevish objections to the muni-

tions plant in the original undercut her final acceptance of it. The unity of
father and daughter is made clearer while the ideological conflict of realism and idealism is made more vital through the strengthening of Cusins.
There is no ambiguity about the philosophical meaning of the play: that is
clear and consistent. The only question remaining at the end of the play is
whether Cusins, the moralist, will change. Much depends on the answer. If
he does not, if we go on dividing the human race into the righteous and the
unrighteous, we will perpetuate evil rather than exterminate it. Barbara
knows you cannot cure evil by either hiding or punishing. Only by facing
it—with strength but without vindictiveness—can we begin to challenge
the multitude of social evils our bungled and hysterical attempts at civilization have brought upon us. That is what *Major Barbara* is about.

6

Ethics, Economics, and Government

ETHICS

Anarchism to Organization

It was important to Shaw as artist to develop a dramatic form that was true
to his creed, both in form and content, but it was even more important that
his creed fit the facts. A realist religion must not only be true to the facts of
experience, but must also be a guide to living. It must, that is, be true to
future possibilities as well as present facts. If it is honest, it must provide a
basis for social and political organization and not simply be ignored when
inconvenient. It must not impel us into such hypocrisies as preaching
peace while waging war. The easiest way to avoid hypocrisy is to set your
sights very low, which is exactly what many self-declared "realists" do.
Declare that all men are beasts, expect no more of them than bestial behavior, and you will not be disappointed. If, however, you propose to eliminate
all law and regulation, as the strictest anarchists do, you most certainly *will*
be disappointed. Such attempted "total" freedom devolves in practice into
the freedom of the powerful to devour the weak; that form of liberty becomes license: freedom for the unscrupulous or powerful and slavery for
the honest and weak. How is it possible, then, for Shaw as an advocate of
the supremacy of the individual will *and* of equality to promote the kind of
social organization necessary to protect the rights of the weak without
committing the very hypocrisy he insisted an honest creed must avoid?

Andrew Undershaft claims that brutal economic realities led him first
to violent anarchism and thence to social cooperation organized by a
strong central authority. His egoism was the foundation and necessary
precursor of his altruism. He swore that he would have his will in spite of
law or the lives of other men, and when his will was freed by this declara-

tion of anarchism he found that he wanted the same freedom from want for all others. Accomplishing that goal necessitated cooperation, organization, and laws to enforce them. His social odyssey parallels Shaw's intellectual journey from moral anarchism (he would call it "Protestantism") to a faith in pervasive government so strong as to see fascism, however flawed, as an advance over liberal democracy. The link between the two extremes is economic reality. The production of wealth in our society, Shaw realized, is socialistic. It is the product of the social organism, not of individuals acting individually. We cooperate in the creation of wealth, then fight like jackals over the product. The result is a shocking waste of goods, resources, and human spirit: the poverty, degradation, misery, and destructive competition that characterize modern capitalism. The solution, for Shaw, was a regulated economy run by the state for the benefit of all.

Shaw did not simply abandon his anarchistic moral concepts when he converted to socialism; his ideas about economics and government grew from the seed of his faith in the individual will in the harsh soil of economic and political reality. For Shaw, an ethics based in the satisfaction of the will led to cooperation and harmony, and love of freedom demanded law and government. The liberty demanded by the economic anarchists confers irresponsible freedom on the few by destroying freedom for the many. It violates J. S. Mill's famous principle that the individual's perfect right to freedom ends when he proposes to do harm to others.

Relativism and Subjectivism

Shaw rarely lost an opportunity to declare himself an enemy of morality. What he really meant was that his faith was in conscience rather than codes. Put that way, it seems rather harmless, but the realist view, honestly followed, provides disturbing surprises to those who protect their consciences with ideals—that is, to most of us. Shavian ethics are frightening because they are relativistic and subjectivistic. Those terms are sometimes confused because both suggest the abandonment of absolute moral truth, but they describe two distinct aspects of moral thought. Each also includes a broad range of ideas, while Shaw's view of both is original.

In the simplest sense we are all—whatever we might protest—moral relativists. We daily, even hourly, make choices between relative good and ill. We may forgo a lesser good for the sake of a greater or accept a minor evil to avoid a major one. Shaw insists only that we be consistent and honest about this even in the most trying of circumstances and faced with the most painful decisions. That is the realist stance. For an idealist some decisions are too painful to be faced this way. For instance, in the hope of preventing social evils such as murder and rape we inflict terrible injuries on persons we believe to have committed these offenses. We have chosen one evil to prevent another, but, as Shaw notes, frankly to call it that "provokes a stare of surprise, followed by an explanation that the outrage is punishment or justice or something else that is all right" (Pref. *Major Barbara* 3:24). We cannot bear to think that our choice is merely the lesser of two evils; we must somehow transform it into a positive good. This willful blindness to what we actually do is provoked by our humanitarian instincts—we do not wish to brutalize others—but leads to greater inhumanity than honest realism would. Faith in justice and punishment may blind us to the knowledge that there are better ways to prevent rape and murder than to brutalize the perpetrators and then turn them loose again.

The confusion surrounding the common use of the expression "the end justifies the means" provides an excellent illustration of idealistic refusal to accept responsibility for choosing a lesser but necessary evil. Originally, the phrase meant that means must always be justified by their ends. This is common sense: one does not burn down a house to get rid of a fly. To put the question in commercial terms, Is the product worth the price? Nowadays one hears that "the end justifies the means" is a pernicious, cynical Machiavellian doctrine. But how else can means be judged except in light of the ends they aim to facilitate? If a surgeon cuts off a man's leg, you ask him why. If he says he did it to save the man's life from a cancer that would otherwise have spread to the rest of his body, you may accept his answer. If he says it was the only way to remove an unsightly birthmark, you should seek to revoke his license. No one believes that any means can justify any end. Yet there may be *certain* ends that might justify any means. In the same way, it is always possible that *some* means should never be employed regardless of the goal they achieve. Once you accept the idea of a hierarchy of potentially conflicting values, there is a possibility either that certain goals will be deemed worth any price or that certain means must never be employed regardless of their result. There is always the possibility that some value will surpass all others. We may hope that we never have to choose between our most cherished values, but the possibility exists. Extreme circumstances might force such choices on us, as illustrated by the film *Sophie's Choice,* but for some people, like Dr. Ridgeon of *The Doctor's Dilemma,* such alternatives can be fairly common.

The dread of the doctrine that the means justify the ends arises from a form of moral idealism and is naturally at odds with Shaw's ethical realism. The idealist follows moral principles; the realist looks at the outcomes of actions. Whether Shaw was explaining Ibsen in the *Quintessence*, defending his own method in "A Dramatic Realist to His Critics," or proposing socialist reform, his question was never how to be true to his principles but how to achieve certain ends. In the battles between the purists and compromisers of socialism, Shaw insisted that his "own side in the controversy was the unprincipled one, as Socialism to me has always meant, not a principle, but certain definite economic measures which I wish to see taken" (*Impossibilities* 3).

The distinction can lead to significant differences. We are not talking about instances in which the apostles of principle and the followers of product, or final result, have different values. If their *values* are opposed, the principled men will fight among themselves, and the realists will do the same. The crucial test comes when the values of the idealist and the realist are identical. Suppose that we are faced with a choice between two profoundly unpleasant outcomes. We will give them the labels "A" and "P." No other alternative is possible. Idealist and realist agree that, considered strictly as outcomes, P is much worse than A. Let us say that A = (one man dies), and P = (one hundred men die). Circumstances do not permit us to console ourselves with the belief that any of these unfortunates deserve such a fate; they are equally admirable. So far there is no disagreement between idealist and realist. But let us suppose further that P will result from doing nothing and that A involves an active choice. Your choice is then to do nothing and passively accept the demise of one hundred men, or to save them by actively participating in the death of one. You must kill one man to save one hundred. The realist will be certain to assure herself that these are indeed the only two alternatives and that no other complications affect the decision (for example, that the man's death, while sparing the one hundred in question, may start a riot in which a thousand die). Then she will choose based on the perceived outcomes. The idealist will seek a rule, and a rule that comes to mind is "Thou shalt not kill." He thus chooses to avoid violation of the commandment and accepts the death of the one hundred as something he could not prevent without becoming tinged with personal evil.

There is no certain, rational way to choose between these exceedingly unpleasant alternatives. The idealist could argue that there are certain acts—such as murder—that are so vile that they are inexcusable regardless of the total outcome. The realist can say only that while she would rather save one hundred one lives, one hundred is unquestionably preferable to only one. Of course, she might also, if her ire was roused by the idealist's tone of moral superiority, borrow a line from Andrew Undershaft and accuse him of "lusting after personal righteousness." She might even declare that to demand the lives of 100 other men in satisfaction of that lust is an act of extreme egoism and selfishness. Or she might be reminded of the lesson of *The Doctor's Dilemma* and realize that she cannot be sure of her own motives: there is no such thing as a completely objective decision. I stress again that there is no rational way to arbitrate between the choice of the idealist and that of the realist, but in this instance the quest for personal righteousness would certainly exact a high price.

Moral Development: Male and Female

There is a reason for the identification of the idealist as male and the realist as female, beyond an acknowledgment that both men and women make moral decisions. Modern thinking about moral development has caught up with Shaw in interesting ways. Until recently, ideas about the moral development of children were dominated by the theories of Lawrence Kohlberg, who developed a hierarchy of moral development in children that placed abstract principles as the last and presumably highest stage. Boys did better than girls on this scale. One of his students, Carol Gilligan, has made her reputation revising these theories. She did not reject Kohlberg's empirical findings, she merely looked at them through different eyes—a woman's eyes—and showed that there was no reason why the moral development of boys should be regarded as normative or superior to that of girls. The moral criteria that girls used were different, but no less sophisticated and thoughtful, from those generally employed by boys. Whereas the boys applied abstract rules, the girls asked how much suffering would result from a given action. Then they would choose the action that produced the least harm. Gilligan does not go as far as Shaw; she merely says that the criteria of the girls is as valid as that of the boys, whereas Shaw would have declared it superior.

The simplest form of moral relativism can spark conflict between idealists and realists, but a particularly sensitive area is cultural relativism, which sees moral values as dependent on the culture in which they exist. Like moral subjectivism, cultural relativism seems to question the very validity of moral standards by suggesting that they are entirely arbitrary and conventional. This objection is more serious than relativists and subjectivists generally acknowledge. Cultural relativism suggests that good and ill are whatever the society says they are; moral subjectivism suggests that they are whatever the individual says they are. From the Shavian perspective, neither of these easy assessments is precisely true. The moralists are rightfully concerned about the trivialization of ethics but wrong about its cause. The mistake is believing that the promptings of the human soul are either capricious or, worse, actively evil. Traditional religion teaches the latter, while the former is one of the most regrettable legacies of the worship of science. For Shaw, the source of ethical values was necessarily within us, but it arises from the strivings of an imperfect and immanent deity to express Itself through us. The choice perceived by many modern intellectuals is between an absolute code of conduct imposed on sinful mankind by a transcendent and perfect God, and a collection of conventional ethical systems derived ultimately from the capricious dance of indifferent atoms. Shaw understood that a subjective morality need not be a capricious one. Ethical promptings from within might be as orderly and knowable as the laws of physics. They are simply teleological rather than mechanical; they are the laws of God and not those of the machine. Beliefs about the nature of ethics are unavoidably related to metaphysical assumptions; Shaw's metaphysics—his religion—differed from both traditional religion and modern scientism and produced a correspondingly distinct ethics.

Ethics and Anarchism

When Shaw spoke of his religion, he sometimes provocatively called himself a Protestant (for example, "On Going to Church" 389). He was not referring to the faith of his birth but to his profound belief in the authority of the individual conscience. He was a Protestant in the sense he used to describe Siegfried; that is, "a totally unmoral person, a born anarchist" (*Perfect Wagnerite* 44). How does a born anarchist develop into a passionate socialist? Shaw's most succinct answer to that question is the brief section of *The Perfect Wagnerite* called "Siegfried as Protestant." We need to be governed because, he said, we are not all Siegfrieds. If we were, government would be impossible as well as unnecessary. It would not necessarily be a good thing if we *were* all Siegfrieds. The abolition of laws and codes, Shaw goes on to explain, is no more a panacea than their strict enforcement. The point is worth stressing because Shaw's plays could be interpreted as evidence that he thought otherwise. His plays are filled with characters like Siegfried, whom Shaw describes as

a type of the healthy man raised to perfect confidence in his own impulses by an intense and joyous vitality which is above fear, sickliness of conscience, malice, and the makeshifts and moral crutches of law and order which accompany them. Such a character appears extraordinarily fascinating and exhilarating to our guilty and conscience-ridden generations, however little they may understand him. The world has always delighted in the man who is delivered from conscience. (57)

Shaw's own Siegfrieds have little in common besides freedom from the tyranny of the superego. Such freedom, however exhilarating and even awe-inspiring to observe, is no guarantee that its possessor is at the highest possible evolutionary level. The public generally assumes the reverse, and the public is not always wrong. The examples that Shaw provided were usually on the advanced side of the scale (Louis Dubedat in *The Doctor's Dilemma* being a notable exception); he was not interested in satisfying the taste for conscience-free villainy. But they are not alike, and they do not resonate at the same pitch on the evolutionary scale. Candida is an excellent case in point. In a famous letter Shaw called her "that very immoral female" (*Collected Letters* 2:414). This supreme compliment from the author to his creation has unaccountably been regarded as a repudiation. Her immorality links her not only with Siegfried but with Andrew Undershaft, his daughter Barbara, Lady Cicely Waynflete, Julius Caesar, Epifania Ognisanti di Parerga, and Saint Joan of Arc. It is the source of her fascination, the light that so blinds the men who worship her that they imagine her to be something impossible: an Ideal Woman. This ravishing defect in her character conceals from Morell, Marchbanks, and the various "Candidamaniacs" in the audience the fact that she is otherwise a very ordinary person: a Philistine, as Arthur Nethercot has correctly if provocatively said (14). Critics are right to object to this epithet, if, and only if, it is interpreted as a pejorative. Objectively speaking, Candida *is* a Philistine. She has no sympathy with art, no interest in poetry (not even Eugene's), and is thoroughly happy catering to the needs of the big baby Morell while reigning over what Eugene comes to see as a "greasy fool's paradise" (*Collected Letters* 2:415). She is also a thoroughly amiable, intelligent, and interesting person. Shaw was doubtless fond of her, and if he betrayed a certain impatience in exposing her true nature, it was inspired by annoyance, not with her but with those who insist on idolizing her despite the insistent and transparent lesson of the play: that such idolatry is folly.

Shaw stressed that "without brains and strength of mind she would be a wretched slattern & voluptuary" (*Collected Letters* 2:415). The world is not to be saved by the immoralists, however needed they are to save us from the opposite delusion. Most people are like Wagner's giants, Fasolt and Fafnir, and need the authority of law and social convention. Not wicked monsters who must be restrained, they are honest, hardworking creatures who need the guidance of those with greater intelligence and imagination. They need not be stupid, as examples from Shaw's work show. They may be like Mr. Knox in *Fanny's First Play*, whose wife tells him: "If you have that [guiding spirit] in you, the spirit will set you free to do what you want and guide you to do right. But if you havent got it, then youd best be respectable and stick to the ways that are marked out for you; for youve nothing else to keep you straight" (4:417). Those who lack guidance within must rely on instruction without. Joey Percival, in *Misalliance*, has imagination and intelligence, and as the son of three fathers he is blessed with a broad education; yet he chooses external restraint because, he says, he wants "to be free" (4:207). He seeks freedom from uncertainty and fear. Shaw rejects both the moralist who would fetter us with iron law because we are intrinsically evil and the Rousseauean anarchist who insists that we would all be naturally good but for corrupt social institutions. To the proposal of the anarchist, Shaw asks:

> But if the natural man be indeed social as well as gregarious, how did the corruption and oppression under which he groans ever arise? Could the institution of property as we know it ever have come into existence unless nearly every man had been, not merely willing, but openly and shamelessly eager to quarter himself idly on the labor of his fellows and to domineer over them whenever the mysterious workings of economic law enabled him to do so? It is useless to think of man as a fallen angel. ("Impossibilities" 14–15)

It is equally useless to think of him as captive devil, incapable of right action except in the condition of slavery. If we are intrinsically wicked, how did the moral codes needed to restrain us ever develop? One popular theory, proposed by cynics since Thomas Hobbes, that moral systems imposed by victors are accepted by the vanquished so that they may be reconciled to their slavery, has some truth to it. If it were the whole story, however, the masters would be free of such moral delusions and one would expect a "higher" level of morality the lower on the social scale one descends. This, as Shaw often pointed out, is not the case. But the freedom from fear that ensues from being born a master allows the conscience to have its say. Revolutionaries usually come from the ranks of the privileged. That is why institutions are necessary; not as prisons but as ethical nurseries. They must be designed so as to encourage and develop the best in us instead of provoking, as they often do, the worst.

Freedom and Restraint

Devising institutional means to encourage the best in us is no simple task, and Shaw's attempts to do it produced his greatest failures. His difficulties were both conceptual and practical. The theoretical obstacles to balancing freedom with restraint are obvious in his essay on the social education of children that forms the preface to *Misalliance*. Throughout the essay he repeats the question, What is to be done? Many of his answers are vague or impossible. At times he seems to suggest that children should be allowed to wander freely, unhampered by restraints or compulsions, assured of food and shelter wherever they might go (4:101–2). Elsewhere he recognizes that children need guidance in their natural thirst for knowledge and understanding and that such guidance necessarily involves restraints. He is clear about the nature of the problem: "We must reconcile education with liberty" (4:76). He knows what we must *not* do, especially that we must cease using schools as prisons to keep children out of their parents' way and break their spirits so they will be docile and unobtrusive when they do return home. He specifies that education must engage the child's natural instincts for socialization and learning in a noncoercive way. But he is not clear how to do it.

Shaw would approve of many of the changes of the past one hundred years in the area of child development, but we have done nothing to remove what he regarded as the most imposing impediment to sane child rearing: "Obstructing the way of the proper organization of childhood, as of everything else, lies our ridiculous misdistribution of the national income, with its accompanying class distinctions and imposition of snobbery on children as a necessary part of their social training" (4:50).

Our exploitive social system is founded on the economic machinery of predatory capitalism, which in turn is founded on an ideology disguised as science: modern market-centered economic theory. The ruling class, which is the class that controls economic power, defines the rules of economic "law" and presents them as inevitable, natural, and scientific. Shaw agreed that any economic system must be based on fact and sound economic theory; he disagreed that economic law shows poverty and inequality to be inevitable. He believed that the facts and sound, scientific theory showed just the opposite: that poverty is entirely artificial and unnecessary. Since the capitalists have entirely captured what passes for economic science in our age, it is worthwhile to look at the economic "facts" as Shaw saw them.

ECONOMICS

Political Economy

Like Undershaft, Shaw arrived at socialism through anarchism. He insisted that the spirit must be freed, but the freedom of competitive anarchism ensures that no man, even the richest, can be wholly free of the fear of poverty. The freedom from want is the first and most necessary of freedoms. "Liberty is an excellent thing; but it cannot begin until society has paid its daily debt to Nature by first earning its living" (*Perfect Wagnerite* 69). The Life Force must master political economy.

Shaw's economic ideas, unlike his purely philosophical and religious beliefs, were largely borrowed from others, but they were important to the implementation of his philosophy.[1] His socialism, like everything else, was realistic rather than idealistic. Thus he recognized first that socialism is "founded on sentimental dogma, and is quite unmeaning and purposeless apart from it," and second, that if socialism is to be successful it "must come into the field as political science and not as sentimental dogma" ("Illusions" 412). These concepts are not contradictory; they simply acknowledge that the goal of socialism stems from a nonrational and passionate desire to change the way we distribute the national income but that the *means* to achieve this redistribution must be based in fact and reason.

Shaw believed that socialist theory should be based on scientific economics, and he argued that the theories of two laissez-faire economists, David Ricardo (1772–1823) and William Stanley Jevons (1835–82), provide a compelling case for socialism: Ricardo's *theory of rent* and Jevons *theory of marginal utility.* Silent testimony to the wisdom of Shaw's observation is that contemporary textbooks on economics (which have an overwhelming right-wing, capitalist bias) rarely mention either of them, although marginal utility is the basis of the law of supply and demand and economic rent is the principal force determining how wealth is distributed. Unfortunately, they are not simple to understand. Shaw insisted that Marxist theory (although clearly wrong) was favored by socialists because it is simple and dramatic, while the correct theory is technical and difficult. His rejection of Marx's theory of surplus value, which was based on the labor theory of value promulgated by David Ricardo, was again realism abjuring idealism. The theory of surplus value appeals to socialists because it seems to provide a factual basis for the "sentimental dogma." It purports to show that the difference between the subsistence wage of labor necessary to produce an item and its actual price naturally "belongs" to the worker and is "stolen" by the capitalist. Unfortunately, the labor theory of value is false.

A disciple of Adam Smith, Ricardo helped establish economics as the "dismal" science, particularly with his "iron law of wages." The "iron law" followed Thomas Malthus in proposing that wages must stay at subsistence level because any rise in wages increased the population of the poor, glutting the labor market and bringing wages down again. This "law" is the foundation for Ricardo's labor theory of value, which holds that the value of an item is the cost of its production, which in most cases is the cost of the labor necessary to manufacture it: subsistence wages. Karl Marx reasoned that while value is created by labor, the actual price received in exchange was always higher than the subsistence wage provided the worker. The difference was surplus value, which belongs to the worker because it was created by his labor but is stolen by the capitalist. The fallacy in this theory, as Shaw often pointed out, is that value is independent of labor; it is simply the result of people's desire for something. Defective goods will be worthless regardless of the labor that went into their manufacture, whereas a diamond casually picked out of a crevice could be worth millions. The truth is that value causes labor, not the other way round.

Margins of Utility and Production

Shaw rejected the *value* theories of Ricardo and Marx, accepting instead Stanley Jevons's theory of marginal utility, which modern economists still regard as valid in outline. Utility, although an extremely important economic concept, is not familiar to most people.[2] They have heard about Supply and Demand and know that together they determine the price, or "exchange value," of things. They probably know that when Demand goes up or Supply goes down then Value goes up. (Capital letters in this section merely signify that the word is being used in a special, technical sense that might be quite different from its everyday meaning). It may seem intuitively obvious that high demand would produce high prices and an increase in supply would bring prices down, and most people never go any deeper into the matter than that. Utility is an attempt to analyze the foundation of demand by giving a measurement to what might be called "intrinsic value," as opposed to the Exchange Value. In simple terms, Utility is jargon for "desirability" and represents an attempt to quantify what is essentially subjective. It also varies considerably according to circumstances. It refers to the amount an individual would be willing to pay for an item if there were a choice between paying that price and doing without. You do not have to think about it much to realize that for most of us a gallon of unpoisoned water has far greater Utility than a flawless twenty-caret diamond. Or at least it would if we did not have any water. If we already have an unlimited supply (or even a very large supply) the case is altered. If water is so plentiful that it can be had for the asking, its price (and in this technical sense, its Utility) is nothing. So there really is no such a thing as a fixed, "intrinsic" value for anything, because desire for something varies as circumstances vary but certain things (like drinkable water) are more likely to have greater Utility than others.

Utility is the highest price you would pay if you had no other choice and is clearly a better indication of the importance of a commodity (or service) than is its price, but it is also fluid and variable. It varies not only between individuals but also from moment to moment for a single person. A loaf of bread has more Utility to a starving man than to the gentleman who has just gotten up from a huge Thanksgiving dinner. But once that starving man has devoured his first loaf of bread, the next will have less Utility and the one after that even less. If he keeps getting more bread, eventually even the (once) starving man will reach the point at which he cannot stand so much as to look at another loaf of bread. It now has no Utility at all. And this change in the Utility of an item does not follow a smooth, continuous line. Think about what Utility a particular item, say an umbrella (to adapt an example Shaw uses), has for you. If it looks like rain, and you do not have one, you might be willing to pay, say, ten dollars for an umbrella. A second umbrella is much less attractive: you might give a dollar. It might be nice to have a spare. But a third one would not rate more than the smallest of small change—perhaps a nickel.

Utility is exceedingly important because it is the basis of the "law of supply and demand" that the capitalist economists are always citing. To understand it is to understand that supply and demand is not the simple matter the capitalist would like us to imagine. I will illustrate with a purely hypothetical example. Let us suppose that you are walking about town, doing weekly shopping, and you notice that it looks as though it might rain. So you head for the nearest mall to buy an umbrella and miraculously find there are three umbrella stands that reflect the different Utilities that an umbrella might represent to you personally. One has a sign declaring: "First Umbrellas: Ten Dollars"; the next's sign says: "Second Umbrellas: One Dollar"; and the last proclaims: "Third Umbrellas: Five Cents." So what do you do? Unless your conscience is particularly sensitive and troublesome, you will probably buy from the third stand without bothering to mention that you do not actually have two more like it at home. Of course, you are not likely to see three such stands. If the quality of the products is the same, the price will be either the same or very close to it. Every stand owner wants to make as much as possible from each umbrella but does not want to price his merchandise so high as to drive all the customers away. If he lowers the price he will sell more umbrellas (but make less on each); if he raises the price he will make more for each umbrella but sell fewer. If his price is grossly higher than that of his competitors, no one will come to his stand. So the price of the market is effectively set by the person who is willing to accept the least. But which price? That depends on the total Utility these umbrellas represent to all the people in this market.

For the sake of simplicity, let us assume that everyone is just like you: none already has an umbrella, and they all value first, second, and third umbrellas as you do. What happens if there are one hundred umbrella shoppers and each stand has thirty-three umbrellas. Clearly, no one will want to sell for less than ten dollars because all the umbrellas will be gone before the highest (ten dollar) Utility is exhausted. But what if there are more than one hundred items for sale? If each retailer gets his umbrellas from the same wholesaler (so that any stand could conceivably sell all available items) you might think that everyone would just sell at the highest price until there were no more takers, then sell at the "second umbrella" price. If all the stand owners can agree, that might happen. That is what OPEC tried (for a while successfully) to do. But greed tends to take over; someone is apt to figure that if he can sell *lots* of umbrellas for just a little bit less money, he will do better than if he sells his "share" of the first umbrella market (one-third of one hundred) and then is forced to sell at the "second umbrella" price. It does not matter greatly how much of the "second umbrella" demand is matched by the supply—whether, for example, there are two hundred or one hundred fifty umbrellas for sale—so long as it is important to everyone to sell all or nearly all of the available umbrellas. In the competition to sell more of an item, the sellers will lower the price until it reaches the level of the Utility of the buyers' "second umbrella." This is the Final or Marginal Utility. Jevons declared that the price in any given market would automatically drop to the level of the least utility, that is, in this example, if there are between one hundred and two hundred umbrellas available, the price would be one dollar. He called this the "law of indifference": no one will pay more for an item than the lowest price in the market. In his words, "in the same open market, at any one moment, there cannot be two prices for the same kind of article" (91). So, as the economists put it, the Exchange Value is determined by the *force of demand at the margin of utility* (sometimes they say "margin of supply" because the price is where the level of supply meets the final Utility). Another way of putting it is to say that price is determined by the Utility of the last item consumed ("Final Utility").

This is one of the foundations of Shaw's economic ideas; let us put it into the perspective of the Shavian religion. The Life Force must take command of the facts of its existence, which includes the facts of political economy. The concept of Utility is, to some degree, an attempt to express in economic terms the needs of the Life Force. It is so only to a degree because Utility is a measure, strictly, not of how much one desires something but of how much one is willing to pay, which in turn is controlled by how much one has. Equal incomes, Shaw realized, would allow the operation of economic law to reflect human need more closely. The other important point for Shaw is that the notion of Marginal Utility makes glaringly clear how arbitrary exchange value really is. Utility merely sets an upper limit on the exchange value of an item; it can drop from that point all the way to zero as the supply grows and finally exceeds the demand. Conservative commentators, who ignore Utility, like to pretend that exchange value, particularly in the case of labor, is an indication of intrinsic worth. They imagine that there is natural justice in the difference between the income of a janitor and that of a physician. But if the supply of physicians expanded beyond the demand, their incomes would also drop to subsistence. And if the talent for janitorial work were rare, we would doubtless pay our custodial staffs far more than we do.

Shaw, like the capitalists, was interested in the laws governing supply and demand, but for Shaw that meant mastering economics so as to serve the Life Force better, while for the capitalists it means using economic theory fallaciously to support their Social Darwinist metaphysics and justify their predations. Understanding Utility means understanding that competition in the marketplace, the virtues of which the capitalists are forever praising, could work as it should only if incomes were equal.

Economic Rent

Even if the market were competitive in the way imagined by free market theorists, things would not be so simple, for Supply, like Utility, has its margins. Just as Utility varies with individuals and with circumstances, the efficiency of production varies. In many cases, as supply increases, efficiency drops. Nineteenth-century thinkers, including Shaw, assumed that this was virtually always true. Their reasoning was simple: imagine an uninhabited fertile valley; the first settlers will take the best, most productive land, and as others move in they will be forced to occupy *increasingly less productive land*. In competitive circumstances, demand tends to drive prices down to the level at which the producers no longer regard it worthwhile to produce. If the land were all equally productive, that would be essentially subsistence level (assuming the farmers had no other employment opportunities). But in this case the price is driven down to the subsistence level at the *least productive farms*. By superimposing a graph of price and supply (margin of utility) on one showing cost and production (margin of supply) we determine the actual exchange value in a particular market: the point where marginal utility meets the margin of supply.

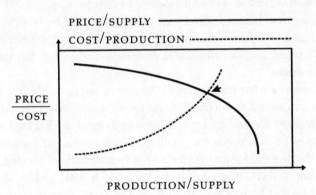

The unbroken line, showing the price (the vertical dimension) at a given level of supply (determined by the Final Utility and represented by the horizontal dimension) tells us that the price will come down gradually until the market becomes glutted, when it begins to drop precipitously. For the broken line the vertical represents the cost of production at the least efficient sites and the horizontal the level of production. It tells us that (in this case) inefficiency rises more or less geometrically as more land is brought into production. As production and supply are commensurate, a horizontal line drawn on the graph anywhere to the left of the point at which the two curves cross represents a given level of production and sup-ply that is unstable. Price exceeds cost of production, so more (presumably less productive) land is cultivated. At these new sites, costs are higher, but because more goods are produced, the price goes down. When costs and price begin to meet, new production ceases. One never moves to the right of the crossing point as costs would exceed price and new producers would be operating at a loss.

Of course, not all farmers have poor land, but the Law of Indifference ensures that they all get the same price. Let us say that grain is selling for a dollar a bushel. That bushel costs Farmer A (the first to arrive) twenty cents to produce; it costs Farmer Z (the last to arrive) ninety-five cents. Farmer A makes seventy-five cents a bushel more than Farmer Z. He works no harder, is no more virtuous or talented, but he makes more all the same. In fact, he need not work at all. If the population is increasing, the newcomers will be occupying even less productive land, so he can make them an offer they will not refuse: "Work my land," he will say, "and I will give you six cents a bushel for all you produce." That is slightly more than he could make on his own, marginally productive land. So whether Farmer A farms his own land or gets someone else to do it for him, the difference between the cost of his production (including subsistence for whoever does the work) and the price determined by the *margin of production* (at Farmer Z's place) is called *Rent*. It is essentially something for nothing: unearned income.

Please observe what happens next. Farmer A can not only live better than Z, he can afford to "invest." Anticipating an increase in population and a consequent demand for land, he buys up as much of that land no one now wants as he can. When the predicted population boost happens, not only does the demand for grain increase, but so does demand for land. Thus is the saying of the Gospels fulfilled: "For he that hath, to him shall be given: and he that hath not, from him shall be taken even that which he hath." Limited resources are a boon to those who own them, whether land or capital, and the hungrier the propertyless are, the richer the fortunate become. So wealth tends to gravitate to the already wealthy. Perhaps it is clear now why the capitalists always claim to believe that there are no limits to growth—even of population. As people become hungrier, wages go down and rents go up. To the rentiers and their apologists, that is the definition of Paradise.

Rent, in short, is the economic advantage that accrues to an individual merely by virtue of owning valuable resources. That applies to talent as well as capital or land; then it is called the *rent of ability*. There is no moral reason that the talented person should have more than the untalented one, but people won't pay as much to hear an untalented person sing as they will pay Pavarotti. Talent is a gift, something its possessor has done nothing to deserve. If earning is working, then rent is unearned income. When told that genius should receive preferential compensation, Sidney Trefusis replies that "genius cost its possessor nothing; that it was the inheritance of the whole race incidentally vested in a single individual; and that if that individual employed his monopoly of it to extort money from others, he deserved nothing better than hanging" (*Unsocial Socialist* 106). True, you generally must work yourself to get the benefit of the rent of ability, but rent, technically, refers to that extra that your talent provides you above what others doing the same thing would earn. If that were the case with all forms of rent, however, rent and inequality would be limited although not eliminated. In other words, if no one could own more of the means of production than they could work themselves, there would be little problem even with some continuing inequality. But that is not the case. All productive economic activity involves both labor and resources. When a society is divided into those who own and those who work, as ours is, injustice and poverty are inevitable.

Why Property Is Theft

Throughout his long life Shaw was fond of repeating Proudhon's famous aphorism: "Property is theft." That, for Shaw, summed up the central truth at the heart of socialism. People still are shocked—perhaps even more now, in an age that has forgotten all of the economic dialectic of the nineteenth century and accepts unthinkingly the current conventional wisdom that communism is wicked and the right to private property is sacred. So perhaps a bit of clarification is in order. First, in economic terms "private property" is not the same as "personal possessions." A man who owns a toothbrush and the shirt on his back is not a man of property. "Property" means land and capital: the means of production. It is not a question of some people having more goods, or more expensive toys, than others. The great evil of private property arises because society is divided into the haves and have-nots, and what the haves have is the right to live at the expense of others, while what the have-nots lack is the right to live at all except insofar as they are useful to the haves. Workers have no right to work for themselves, only for the owners of property. We have come to accept this concept so thoroughly that we nod mechanically when we are told to be grateful to property owners for "creating jobs." The pernicious effects of this system are not obvious to most of us as long as the ownership of property is widely distributed. Then there are usually many opportunities, at least for those with cultural and educational advantages. There are times, however, when its evil effects become especially obvious and disruptive: when the owners of property realize that they can use their resources more profitably with less labor. That happened in England in the fifteenth century, when expanding trade increased the demand for wool. Landlords "inclosed" their land, drove off the peasants who farmed it, and converted it to sheep pastures. Thousands of people were left without a livelihood. Many became vagrants or outlaws. The authorities did what they always do when their relentless robbing of the poor leaves a class of dangerous people who have nothing to lose: they passed laws against the poor, in this case laws against vagrancy or "masterless" men. In our day we build more prisons and demand mandatory sentencing. The recent much touted "economic miracles" of Latin America actually left the poor in those countries (who were wretched to begin with) worse off than they had been. Why? Because land was converted to the production of high-profit, low-cost export goods that enriched both local owners and foreign "investors" while displacing those who traditionally eked their existence from the land.

The simple truth that the right to withhold valuable resources from the community is legal theft was at the heart of Shaw's socialist convictions. This is what he meant when he said that the power of the property owner is like that of the "highwayman who puts a pistol to your head and demands your money or your life" (*Intelligent Woman's Guide* 71). When society is divided into those who own the means of production and those who do not, the owners can—and do—say to the proletarians: "We will allow you to live, if, and only if, you make yourselves useful to us." Since the proletarian cannot produce without land and capital, he must work *for* the owners of these things, who regard this as a perfectly fair and natural transaction. If you regard the right to produce so that you might consume to be as sacred as the right to life, the transaction is like that offered by the highwayman. Goods and services must be produced daily by labor; the landlord forces the laborer to yield his labor in the same way the thief takes money at the point of his gun.

This situation is obvious only when labor is so abundant that its price is driven down to subsistence—as it was in the nineteenth century. (Shaw maintained that as long as there are more workers than are needed the actual price of labor is nothing—which is technically true, for the subsistence wage given unskilled labor was really just the cost of keeping the brutes alive.) When supply exceeds demand, its value (final utility) drops to zero. The exploiters of natural resources were protected from this misfortune by their own inefficiency, or rather by the inefficiency of the least effective production sites. Unskilled laborers in nineteenth-century England had no such protection. As long as there was widespread unemployment, workers could be had for the asking; the subsistence wage was really only the cost of maintaining a slave or providing fodder to draft animals. Shaw went further than Ricardo in this; Ricardo maintained that the value of labor always fell to subsistence. It was necessary only to maintain them as one would livestock. Actually, said Shaw, the employer had less incentive to provide for such workers than he would for slaves or draft animals because there was no capital investment to protect ("Economic Basis" 18). They were paid what amounted to a subsubsistence wage, and when they were worn out they were sacked. Laborers were a disposable commodity. Because this situation kept wages at the absolute minimum, employers convinced themselves that it was a necessary condition of economic health, and they spoke righteously about the economic necessity to maintain, in Marx's famous phrase, a "reserve army of the unemployed."

Unfortunately, as we have seen, disparities in wealth are inclined to grow if left alone, and property tends to accumulate in fewer and fewer hands. The fewer people who own property, the less they are inclined to use their property productively. This becomes clear if you consider what would happen if only one man owned everything. He would need to employ just enough people to supply his own wants (and his servants' bare necessities) and, of course, a huge army to keep the hungry, dangerous poor at bay.

The apparent difference between the relation of gun-wielding highwayman to victim and that of property owner to worker is entirely conventional. We do not grant that a man with a gun has the right to deprive others of life. We do grant the property owner the right to deprive the propertyless of the means to live. Once the wielders of weapons were accorded greater right by society. It was called the "right of conquest." We have ethically grown so far as to realize that the "right" of conquest was in fact a colossal wrong. To progressive thinkers of the nineteenth century, like Shaw, it was equally clear that the "Sacred Right of Private Property" is an even greater evil. It is the source of all poverty and most injustice; it is the foundation of imperialism and slavery and the infection that gives rise to drug abuse, crime, and all manner of social disease.

The Nonwork Ethic and the Idolatry of Parasites

Ricardo saw this system as unfortunate but inevitable; Shaw knew it was arbitrary and evil. The disease afflicts both upper and lower classes: "What is the matter with the poor is Poverty: what is the matter with the rich is Uselessness" (*Man and Superman* 2:794). Both are spiritually debilitating. Parasitism as well as poverty produces atrophy of soul. The poor are brutalized by want and disease; the lesions of surfeit and ease are more subtle but still profound. "The right to live is abused whenever it is not constantly challenged" (2:793), yet the artificial rights conferred by property produce a class that regards parasitism as the definition of gentility. Members of this class regard it as dishonorable to help in the production of what they consume; they insist that their right to live should not be challenged by even the necessity to produce their share of life's sustenance. The gentleman parasite "is necessarily the enemy of his country" because he preys upon it (2:739).

The class system is not objectionable for making distinctions between people because distinctions are the inevitable result of differences; it is objectionable because the distinctions it makes are destructive and artificial. Sidney Trefusis, the Unsocial Socialist, insists on "the natural inequality of man, and the failure of our artificial inequality to correspond with it" (*Unsocial Socialist* 160). People naturally differ in their talents and abilities, but these differences are suppressed by an artificial hierarchy based on the possession of money. Money becomes the sole measure of value. The system is self-justifying. Depriving people of the means to live well degrades them, and their degraded condition is used to justify their deprivation. Sartorius justifies refusing to improve his slum, saying that "these poor people do not know how to live in proper dwellings: they would wreck them in a week" (*Widowers' Houses* 1:92). Sartorius, who has experienced poverty, is more understanding than most; his daughter's attitude is more typical: "Oh, I hate the poor. At least, I hate those dirty, drunken, disreputable people who live like pigs" (1:110).

Breakages, Limited, and the Accumulation of "Illth"

Capitalist inequality is economically destructive in several ways. By placing the parasite at the top of the hierarchy, it debases productive labor and ensures that everyone will strive to do as little worthwhile work as possible. Even if the worker preserves some pride in his work, in spite of the prevailing nonwork ethic, he is aware that he is working for the benefit of someone else. For him, the more one does, the more one is robbed. Like

Snobby Price, he will be tempted to imitate the capitalists by taking as much as he can and doing as little as possible for it (*Major Barbara* 3:96). The economic competition central to capitalist theory is itself destructive, for it is easier to sabotage the competition than to create a better product. The system favors the likes of Boss Mangan, who admits: "I may not know anything about my own machinery; but I know how to stick a ramrod into the other fellow's" (*Heartbreak House* 5:164). And the unbridled operation of the laws of supply and demand ensures that everyone has a vested interest in reducing the supply of the goods in which he deals.

> Individuals are constantly trying to decrease supply for their own advantage. Gigantic conspiracies have been entered into to forestall the world's wheat and cotton harvests, so as to force their value to the highest possible point. . . . All rings, trusts corners, combinations, monopolies, and trade secrets have the same object. Production and the development of the social instincts are alike hindered by each man's consciousness that the more he stints the community the more he benefits himself. ("Economic Basis" 16–17)

Many people, particularly in the professions, have even greater conflicts between their interests and those of the public. The consequence is that "all professions . . . are conspiracies against the public" (Pref. *Doctor's Dilemma* 3:237). Contrary to capitalist theory, the pursuit of maximum individual gain results in a *reduction* in the public weal.

> And as the use of a plot of land for growing wheat, or as the site of a cathedral or college, may be less lucrative to its private owner than its use as a site of a totalizator, an able merchant may make more money out of the vices of mankind than an inventor or philanthropist out of its needs and virtues. In England a surgeon can earn hundreds of pounds by a major operation, and three guineas by declaring it to be unnecessary. A doctor who cures his patients loses them. A victualler's "good bar customer," meaning one who drinks more than is good for him, is a bad citizen. The prudent plumber takes care not to make his repairs too permanent. It is therefore disastrous from the public point of view to give any person a pecuniary interest in disease or in mischief of any sort. (*Everybody's Political What's What?* 316–17)

But that is what capitalism does. The profitability of waste, inefficiency, and destruction is embodied in the ubiquitous Breakages, Limited, the malign de facto center of power in *The Apple Cart*. Because its profits depend on breakdowns, accidents, and waste, it effectively suppresses all inventions and innovations that would create greater efficiency or make durable goods truly durable (6:328–29).

Artificial inequality even distorts the market forces of supply and demand idolized by capitalist theorists. Because what is called "effective demand" depends on having money to offer, starvation does not create "demand" if those starving have no money, while idle people with more money than they need to satisfy their genuine needs begin to lust after luxuries: useless toys that society calls "status symbols." The economy is diverted from the production of genuine wealth and devotes itself to producing what Shaw called "illth." "Exchange value itself, in fact, has become bedevilled like everything else, and represents no longer utility, but the cravings of lust, folly, vanity, gluttony, and madness, technically described by genteel economists as 'effective demand'" ("Economic Basis" 21).

Money, Idolatry, and Civilization

The artificial inequality produced by unequal distribution of society's goods has a purpose:

> There is a solid reason for such inequalities in all societies which, like our own, are based on Idolatry. It is absolutely necessary, if you are to have an ordered society at all, that Bill Jones, who may possibly be a more muscular man than Jack Smith, should nevertheless obey Jack Smith even when he has not the least notion of what Jack Smith is driving at. To induce him to do it, you must somehow contrive to make him idolize Jack Smith. . . . If that is to be done, you must put a crown or a tiara on Jack's head; prevent him from ever doing—or at least letting anyone see him doing—anything that Bill does; give him much more money and quite different clothes, besides lodging him in a much finer house and surrounding him with minor idols to set the example of worshipping him. ("Simple Truth" 161–62)

It would appear that inequality, despite its terrible attendant evils, is necessary "if you are to have an ordered society at all," but it makes sense only if the idolized actually do the superior work: if the governing class actually governs and does not just live in idle uselessness. The difficulty is that the system is artificial and cannot guarantee that the most competent will have the reins of power. The idolatrous awe of money obscures true distinction, but the competent have a power apart from that conferred by wealth. The authority of the tertiaries in *Back to Methuselah*, like that of Andrew Undershaft and *Too True To Be Good*'s Private Meek, derives from competence. There is a reality behind superstitious idolatry of rich persons: it is the power of money, which is the power to deprive others of a livelihood. We obey rich people for the same reason that we obey the thief who puts a pistol to our heads. "But that is not obedience to authority: it is submission to a threat. Real authority has nothing to do with money" (*Intelligent Woman's Guide* 71).

Competent or otherwise, the rich will use their power to maintain their own privileges. Indeed, one of the worst aspects of the exploitative capitalist system is that its evils are self-perpetuating. This, Shaw always insisted, was not because the capitalists and landlords are evil but because they, like the rest of us, are subject to the enormous power of the will-to-believe. People believe mostly what they want to believe.

> If by inequality of income you give your doctors, your lawyers, your clergymen, your landlords, or your rulers an overwhelming economic interest in any sort of belief or practice, they will immediately begin to see all the evidence in favor of that sort of belief and practice, and become blind to all the evidence against it. Every doctrine that will enrich doctors, lawyers, landlords, clergymen, and rulers will be embraced by them eagerly and hopefully; and every doctrine that threatens to impoverish them will be mercilessly criticized and rejected. (*Intelligent Woman's Guide* 498)

Natural Eugenics

The artificial inequality produced by property and rent is the enemy of the Life Force, as well as of present social welfare. If the human race is to be improved—and it needs improvement—we must be better bred. We must concern ourselves with eugenics. That word has acquired some highly unpleasant baggage, so we need to explain carefully what it is that Shaw meant by the term, which is capable of producing near-hysterical reactions in otherwise levelheaded people. These people seem to believe that because eugenics was evoked to justify Nazi genocide, eugenics must necessarily be evil. The well-intentioned people who wished to rid the world of congenital defects cannot be held responsible for racists who promoted genocide, and the attempt to tar Shaw with that brush is simply stupid. His statements on eugenics were consistent throughout his life: he maintained, first, that better breeding was essential and, second, that only the Life

Force could be trusted to select the pairs. This is what he said in 1910, but the same opinion is in *The Intelligent Woman's Guide* and *Everybody's Political What's What?*, among other places:

> An improvement by direct breeding is impossible, not because there is the smallest rational objection to a human stud farm, but because if we set up a stud farm we should not know what to breed. The Eugenic Society feels quite sure, apparently, that it can make a beginning by at least breeding out tuberculosis, epilepsy, dipsomania, and lunacy; but for all we know to the contrary, the Superman may be tuberculous from top to toe; he is quite likely to be a controlled epileptic; his sole diet may be overproof spirit; and he will certainly be as mad as a hatter from our point of view. We really know nothing about him. Our worst failures today may be simply first attempts at him, and our greatest successes the final perfection of the type that is passing away. Under these circumstances there is nothing to be done in the way of a stud farm. We must trust to nature: that is, to the fancies of our males and females. ("Simple Truth" 186)

All we can do is remove the artificial barriers we have erected between potential mates through artificial inequality. Shaw's program of eugenics can be summed up in a single word: equality.

Natural Solutions in a Controlled Environment

Equality is Shaw's answer to *all* of these evils of capitalism. Specifically, you must equalize incomes, as "you cannot equalize anything about human beings except their incomes" ("Case for Equality" 122). He took it for granted that the achievement of such equality required that the state, as representative of all the people, take possession of the means of production and administer the distribution of the national income. The goal, however, was not far different from that of the communist anarchists: a cooperative society with the maximum possible freedom. Shaw's contention was that moral freedom could achieve social good only under socialism and equal incomes. Vice and virtue are branches of the same tree. They are merely injurious and beneficial effects of the same human propensities. "Human nature is only the raw material which Society manufactures into the finished rascal or the finished fellowman, as the case may be, according to the direction in which it applies the pressure of self-interest" ("Socialism and Human Nature" 96). The "natural cure" for vice "is the resistance of the victims" (97). The "pressure of self-interest" works to restrain antisocial behavior but only when the victim is on an equal footing with the culprit. The operation of self-interest as a guide to the betterment of society as a whole sounds curiously like the invisible hand of Adam Smith, but Shaw insists that it could be possible only when incomes are the same.

One of the beneficial effects of equalizing incomes is that "of securing promotion by merit for the more capable" (*Intelligent Woman's Guide* 101). Promotion by merit is not merely a different way of ranging the human population on a scale of worth, from contemptible to revered. Equality of income is a way of securing equality of respect. Shaw did say that socialism would make possible a natural aristocracy, but it was not an aristocracy of dominance, or intellect, or any of the gifts from God to the human race that happen to be vested in one individual. Shaw's last word in his address to the Intelligent Woman was that under socialism the title of "lady" would no longer be the distinction of the parasite but the mark of "she who, generously overearning her income, leaves the nation in her debt and the world a better world than she found it" (500). This, he points out, is a distinction within the grasp of every able-bodied person.

Idiots and Inequality

One would think that this concept of "aristocracy" would be attractive to the many, but Shaw suggested a discouraging reason why it is not so. At the beginning of his conversion to socialism, Shaw and other socialists thought the advantages of socialism were so obvious "that Socialism had only to be put clearly before the working-classes to concentrate the power of their immense numbers in one irresistible organization" bring about the revolution immediately ("Transition" 173). It seemed merely a matter of educating the proletariat, organizing them, and letting their self-interest do the rest. The workers shocked their would-be benefactors by repudiating socialism. Many socialists refused to believe that the workers could be so blind. Shaw accepted the truth (with an occasional note of bitter irony) but imagined that it was largely a result of the short-term interests of the "parasitic proletariat"—those whose income was derived from catering to the idle rich. A more important reason may be found in one of Shaw's little-noted observations: "Between persons of equal income there is no social distinction except the distinction of merit. Money is nothing: character, conduct, and capacity are everything. . . . That is why idiots are always in favor of inequality of income (their only chance of eminence), and the really great in favor of equality" (*Intelligent Woman's Guide* 102). Shaw should have noticed that the idiots are in the majority. He often characterized the temperament opposed to socialism as the gambling temperament ("Economic Basis" 3–4). As long as eminence is identified with wealth and capitalism holds out a gambler's chance that anyone might become wealthy, people will prefer the remote possibility of artificial distinction to the certainty of natural mediocrity. Shaw knew that although capitalism glorifies the rich and debases the poor, "it gives to every poor man a gambling chance, at odds of a million to one or thereabouts, of becoming a rich one," which gives a reason to hope (*Practical Politics* 169).

Government

Salvation Through Government Organization

Another obstacle to equality and the establishment of Shaw's natural aristocracy of service is intense fear of government involvement in our individual lives. Shaw did not share this fear. His attitude toward government has provoked heavy criticism, even from his supporters. The political tumult of the latter half of Shaw's life has left scars on our collective psyche that are still so sensitive that we cannot, even now, bear to have them touched. Shaw's reactions to those events continue to probe those old wounds, and we still wince. Shaw was seriously wrong about many of the people and events of that period, but our sensitivity to the evils of that time have led us to profoundly misunderstand the nature of, and reasons for, his mistakes. Because his mistakes involved Hitler, Stalin, Mussolini, and the Holocaust, which have become icons of evil to our age, it is necessary to make careful distinctions. I am not concerned with Shaw's personality or psyche but merely with the relevance of his philosophy. Arnold Silver, for example, is convinced that Shaw harbored hidden homicidal tendencies. He may well be right, but whether he is right or wrong is irrelevant to my concerns here. Or it can be argued that Shaw's political mistakes of the period between the world wars were a direct consequence of his philosophical premises, that his conviction that there are no good men or scoundrels blinded him to the real evil of Stalin and Hitler. If true, that would constitute a fatal flaw in Shaw's religion of moral equality. It is thus an issue that must be addressed.

Most of the casual judgments about Shaw's mistakes are themselves mistaken. Shaw, it is said, was seduced by his fascination with great men into believing them the salvation of the world. He was an elitist. He was an authoritarian. He was an enemy of democracy. All of these charges are flatly false. When it is pointed out that Shaw vigorously attacked each of these positions he is accused of espousing, the critics claim that he was confused and contradictory. On the contrary, the misunderstanding arises because Shaw was thoroughly true to his beliefs. If anything, it is the critics who are inconsistent.

It is true that Shaw was fascinated with exceptionally intelligent, clever, talented, and self-assured women and men; so is everyone else. Barbara Undershaft is infinitely more interesting than her sister Sarah, just as many people prefer Antigone to Ismene. That is not the same as believing that these men and women are the salvation of the world, a position Shaw specifically and emphatically rejected in *The Intelligent Woman's Guide* and elsewhere. His desire to point the way to the future led him to prefer superior persons as dramatic subjects; when, in *Widowers' Houses,* he held the mirror up to common natures, those ordinary folks shrunk in horror from their unfamiliar images and demanded that Shaw cease assaulting them with immoral human monsters.

Shaw was also, in the same trivial way, an elitist. We are all elitists with respect to airline pilots. The airline that challenged this assertion by announcing that, henceforth, the passengers on each flight would elect their pilot from among themselves would soon be out of business. That is exactly Shaw's elitism: he believed that government was a difficult and sensitive job that required particular aptitudes and special training. He wanted the ship of state to be piloted by those best qualified. But if an elitist is someone who believes that "inferior" people should serve the needs of the "superior," then Shaw was the opposite of an elitist. His governmental "elite" was to be women and men who were self-chosen because of a concern for the public welfare, not a lust for power. Shaw told his imaginary protégé, in his earliest literary effort: "Ridiculous as it may seem to you, my dear Dorothea, the scullery maid is every whit as good a person as you are, unless you can surpass her by learning more, being kinder and controlling your temper better, and by doing work that requires more thought than washing dishes. Such superiority alone deserves admiration and respect" (*My Dear Dorothea* 44).

Shaw insisted that legislation must be by the "quality" rather than the "mob," but he went on to point out that those terms refer to the same persons in different capacities:

In literature and drama, for instance, I belong to the quality. In mathematics, athletics, mechanics, I am one of the mob, and not only accept and obey authority but claim a neighborly right to be told what to do by those who know better than I do. The best of us is nine hundred and ninetynine per cent mob and one per cent quality. . . . In championing the rights of the mob I champion my own. (*Everybody's Political What's What?* 30–31)

Shaw's position was directly opposed to that of those who have fretted publicly that laws to prevent corruption in government will make it difficult to attract talented persons into the service of their country (on the strange theory, one supposes, that a clever thief is more desirable than a foolish one). Our legislators and administrators should serve us as priests, nuns, and monks are supposed to serve God, drawn thither not by bribes of power, wealth, and privilege but by the promptings of an inner vocation (Pref. *Too True to Be Good* 6: 415). Private Meek is the type. Shaw's elite wants to serve its community, not to be served by it.

Finally, anyone convinced that Shaw was an authoritarian should look carefully at the preface to *Misalliance.* Government, he believed, is necessary to ensure the maximum possible freedom, and the instinctive fear and hatred of masters that is always leading us to thwart government is the most certain prescription for slavery. He reasoned that the checks and balances of the American Constitution and those of the English party system were devices that, by making it impossible for government to accomplish anything, delivered us into the hands of the plutocrats, who were motivated by the narrowest and basest of motives.[3] Pseudo-democracy serves the narrow, selfish interests of "irresponsible private enterprise" by disabling the government, whose function is to serve the community. The appeal of dictators is that they can break the chains with which the private interests have bound government and get things done, but dictators bring their own problems: "The only sane course is to take the step by which the dictatorship could have been anticipated and averted, and construct a political system for rapid positive work" (Pref. *Apple Cart* 6:255). Shaw's "authority" was to have been a bureaucracy of experts, equipped with the knowledge and skills to solve the problems of their society and driven by a passion to serve. In his ideas about government, as in everything else, Shaw knew the importance of distinguishing between the will and the way. The will of Mr. Everybody—the "mob"—must prevail. That is the nature of true democracy. The way is another matter: "It is on the question of method that your expert comes in" (Pref. *Getting Married* 3:479). One of the most important duties of the expert is to educate the public as to the soundest way to achieve its will. "It is said that every people has the Government it deserves. It is more to the point that every Government has the electorate it deserves; for the orators of the front benches can edify or

debauch an ignorant public at will" (Pref. *Heartbreak House* 5:16–17).
Pseudo-democracy, which stops at providing votes for everybody, is a disaster because it assures the election of demagogues and frauds who have
no interest in educating the public. Their purpose is to exploit, not to serve.

Government by the Best Does Not Mean Inequality

Shaw lacked a common assumption most of us share: the idea that
"bosses" have some sort of God-given, natural rights of ownership over
those they boss. We assume that employees work *for* their employer, that
children *belong* to their parents. For Shaw the relation of boss and bossed
was necessary and potentially beneficial while that of master and slave was
useless and destructive. We reluctantly accept the need for bosses (in no
area of group endeavor have we managed to do without them), but because
of our unwarranted assumptions about their rights we constantly rebel
against them. Our anarchistic ideals conflict destructively with our idolatry of power. Perhaps we should revise our thinking.[4]

Dictators and Democracy

Shaw trusted government, not because he placed all his hope in tyrants but
because he had faith in people. The average person is not capable of government; neither is she capable of making a decent pair of boots, but she
can recognize good boots when she sees them. More important, she allows
the cobbler to go on about his business. She does not criticize every stitch
and rivet or hamper him at every step because she does not trust him to do
his job. If we turn legislation and administration over to those with the
capacity for it, Shaw felt, we have as good a reason to trust them as to trust
the shoemaker. Governments are limited by the superstitions and ignorance of the citizenry, just as the professions are confined by the follies of
the laity and cobblers constrained by the tastes of their customers. That is
why all change must come ultimately from the laity (Pref. *Doctor's Dilemma* 3:296–97). The ignorance of the people is always an obstacle to
progress. The obvious answer is to educate them. People could not govern
themselves, even if perfectly informed, not because they are intrinsically
depraved or vicious but because the people cannot do anything in the mass
except as a mob does it (*Sixteen Self Sketches* 52). It is true that the consciences of most people are not well-developed and suffer more or less
severely from myopia. Leaders must not only be talented; they must have
larger consciences. They must be moved by a sense of responsibility for the
community at large. "Government presents only one problem: the discov-

ery of a trustworthy anthropometric method" ("Revolutionist's Handbook" 2:782). Our habits of mind lead us to believe that this means finding those who ought to have natural rights of possession over the rest of us; Shaw had in mind the discovery of his natural aristocracy of service.

Belief in a natural aristocracy of service does little to explain Shaw's pronouncements on the disturbing political events in Europe between the world wars. The topics that people find most upsetting in Shaw's writings are, understandably, Stalin, Mussolini, Hitler, and the Holocaust. He was wrong about all of them, but how and why he was wrong is important. Stalin fooled Shaw into believing that he was exactly the sort of ruler Shaw most admired: pragmatic about means and realistic about ends (*Collected Letters* 4:269). Shaw knew we are all, however perceptive, blinded by our biases; everyone is an "idiot" about something. "I do not know what I am an idiot about or I should not be an idiot about it; but no doubt I share the common lot" (*Collected Letters* 3:839). He was an idiot about Stalin. He was not the only one, as Stalin was immensely successful in deceiving even those close to him (Pipes 14), but those who admire Shaw in other respects would expect greater perception from him. Probably nothing has done more to damage Shaw's reputation than his wholehearted endorsement of Stalin. He even goes so far as to defend Stalin's "liquidation" policies in the preface to *On the Rocks,* where he justifies "extermination" as not only necessary but inevitable. Much of that essay, despite the deliberately provocative word used, is in harmony with what he says with less inflammatory rhetoric elsewhere. He uses the word "exterminate" to mean both killing and more benign methods of elimination. Socialism would "exterminate" both the poor and the idle rich but not necessarily by killing them. He does make it clear that he views killing as appropriate if other means fail. All societies, he argues, make distinctions between the tolerable and the intolerable. A new society with a socialist ethic could not tolerate individuals who insist on engaging in what that society deems "theft." Such a society must "exterminate" such individuals or be itself exterminated. It is—at least from our perspective—astounding that Shaw imagined that was the full extent of Stalin's activities. He actually believed that Stalin was his kind of "realist": a pragmatist with lofty socialist goals. He imagined that the Soviet leadership was the new "priesthood": those drawn to serve the public by the prompting of an inner vocation. He was not horrified by the impromptu executions by police, apparently believing that no one would do such things unless public safety and the survival of the new order demanded it. In a way, this also is characteristic of his thinking throughout his life. He was also stressing the need to face the necessity of killing and dismissed, almost as unimportant, the need to be certain that *only* those whom society genuinely *cannot* tolerate are thus harshly treated. He certainly knew how stupidly cruel his fellow citizens could be, as he often inveighed against them for those very qualities. Could he imagine that the Russian leadership was immune to the follies he testified against in the English government? Or for that matter, the German and Italian leadership? It is true that his mistakes about Hitler and Mussolini were of a different order. He did not endorse them, as he did Stalin, but he did oppose demonizing them as hysterical jingoism. Still, he failed to understand the danger they posed. One suspects that he may have been a jingoist in reverse, believing that foreigners were free from the cruelty and self-delusion so obvious to him in his countrymen. Shaw's failure, at any rate, horribly illustrates the danger of relativist morality. The realist, like the one in the example at the beginning of this chapter, who chooses to participate actively in a lesser evil rather than passively allow a greater one had better be very certain it is indeed a lesser evil. One must adopt an attitude of extreme skepticism about one's own knowledge and understanding, but Shaw's favorable judgment of Stalin was as cocksure as it was dreadfully wrong.

His reaction to the Holocaust is particularly revealing. He simply did not believe it. He did not believe it because he could not believe that people could do such things, even though Nazi ideology emphatically labeled Jews as "intolerable." Perhaps he imagined that, like the Chaplain in *Saint Joan,* the Nazis would recant in horror when brought face to face with the real effects of their rhetoric of hate. Or perhaps he was repeating earlier pronouncements in what would turn out to be very different circumstances: he had dismissed as propaganda the stories of German atrocities during the first Great War, and he was right then. He was wrong now. What had changed? There is irony in the answer because in the intervening years, as we all have come somehow to accommodate the horror of the Holocaust within our view of ourselves as human beings, we have learned that one of the "ideals" with which it was justified was that very "Science, with a capital S," which Shaw had denounced because it "claimed exemption from all decent and humane considerations" (*Sixteen Self Sketches* 123, Proctor, passim).[5] Shaw did not believe the stories about the death camps because they appeared to violate his most fundamental assumptions about the world: the creed of Major Barbara that we are moral equals, all children of one father. He did not acquiesce in the calls to treat the dictators as devils partly because he knew that the surest way to make someone act like a devil is to treat him as one and also because he genuinely and profoundly did not believe in human devils. When he countered the accusations made against Hitler and Mussolini, it was invariably by admonishing his countrymen to cast out the beams in their own eyes before ranting about the mote in their neighbor's eye. Julian Kaye is shocked that Shaw insisted on treating Hitler as a gentleman and that he opposed punitive "justice" to be exacted of Mussolini and the Nazis (194–95). A sympathetic critic observed in a similar vein that Shaw "wrongly but honorably opposed punitive treatment [for the Nuremberg defendants], much as he rightly opposed punitive reparations against Germany after World War I" (Rawson 3). Shaw's belief was that vengeance, in whatever guise, was wrong. Any exception destroys the argument. Shaw's position admits of no shadings: you either believe that two black eyes make a white one or you do not. Shaw thoroughly and honestly believed that all men were his brothers and all women his sisters. "Everybody says it: nobody believes it—nobody." Nobody but Shaw. As for the rest of us, hypocrisy has become so completely second nature that when someone acts on a belief to which we all give lip service we literally cannot understand it. We search vainly for an explanation we *can* comprehend: hero worship, authoritarianism, elitism—anything but the truth staring us in the face. Naive, Shaw may have been; credulous, in some ways he undoubtedly was; but inconsistent he was not.

Shaw underestimated the human capacity for cruelty and destructiveness. He was wrong. But if Shaw, judging by his own nature, believed the race of humans could not be capable of conscientiously systematic mass slaughter, and we, using the same method, actually knew better than he did, it is not an occasion for self-congratulation. If Shaw did not believe in the Holocaust because he could not imagine that the Germans, his brothers, would be capable of something so horrendous, then his error certainly was honorable. Those who would condemn him because German neo-Nazi revisionists—for very different reasons—also deny the fact of the Holocaust are assigning guilt by association, and that error is not honorable. It is not even sensible.

Shaw's Credulity

Shaw may legitimately be faulted for overestimating human beings. He was amazed that the Ulster Protestants would have chosen division and strife rather than joining a united Ireland. "I guessed ahead, and guessed wrongly, whilst stupider and more ignorant fellow-pilgrims guessed rightly" (Pref. *John Bull's Other Island* 2:874). Guessing again, he believed that dictators would be held in check by a natural democracy, by the people who knew good shoes when they wore them but did not know how to make them. He assumed that dictators would be less dangerous than ordinary rulers because they would be stripped of idealism and its accompanying aura: the "divinity that doth hedge a king" which is the last refuge of tyrants. Thus stripped naked, the dictator would be tolerated only as long as he did a good job. It did not turn out that way. Shaw also assumed that the reports of the death camps were hysterical, jingoistic exaggerations. He was wrong. These conclusions were not the confused distractions of a senile old man; they were entirely consistent with the most fundamental principles of Shaw's philosophy.

The question is inescapable: was Shaw fundamentally wrong? Did he merely appear to be right in the limited context of nineteenth-century civilization? Is the world divided after all into good men and scoundrels? Or perhaps there are only scoundrels, and the best hope for our moral pride is to claim pathetically that we are not as nasty as some of the other scoundrels. I know of no satisfactory refutation of this position. Conscious of the terrifying force of that argument and the teeming evidence behind it, Shaw could only counter that there is nothing worse than the council of despair. There is nothing worse because it is a self-fulfilling prophecy; because for evil to succeed it is necessary only that good people do nothing, as they must if they believe they *can* do nothing. There is nothing worse because the council of despair is a declaration of irresponsibility; it is Pilate washing his hands.

And there is reason to hope. The moralists who cry out that without the restraint of absolute moral strictures and draconian penalties men and women will lapse instantly into viciousness and depravity give the lie to their own arguments, for the common chord struck by their moral hysteria is a measure of the fact that we fear sin at least as much as we covet it. Doubtless, as Shaw maintained, most people need some external restraints because they lack the internal moral strength to go it alone, and perhaps the lesson of the dictators and their dupes in the social chaos that followed the Great War is that most people are moral sheep who become easy prey to wolves in shepherd's clothing when left on their own. If that is true, the moral abnegation of the intellectual nihilists is all the more reprehensible.

At all events, the attacks on Shaw by liberal idealists are mistaken. They accuse him of inconsistency, of a naive and futile optimism, and of a snobbery that led him to idolize "great men" who turned out to be glorified hoodlums. Shaw is consistent and his critics inconsistent. Eric Bentley, for example, berates Shaw both for his optimism and for his presumed snobbish dislike of the common people. But when Bentley declares on the one hand that human beings are incapable of improvement and on the other that political salvation will come from the common people, it is Bentley, not Shaw, who is being inconsistent (*Thinking About the Playwright* 86–97). It is just not sensible to declare both that human beings are corrupt and depraved and that political salvation can come only from those least equipped in education and culture. Shaw is surely right to maintain that government *by* the masses is both impossible and undesirable and that the only sensible goal is to have things run by those persons most competent to run them, making certain that they are held fully accountable. Shaw failed to come up with a convincing plan for making that happen, but then so has everyone else. Shaw may have been naive, but he was not so naive as to put his faith in "a unionized work force" in charge of everything (Bentley's solution).

Natural Democracy and the Dictators

Of course, from the point of view of the sentimental idealists, the most damning charge against Shaw is that he was an elitist who had faith only in the exalted few and had contempt for the masses. This, they say, is why he endorsed Stalin and winked at Hitler and Mussolini. But Shaw's own explanation, though it may appear naive to us, is consistent with both his philosophy and the other judgments he made throughout his life. He insisted that, whatever their faults, they represented an advance on capitalist plutocracy. Part of his reasoning has to do with his concern for responsibility. In his exegesis of *The Ring*, Shaw portrays Siegfried as an advance over Wotan because the latter had become the slave of his own godhead; that is,

> the conventional system of law and duty, supernatural religion and self-sacrificing idealism, . . . which is really only the machinery of the love of necessary power which is his mortal weakness. This process secures . . . fanatical devotion to his system of government; but he knows perfectly well that such systems, in spite of their moral pretensions, serve selfish and ambitious tyrants better than benevolent despots. (*Perfect Wagnerite* 34)

The idolatry with which the established, "legitimate" government vests itself becomes a cloak behind which scoundrels can hide. The same is true of pseudo-democracy, or votes for everybody, which destroys responsibility by allowing the leaders to blame their mistakes on the electorate. "A minister of State who accepts and undertakes a public duty on the understanding that if he fails he will be impeached and possibly shot, or at least discharged and discredited, is a responsible minister" (*Everybody's Political* 33). "Better one dictator standing up responsible before the world for the good and evil he does than a dirty little dictator in every street responsible to nobody," as Old Hipney declares (*On the Rocks* 6:719). The dictator could not hide behind sham ruses; his rule must be based on competence. This was naive of Shaw. It was extraordinarily naive in the case of Stalin. He seems to have had no sense of the diligence with which Hitler and Mussolini developed their protective, artificial "godhead" or the effectiveness of military terror in convincing those initially reluctant to go along with it. He imagined that with the traditional garments of authority torn away the dictator would actually be forced into something closer to genuine democracy. This is certainly a flaw in his thinking, but it is not the mistake of authoritarianism; rather, it is a betrayal of his hidden anarchism. He believed that with the bandages of idolatry stripped from their eyes, the people would, acting in their own self-interest, demand responsible leadership. He expected something not unlike Adam Smith's invisible hand to restrain the leaders. He also believed of rulers what he believed of everyone: that you get the best of them by appealing to their consciences. "All this country or any country has to stand between it and blue hell," Hipney says, "is the consciences of them that are capable of governing it" (6:721). He thought the masses, together with their own consciences, would always keep the dictators in line. Either humanity itself—natural democracy—or the devotion of the leaders to the genuine improvement of humanity—"vocation"—was, in Shaw's view, the ultimate safeguard against tyranny. As long as the people were not blinded by self-perverting ideals, they could be counted on to rein in ambition and make power serve their needs. We can see, with the wisdom of our century's experience to aid us, that Shaw was himself blinded by his own ideals. His blindness is remarkable because he understood it so well in others and even—in the abstract—in himself. He knew that we all believe what we want to believe, and he wanted to believe in the essential goodness of human beings. He knew that we are easily turned from the purposes of the Life Force, but he was certain that so long as we are not deluded by ideals or deflected from the general good by self-interest, we would return to the quest for godhead. Just as he thought that the Ulster Protestants would join with their

Catholic brothers and sisters, he was sure that once freed from the humiliation of Versailles, Germany would not seek war because there was no longer need for war. In one important way he was right: both Germans and Ulster Protestants paid dearly for choosing strife. Shaw believed although his faith was forever being disappointed. And he knew it. He knew better than most how frail a straw the human conscience is, often remarking that few people have more than one strong point of honor and observing that "the human conscience can subsist on very questionable food," yet he persisted in believing that his sisters and brothers would behave more honorably and sensibly than they in fact ever would (Pref. *Doctor's Dilemma* 3:244). That is why he was convinced that "natural" democracy would be an effective curb to dictatorship. The final irony is that, despite entrenched conventional wisdom, Shaw did not have too little faith in the people. He had too much.

III

God and Science

The Marriage of Science and Religion

SHAW AND SCIENCE

It is difficult to imagine a notion more at odds with the respected, unquestioned wisdom of our age than Shaw's contention that Creative Evolution provides a faith that is not merely consistent with science but true to the spirit of science: a scientific religion. His argument is cogent, his reasoning sound, and his premises almost unarguable, but his conclusions are still dismissed out of hand. In a certain sense, Shaw was being even more scientific than the scientists, while at the same time he was utterly out of harmony with the way scientists now see the world. The fundamental difficulty is that the metaphysics of deterministic materialism have become so ingrained in our thinking that they are unconsciously accepted even by those who attack science. No one, however—including Shaw—has presented an alternative that is rigorous, systematic, and demonstrably in harmony with the goals of science. We do not have a "science of spirit," but it is possible to provide a logical sound metaphysical basis on which such a science could be built. Unfortunately, many walls of weighty received opinion must be torn down and cleared away before this will become apparent. There are three main areas of misunderstanding: the nature of science and "true" scientific thinking, the "natural" relation between science and religion, and finally the logical foundation of Shaw's "vitalism" and its susceptibility to scientific analysis.

Shaw and the Scientists

Shaw is commonly thought of as an outright opponent of science. Bertrand Russell, for example, said flatly that "Shaw's contempt for science was indefensible" (*Portraits* 79). He went on to claim that the playwright's passionate opposition to vivisection was based on "not any sympathy for animals, but a disbelief in the scientific knowledge which vivisection is held to provide." The facts contradict the latter statement, for Shaw invariably insisted that opposition to vivisection should be divorced from the question of whether any useful knowledge is gained in the process; the humane considerations simply outweighed any knowledge that might be acquired (*Shaw on Vivisection* 55). Closer to the truth is the more moderate assertion of some of Shaw's scientific friends that he "had a hopelessly unscientific mind" (Pearson 234). He did not think like most scientists, and the difference made communication difficult or impossible. Yet as Thomas Postlewait and Desmond J. McRory have made clear, he always insisted on the importance of science and was opposed only to scientific arrogance, scientific credulity, and the treatment of scientists as infallible priests with direct access to the mind of God. He thought of himself as having a scientific disposition and insisted that his background "made it impossible for me to believe anything until I could conceive it as a scientific hypothesis" (Pref. *Methuselah* 5:338). He meant that he could not believe anything that was inconsistent with the facts and with reason, not that he subscribed to the fashionable scientific worldview. In spite of the marked differences between his way of seeing the world and that of most scientists, there is a crucial similarity which is at the core of his insistence that his was a "scientific" religion. He and the scientists conceive the universe as operating according to a single set of predictable, comprehensible rules. Such an assumption is necessary for the enterprise of science. The difference is that for Shaw those rules are in part teleological, and the scientists cannot imagine them as anything other than strictly mechanistic. He rejected the scientific dogma that everything in the universe can be explained in mechanistic terms because it ignores the plain facts of consciousness and will. In that sense he thought himself more scientific than the scientists: they, he thought, were blinded by their total faith in the materialistic dogma whereas he was acknowledging the facts. That is why he claimed that now "Religion is Science, and Science is Witchcraft" ("Science and Common Sense" 196). Science is bent on denying truths that are central to religion and obvious to common sense. Traditional religion, unfortunately, ignores truths central to science. Refusing to choose between the two, he said that we must have a religious science and a scientific religion (*Everybody's Political What's What?* 363). All questions are scientific questions (*Everybody's Political What's What?* 203) and "all truths . . . are divinely inspired" (*Black Girl* 59). Scientists claim to be open-minded and skeptical, but they actually are incapable of saying "I don't know" ("Science and Common Sense" 197). Specifically, science denies the existence of anything it does not understand; it does not understand the mind, so mind must be banished from the universe (*Everybody's Political What's What?* 203). While it is natural to assume that the scientists know better than Shaw what science is all about, there is actually much to be said for Shaw's critique of science. More important, his insistence that science and religion are compatible is based on an understanding of a fundamental weakness in scientific thinking that Shaw actually understood more clearly than the scientists.

First Mistake: The Nature of Science

Shaw's idea of what science ought to be about was overly simplistic but had the virtue of clarity and logic. He essentially accepted the "mythical" view of science, the view scientists like to take of themselves, and faulted the scientists for not living up to it. Science should have perfect respect for the facts and be ready to scrap any theory, no matter how lovingly constructed or how deeply invested with time and energy if, in Andrew Undershaft's words, it "turns out just a hairsbreadth wrong after all" (*Major Barbara* 3:170). Shaw thought that the mind and its will were obvious, undeniable facts; science saw that they did not fit the theory and so insisted (indeed still insists) that they do not exist. For Shaw, that meant science was behaving unscientifically.

Shaw's point of view is so heterodox that many find it impossible to conceive that it is even remotely rational. They are not even capable of hearing arguments in its favor, for they "know" in advance that it must be wrong. Indeed, a careful examination of the literature regarding the debate between the materialists and antimaterialists is enough to convince any skeptic of the truth of Shaw's observation in the letter to Chapman quoted earlier: "Every man sees what he looks for, and hears what he listens for, and nothing else" (*Collected Letters* 1:301). Attentive reading of the various disputes makes it clear that the proponents of different views do not really hear each other. It is as if they lived in different worlds and saw different things, so that the disciples of each view become perfectly convinced that their opponents are talking—not merely nonsense—but *obvious* nonsense. Indeed, there are those who become huffily indignant that such questions are asked at all, because the answers are, to them, transparently obvious. Unfortunately, different people propose totally different "obvious" answers. Under such circumstances one despairs of achieving anything like effective communication, but if Shaw's dream of a vitalistic, teleological science is ever to be realized, it is necessary to try.

Perhaps one should start with a recognition of the deep emotional needs that underlie the "will-to-believe" on both sides. The vitalists are horrified by the cold, soullessness of materialism. They have come, in no small part at the insistence of scientists, to associate materialism with the entire enterprise of science; they have thus come to be distrustful of science generally. For their part, the scientists and materialists who boast a scientific point of view see vitalism as a crackpot attack on reason, order, and the very knowableness of the universe. It seems to them a know-nothing assault on science itself. The vitalists need to be convinced that vitalism and teleology are not incompatible with determinism; that the true object of their fears is not determinism, but mechanism. The materialists must be persuaded that a teleological universe is both orderly and knowable. The first step will be to show that their materialism is actually in conflict with their vaunted values of objectivity, logic, and skepticism and that science, though unquestionably constrained by the restrictions of reason and empirical observation it places on itself, is also subject to the same irrational pressures that afflict ordinary mortals.

Karl Popper

Despite the impression one gets from Shaw, the idolatry of science did not reach its apogee in the nineteenth century but in the 1920s, when Logical Positivism became popular. The heir to Auguste Comte's positivism, this movement was stronger in its adulation of science than anything proposed by Comte or his followers. It saw science as a slow, patient, but inexorable accumulation of certain facts. Science could be trusted because it conscientiously abstained from saying anything that could not be verified. They took as their motto Ludwig Wittgenstein's famous aphorism "Wovon Man nicht sprechen kann darüber muss Man schweigen" (If you have nothing to say about something, you should hush). Declarations about anything that could not be verified were regarded as empty metaphysical speculation, and metaphysics was derided as literally nonsense: devoid of sense. It was a mere abuse of language. The verification principle, which described the method by which facts were to be ascertained, was to have been the iron hoop that bound solid facts to the granite pillar of certainty. The verification principle proved illusory, and the hoop of iron disintegrated into rust. The weakness of the principle was evident almost from its promulgation, but it was torn apart by Karl Popper. Popper pointed out that science cannot actually verify anything except possibly the most trivial of individual facts. It relies on abstract theories that cannot be verified because they are complicated systems of inference, and it has been understood, at least since Hume, that no inference can ever be made with absolute certainty.

But science does have an effective means of testing hypotheses. While it cannot verify, said Popper, it can *falsify*. No theory can be absolutely verified because a single counterinstance can always disprove any theory. The theory that perpetual motion is impossible could be disproved, for instance, with the construction of a single perpetual motion machine. This provides science, however, with a criterion for distinguishing a good scientific theory from a bad one: a good theory is one that is easily subjected to potential falsification and has actually survived many attempts to falsify it. A bad scientific theory is one that is immune to falsification, one that provides an answer to any possible set of circumstances. Freudian psychology is, by this standard, a bad theory because it provides an answer to any conceivable objection by its critics. If you protest that you do not harbor homicidal feelings toward your father or lustful ones about your mother, the Freudian can smile a superior smile and say: "Of course not: You have repressed these desires and forced them into your unconscious." There is no way to prove him wrong. When Creationists dispute the fossil evidence for the age of the earth or the evolution of life by saying that God placed misleading evidence in our way as a test of our faith, they securely protect their theory from falsification. But such theories should not be automatically dismissed as "nonsense," as the Logical Positivists insisted, for they may have important heuristic value; they may lead us toward truths that are presently inaccessible to more rigorous methods. Indeed, they may even be perfectly true; they merely are not scientific.

While Popper's observations may seem like a warning to science against assuming to know too much, in another way they flattered the scientists by reinforcing part of the scientific myth. That is the myth that science is profoundly skeptical, always doubting, probing, and testing its own theories, ever ready to discard its most cherished beliefs without hesitation at the moment, like Andrew Undershaft with his experimental weapon, if it turns out the least bit wrong. The theory of scientific falsification allows scientists to think of themselves as intellectually humble, courageously open-minded, and ruthless with respect to the flaws in their own thinking—quite unlike the traditional authorities on the nature of the cosmos,

the theologians, on whom the scientists look down with more or less tolerant condescension. Not surprisingly, Popper's notion has been absorbed
into the orthodoxy of science and is incorporated into the image many
scientists have of what they do. It is cited in this way, for instance, by
Stephen Hawking in his popular book *A Brief History of Time* (10). So
while Popper attacked the intellectual arrogance of Logical Positivism, he
flattered the scientists by portraying science as ruthlessly skeptical. After
all, it was philosophers, not scientists, who had insisted that science produced a body of certain fact. And Popper makes explicit what is implied by
Shaw's view of what science should be.

Thomas Kuhn

Then came Thomas Kuhn, a historian as well as a philosopher of science, to
point out that this is not the way science actually works. It could not work,
in fact, because falsification is far more difficult than the theory implies.
The reason is suggested by the old proverb "The exception proves the
rule." The sense of "proves" is "tests" (as in "proving ground"), and the
meaning of the saying is that every rule is tested by apparent exceptions.
Galileo's rule that light and heavy objects fall at the same rate is not falsified by the fact that under normal circumstances a feather and a brick do
not fall at the same rate. Air pressure affects the objects differently, so the
rule becomes manifest (with those particular objects) only in a vacuum.
The trouble is that in nature many different factors influence the course of
events, and one can never be certain, no matter how rigorously controlled
the experiment may be, that all "hidden" factors have been eliminated. If a
single counterinstance were always fatal to a scientific theory, science
would get nowhere.

Science actually moves in a way sharply different from the orthodox
myth of scientific progress. Science is historically a dialectical process in
which periods of "normal science" are punctuated by "revolutions." The
accepted myths about scientific thinking come closest to being realized
during the revolutions, but normal science, which is what most scientists
do most of the time, is entirely different. This historical rhythm is controlled by "paradigms," models of the natural world, or aspects of it, that
serve as a kind of archetype on which scientific investigation is based.
"Paradigm" is somewhat loosely defined and is used to represent both the
fundamental assumptions that are shared by nearly all scientists and the
more narrowly applicable models appealed to by specialists. They are

shared examples rather than abstract "laws," so that Newtonian mechanics, which is a constellation of shared models of the way things work, might be thought of as a paradigm, and so might Newton's second law of motion, which is only part of the first.

The paradigms are the central, focal feature of science. Normal science is conducted under periods of stable paradigms; these are times when the paradigms are accepted *without question*. They are the focus of all research, but they are not tested or subjected to potential falsification: rather, they are "articulated" (23). This means that the labors of scientists under conditions of normal science are directed toward explaining more and more of the world *in the terms defined by the paradigm*. This sort of research is analogous to puzzle solving. It is not an open-ended search for an answer that may or may not exist. For this reason basic scientific research is very different from that directed to solving human problems, such as the search to find a cure for cancer. A cure for cancer may not in fact exist. Every puzzle, however, has a correct answer; the difficulty lies in how to arrive at it. Normal science is a matter of solving such puzzles (37). The counterexample is not then a fatal falsification but a challenge to be overcome. Normal science is like a complex jigsaw puzzle, and the paradigm is the picture on the top of the box. Normal science is occupied with bringing facts that *apparently* contradict the paradigm into its domain. One way in which normal (rather than revolutionary) science approximates the myth of science is that only normal science is truly progressive and cumulative. During periods of normal science more and more puzzles are solved and more and more facts are brought into the fold. The paradigm accretes authority and power. It becomes increasingly immune to doubt. Eventually, however, cracks begin to show. Puzzles prove recalcitrant, impossible to solve. Patterns of unsolvable puzzles develop. Uncertainty creeps into a world of supreme confidence. Doubt emerges, and the paradigm goes into crisis. This new stage, the crisis of the paradigm, is for scientists "a period of pronounced professional insecurity" (68). Ordinarily at this point rival paradigms appear and intense debate ensues until a new paradigm is established in the place of the old. Only when dealing with a full-blown crisis in the paradigm does a scientist "look almost like our most prevalent image of the scientist" (87). "Almost" because although there is intense debate and scrupulous examination of the evidence, the proponents of the competing paradigms do not really proceed rationally and then decide together which best fits the facts. They have different assumptions and in some sense actually see the world differently, so that by and large they talk through each other rather than to each other. The new paradigm is adopted for reasons that have more to do with faith than reason.

Contrary to myth, scientific activity is pervaded by dogmatism, arbitrariness, and irrationality. Kuhn insisted that he was not being critical of science and that these extrarational elements are essential to the proper functioning of science. Even though normal science is based on unquestioning acceptance of the established paradigms, and scientific education is more rigid and narrow "than any other except perhaps orthodox theology," this rigidity provides much of the focus and discipline that are the core of science's strength (166). Normal science builds a background fabric of understanding against which the anomalies leading to crisis appear. In other words, without the somewhat dogmatic devotion to the paradigm that characterizes normal science, the anomalies that precipitate crisis would remain invisible. This process is similar to Popper's falsification but much more complex. It is not the operation of a single counterinstance invalidating a hypothesis but a pattern of anomalies calling a fabric of understanding into question. Even then, no paradigm is considered "falsified" until it can be replaced by something deemed better. "Once it has achieved the status of paradigm, a scientific theory is declared invalid only if an alternate candidate is available to take its place. No process yet disclosed by the historical study of scientific development at all resembles the methodological stereotype of falsification by direct comparison with nature" (77). Simply to reject the paradigm as "falsified" would be to question the entire scientific enterprise. "To reject one paradigm without simultaneously substituting another is to reject science itself. That act reflects not on the paradigm but on the man. Inevitably he will be seen by his colleagues as 'the carpenter who blames his tools'" (79).[1]

All this throws Shaw's quarrels with science into a different light. When Kuhn says that facts that do not fit into the paradigm may not be seen by scientists at all, he sounds a lot like Shaw, who always insisted that facts never meant anything until they were fitted into a theory (Pearson 223; "Illusions" 411–12). But essentially, Shaw complained that scientists were not living up to their own mythology. For him science meant—or should have meant—a willingness to accept change, ruthlessly to throw out old theories when they do not fit the facts, to accept one's own ignorance as the basis for seeking new knowledge, and to display intellectual humility in the face of mystery. Small wonder then, that he "reckoned without the reluctance of the 'man of science' to say 'I don't know'" ("Sci-

ence and Common Sense" 197). He realized that even intelligent and perceptive people will believe what is in their interest to believe, and he did
not exclude scientists from this common fate (Pearson 233). But he did not
realize that for the scientist ignorance is failure. Within his area of investigation, to say "I don't know" is to admit defeat. No professional wants to
be known as the "carpenter who blames his tools." As Shaw often pointed
out, we all believe what it is profitable for us to believe.

Science is more like religion than many scientists are willing to concede.
Not only are faith and dogma crucial to the enterprise, but the mytholo-
gizing process of science welds together two incompatibles: certainty and
doubt. The fundamental myth of science holds that it accrues certainty
through systematic doubt. Neither is true: not the method nor the result,
but the myth is accepted almost without question. Successful enterprises,
like successful nations, rarely doubt their own myths. Americans are
shocked if anyone doubts that their country's destiny is to lead the rest of
the world into political salvation; Europeans, who have been there themselves, look on with patronizing amusement. The amazing success of science in the past few hundred years has led scientists into unreasonable
ideas about their own powers of understanding. They do have every reason
to be proud of their achievements. Even if science is something of a game,
it is a game played by very demanding rules, and these rules, which insist
on rigorous testing and mathematical precision, help to give credence to
the scientific myth. We do not see our weaknesses until taught by failure;
hubris is the besetting sin of heroes, not of mediocrities or losers.

SCIENCE AND RELIGION: SEPARATE BUT EQUAL?

If Shaw objected strenuously to the banishment of mind and value and
the dogmatic acceptance of the materialist metaphysic, he dissented as
well from the view that science and religion occupied separate, watertight
spheres. He passionately believed that it does no good to base your values
on religion, if you continue to maintain that the physical world is entirely
the domain of the mechanistic science. Here, as elsewhere, Shaw is at odds
with those one would expect to be his natural allies, in this case those who
wish to find a place for both science and religion. There is probably no
principle dearer to the hearts of those Darwinists who do not, like Richard
Dawkins and Daniel Dennett, embrace Darwin as a support for atheism,
than the belief that religion and science inhabit entirely separate realms.
Stephen Jay Gould, a good representative of that group, insists that scien-

tists have no reason to be hostile to religion "since our subject doesn't intersect the concerns of theology." The two have nothing to do with each other. "There is no warfare between science and religion, never was except as a historical vestige of shifting taxonomic boundaries among disciplines. Theologians haven't been troubled by the fact of evolution, unless they try to extend their own domain beyond its proper border" ("Darwinism Defined" 70).

Mary Midgley takes much the same approach. She is not so cavalier in dismissing any possible clash between the two, but she is certain that the way to keep peace is to keep religion and science separate. "The religion which does clash with science has left its own sphere, for bad reasons, to intrude on a scientific one. It is bad religion" (12–13). Similarly, when science intrudes on the realm of religion, it is bad science. What, then, are their proper realms? Midgley tries to give the world of fact to science and reserve meaning to religion, but she immediately concedes that this is difficult to do. What we recognize as a fact is determined by the way we give order to our experience, the way we give meaning to it. If religion is to confine itself to values and purposes, how is it to guide us when it is required to be silent on all questions pertaining to the factual nature of the world? For its part, science is not, nor can it be, a mere piling up of facts. As Kuhn makes clear, it must provide meaning or it could not function.

Scientists disagree about just what sort of meaning it provides. There are those, like M. T. Ghiselin and Herbert Simon who insist that science (Darwinism in particular) shows us that we are intrinsically and inevitably egoists. "Scratch an 'altruist' and watch a 'hypocrite' bleed" (247), says Ghiselin. Simon ascribes altruism to "bounded rationality," which is a slightly pompous way of saying that if we behave with less than perfect selfishness, it is because we are a bit stupid (1667–68). Scientists like Gould insist on the segregation of religion and science as a way of rejecting such views. They point out that the sociobiology and social Darwinism of Ghiselin and Simon are based on fallacious reasoning, and they agree with Shaw that natural selection is without moral significance. They generally invoke some version of the naturalistic fallacy. The term was coined by the English philosopher G. E. Moore, but the concept is linked to remarks made by Hume to the effect that people often leap unjustifiably from propositions involving terms linked by "is" to relations described by the word "ought." The simplest statement of the idea is that one cannot derive "ought" from "is." In this commonsense form it has been attacked by philosophers, particularly those who advocate any form of naturalistic or scientific ethics. Clearly certain kinds of statements purporting to describe what is the case can have ethical significance. The statement "God detests adultery," accepted as an assertion of fact, leads to inescapable conclusions about what one *ought* to do. A more careful description of what people mean when they say that "is" does not imply "ought" is that one cannot logically derive conclusions about values from a frame of reference that is value-free. Statements of fact, themselves value-free, can certainly *influence* moral judgments. If you believe that the soul of your father or mother may inhabit a chicken or steer, you may reasonably conclude that you *ought* to become a vegetarian but only if you already had convictions about how you *ought* to behave toward your parents. The mechanistic laws of science, however, are value-free; by themselves they do not imply moral conclusions. Darwinism, being the description of a purely mechanical process, cannot provide us with a guide to correct living. Even if it could be shown that natural selection invariably favors selfishness, that would not mean that selfishness is in any sense "good" or desirable.

If you do not delve too deeply into metaphysical questions, this solution seems at first to work reasonably well to protect ethics from simple Hobbesian egoism, although it does tend toward some form of utilitarianism. The most obvious difficulty is that it does not allow us *any basis at all* for our values. If natural selection, operating on the random products of physical law, is the sole determinant of the forms and behaviors of living things, ourselves included, is it not reasonable to conclude that our moral convictions and religious beliefs are themselves the products of random forces shaped by a nonrandom but utterly valueless principle called natural selection? Viewed this way, values become intrinsically meaningless. They exist only because they are favored by the blind and mechanical operation of natural selection. It thus becomes apparent that if the sociobiologists were true to their basic principles and did not insist on egoism as the one true virtue, their position would be far more formidable. They could merely declare that all values, whether altruistic or egoistic, are illusory. They exist, to be sure, but they have no intrinsic justification. The human conscience has precisely the significance of the tortoise's shell: created at random, it was selected by the mechanical sorter of natural selection. This is why many humane and conscientious people, who also happen to have probing and analytical minds, react with horror to Darwinism. It entails a universe without meaning.

Thus liberal Darwinists like Gould are right to maintain that the sociobiologists incorrectly derive values from the paradigm of natural selection, but because they affirm their allegiance to the central principle of Darwinism, that life is shaped entirely by the blind force of natural selection operating on random events (random because produced by the equally blind laws of physics), they are left without a basis for any morality whatsoever. If the sociobiologists say that we "ought" to be selfish because natural selection requires us to be so, they are wrong; but if they simply concluded that all morality is an illusion and that *ought* is a word devoid of intrinsic meaning, their position would be unassailable, *given their Darwinist assumptions*. Darwinism is objectionable to many people because part of its meaning is the trivialization of value, not because it entails egoism—which it does not do.

There is a deeper difficulty. Darwinism trivializes values by making them the product of blind mechanical forces, but it assumes that they have agency—that values cause behavior. If they did not, they would have no effect on reproductive success and thus would be ignored by natural selection. But if science insists that the physical world is governed exclusively by blind mechanical law, where does human purpose fit in? If purpose does not matter, neither do values. What difference do our values make if they have no power to affect our world? If they cannot supersede mechanistic laws? If Darwinism in any form trivializes value, strict mechanistic reductionism—the claim that ultimately everything in the universe can be explained by the laws of physics—would appear to make it meaningless. The liberal scientists take refuge at this point in "holism," which maintains that when the systems under observation reach a certain level of complexity, entirely new laws, laws not deducible from physics, must be called on. They reject both mechanism and anything that smacks of vitalism. Holism is, unfortunately, an ambiguous term. Some thinkers attempt to make peace between the two camps by espousing something called "descriptive holism," which holds that whether a reductive or a holistic view is appropriate depends on the level of description. In other words, the mating behavior of animals may ultimately be completely governed by physical laws operating on hadrons and leptons, but it would be ridiculous to attempt to describe it at that level. No one doubts that a forest is composed of trees, but it is not appropriate to discuss forests in precisely the same way that one does trees. Critics maintain, with reason, that this is a distinction without a difference, a verbal concession to holism that gives up nothing the holists find objectionable in reductionism. True holism, they say, is *emergent holism*, which holds that entirely new laws, irreducible to more elementary laws, *emerge* in sufficiently complex systems. This explanation is unsatisfactory to scientists because it means disunity in scientific law. It demands a dualistic or pluralistic metaphysics that most scientists find deplorable. So the liberal Darwinists, who wish to maintain their credentials as faithful disciples of science and its fundamental principle of unity, yet seek to avoid the bleaker implications of materialism, tend to dance between these two views of holism. They try to maintain that these emergent principles (which are, at present, entirely unknown) are perfectly consistent with mechanistic science. According to Gould, "new, or 'emergent,' principles are needed to encompass life's complexity; but these principles are additional to, and consistent with, the physics and chemistry of atoms and molecules. They represent, if you will, a higher physics and chemistry appropriate to more complex levels of our natural hierarchy" ("Just in the Middle" 26). What is meant by principles "additional to, and consistent with, the physics and chemistry of atoms and molecules"? Do they supersede the "lower levels" that govern particles or do they not? Is this a form of descriptive holism or is it genuinely emergent? That is, does it entail different causal laws? What is meant by "consistent with" chemistry and physics? That they are *logically* consistent? If the two sets of laws are logically inconsistent, then one or the other must be false. The assertion would appear to be true but trivial. If it means that the laws of physics are never superseded, then Gould is advocating descriptive holism. Either the laws operating at the level of atoms are superseded or they are not. If they are not, then reductionism is true except in the trivial "descriptive" sense. If they are, then the laws of physics and chemistry, considered as a description of the causal relations of the physical world, are incomplete in a profound way. If life follows such holistic laws—laws that override the known laws of physics and chemistry—then Darwinism becomes problematical, for how can you flatly assert that variations in living things arise "by chance" when you do not know the laws that govern life? How can you be certain that all direction in the development of life comes from without?

Peace between religion and science cannot be maintained simply through the expedient of segregation. Each is vitally concerned with both facts and meaning. Exclude religion from the realm of the physical world and confine it to the reservation of values and purpose, and it will ask where these values are to come from and how purpose can change the physical world. Shaw rejected this doctrine of separate but equal; he demanded that religion be scientific and science religious (*Road to Equality* 323). Such unity cannot be achieved through any pat formula because it entails above all the acknowledgment that the formulas offered by both religion and science are inadequate. Religion must learn to accept change, to be willing to discard that which proves incompatible with the facts, and to rid itself of superstition and nonsense. Science must become tolerant of mystery, to accept that there are large and important areas of our experience about which it presently knows nothing. And if science is to avoid nonsense itself, it must learn to recognize the facts about any new subject matter that it undertakes to comprehend. It must, if it wishes to study life and mind, find a place for teleology and consciousness.

Religion cannot avoid being scientific, and science must inevitably be religious in the sense that their territories must unavoidably overlap. If each attempts to ignore the other, the result will be "bad" science and "bad" religion. This is clearest when both claim exclusive domain, but the attempts at segregation, at confining each in a watertight compartment, are logically inconsistent at best and a barrier against the growth of both religion and science at worst.

Conflicts cannot be avoided in advance; they must be faced and resolved as they arise. The segregationists do not really help matters by sweeping controversy under the rug, and the pervasive construal of scientific law as blind and mechanistic, together with its claims of total dominance of the physical world, must inevitably produce strife. Conflicts are especially common because of the claims of two scientific disciplines that have particular relevance to religion: evolution and scientific psychology—as Shaw insisted.

DARWINISM: THE LINCHPIN OF MATERIALISM

The mechanistic, materialistic assumptions of science force it to conflict with religion. And the reason that the dispute about conflict between religion and science invariably turns to Darwin is that Darwinism is the linchpin of materialism. Daniel Dennett likens it to a "universal acid," an imaginary acid that eats through all substances possible and thus cannot be contained. His point is that Darwinism utterly destroys all justification for belief in a teleological universe; it brings everything in our experience into the realm of mechanistic causal law: not merely evolution but psychology, religion, sociology, ethics—everything. It represents the glorious triumph of materialistic atheism, which for Dennett means the triumph of science over superstition.

Unfortunately, discussions of Darwinism are invariably muddled by the kind of "semantic shell game" that Mary Midgley finds in the writings of most sociobiologists (124–31). Dennett is explicit about the philosophical and theological side of Darwin, but when that view becomes embarrassing, he insists that Darwinism is simply a scientific theory. This tactic does not end the controversy. Darwinism is controversial considered strictly as a scientific theory, that is, simply as a hypothesis explaining how evolution came about. As a consequence, Darwinism is a perfect illustration of what Kuhn says occurs when a paradigm goes into crisis because Darwinism is not merely just another scientific paradigm, it represents the metaparadigm most scientists see as the foundation of all science—scientific materialism.

The details of the scientific vulnerability of Darwinism are not relevant to this discussion, but since the scientific community likes to pretend that none but Creationists ever question the certainty of Darwinism, the reader might find it useful to learn something of the nature of the scientific dispute. Darwinism is actually a peculiar theory, seen from the point of view of science. To understand why, it is important to realize precisely what it postulates. Darwinism is not the theory of evolution; it is not even the theory that evolution is shaped by natural selection; it is the theory that absolutely *nothing except* natural selection shapes evolution. This is peculiar because Darwinism requires modification of species to take place in two steps: variants arise and then they are selected. Natural selection can operate only on that which has arisen. Darwinists insist that variants arise through "chance." Although they vociferously deny the importance that chance plays in their theory, it is in fact its most distinguishing feature. No one who accepts evolution denies that natural selection must play a role. If you believe that variant traits do appear from time to time and are passed on from parent to offspring, it is impossible not to believe that traits that enhance reproduction will thrive and those that diminish it will not. The assertion that traits invariably are engendered "by chance" is essentially what distinguishes Darwinism from Lamarck's theory. But a "good" scientific theory, scientists often tell us, is one that makes unambiguous predictions that are empirically testable. It is difficult to say exactly how to test the assertion that some complex set of events—in the past—occurred by "chance." It is not even easy to say exactly what that means. Darwin, who, as Shaw always said, was not a Darwinian, never maintained that variations arose by pure chance. He merely thought that the pressures of survival and reproduction were so important that they would be sufficient to shape life in all of the various ways we see. It was his great insight that the need to survive and reproduce could produce tremendous change regardless of how the variations arose, as long as some of the variations were sufficiently adaptive. As Darwin saw it, one could regard the process as operating *as if* the variations sprang up by chance.

Modern Darwinians do insist on pure chance. But why? What do they mean by asserting—as a positive fact—that inheritable variations are always *random*? Essentially they are saying that it does not matter how the variations arise. It is irrelevant. How do they know that? The biologists have no such knowledge of the forces that produce genetic variation. What they have is a tremendous faith that whatever those forces turn out to be, they will have nothing to do with the direction that life actually takes. The difficulty, from a scientific perspective, is that it is very difficult to test such an assertion. As a result, Darwinism dances on the edge of being "unfalsifiable" in Popperian terms. It is easy to describe what a random result might be in a simple system such as the machines that generate lottery numbers with air pressure and numbered Ping-Pong balls. That is because while it is impossible to calculate the trajectory of an individual ball, we can be certain that all the balls are the same and similar forces are acting on all of them. But what if the balls had slightly different weights and shapes? The outcome would still be random in some sense (it could not be precisely predicted), but repeated trials would produce a different pattern of outcomes. Over time, some numbers would be clearly favored over others. But if your observation of these trials is limited to a very few (as it generally is in evolutionary biology), how can you say if a given outcome is the result of "chance"? Or more precisely, how can you "falsify" the assertion that only chance is operating?

Monkeys and Typewriters

Darwinism does make predictions, although vague, that have been challenged. Several thoughtful, reasoned, and well-informed attacks on natural selection have been made in recent years. Two in particular—Robert G. Wesson's *Beyond Natural Selection* and Michael Denton's *Evolution: A Theory in Crisis*—are notably balanced and informative.[2] Denton looks at Darwinism from the perspective of Kuhn's dialectic of normal and revolutionary science. His contention is that the Darwinian paradigm is in a state of advanced crisis, the state at which anomalies have become inescapable and obvious, engendering heated debate and passion among those in the profession. But as Kuhn maintains, the old paradigm is clung to no matter how glaring the anomalies become until a new paradigm is offered to take its place. And science has not found a replacement for Darwinism. Like a volcano on the verge of eruption after gathering energy during a long dormancy, evolution is a theory waiting for revolution.

This is not the place to describe the many technical objections to Darwinism that have been raised, but it is easy to describe their general tenor. Most of the difficulties are related to the way chance operates in complex systems. As systems increase in complexity, the chances of finding appropriate or viable variation at random plummets at an accelerating rate. Living organisms are enormously complex systems. Most people who are not mathematically inclined have little grasp of the improbabilities involved. One still occasionally hears the assertion, often attributed to T. H. Huxley, that six monkeys randomly pounding away at typewriters could, *given enough time*, produce all the books in the British Museum. While this is literally true, the time required would make the age of the universe look like a nanosecond. Let us take an example somewhat less ambitious than the contents of the British Museum or the works of Shakespeare (also cited as a feasible product of simian labor). Consider the following sentence:

> In the beginning was the Word, and the Word was with God, and the Word was God.

This sentence contains seventy-nine discrete symbols, including letters, spaces, and punctuation. Let us say that the total number of choices is thirty: twenty-six letters (ignoring capitals), a space, period, question mark, and comma (for all other punctuation). A computer programmed to select symbols at random would have a chance of one in thirty of getting the first letter right and the same probability for each successive choice. So the chance of getting the first word (two letters) right is 1/30 x 1/30 or 1/900. The probability diminishes exponentially with each new letter so where n = number of letters, the probability of getting the correct combination is:

$$\frac{1}{30^n}$$

Or in the case of the sentence above:

$$\frac{1}{30^{79}}$$

That gives a denominator, expressed in scientific notation, of 4.93×10^{116}. The number of seconds in a year is 31,536,000 or 3.15×10^7. The age of the universe is presently thought to be about 15 billion or 1.5×10^{10} years.

Thus the universe is only 4.725×10^{17} seconds old. The number of possible combinations of seventy-nine letters is then more than 10^{99} or several trillion trillion *times* the number of seconds in the present age of the universe. Another point of comparison: it is estimated that there are only about 10^{70} atoms in the entire universe.

A random search among all possibilities for this particular sentence, although short and simple, is clearly out of the question. But what if we were not looking for a particular sentence but merely wanted to find a meaningful English sentence. The number of meaningful sentences seventy-nine letters long is enormous. Linguists have calculated an estimate of 10^{25} possible English sentences that are one hundred letters in length, but since the total possible combinations of one hundred letters (counting only the twenty-six letters) is 3.143×10^{141}, you have a ratio of one in 3.143×10^{116} (Denton 310).[3] Looking for a needle in a haystack would be simple in comparison. Probability can be expressed as the number of "right ways" divided by the number of all possible "ways." Those who are not intimate or comfortable with mathematics are apt to imagine that if the number of right ways is huge (as in the case of short, meaningful English sentences) the probabilities must be good, but that is true only if the total number of possible ways is not much larger. In this case it is *vastly* larger. It is also true of much more complex things such as novels in the English language. The number of such possible intelligible novels of less than four million characters (enough to accommodate *War and Peace*) would seem to be infinite, but it is not. It merely is unimaginably huge. But the number of random strings of four million characters is so enormous that if you divided it by the number of conceivable English novels you would still have an inconceivably large number.

But does this premise apply to living things? Certainly the number of possible species is unimaginably large. But surely the number of ways of arranging a large number of atoms and molecules is much larger, something comparable to the ratio of possible combinations of seventy-nine letters and possible English sentences that could be constructed from them. With living things there are so many unknowns that no one knows what the real ratio would be. We do know that at every level, right down to the contents of the individual cell, biological systems appear to be extremely complex. A single cell, invisible to the naked eye, has the complexity of a small factory. Over and over, biologists are forced, much to their chagrin, to explain these systems in teleological terms. They are forced to describe them in terms of their functions. They would like to say such and such a molecular structure follows simply from thus and such a set of chemical laws, but more often than not they can only say, "If it were structured otherwise it would die." There is good reason to believe that living things are actually far more complex—far more "improbable"—than English novels, let alone English sentences. Of course, we do know that all of human complexity is somehow encoded in our chromosomes: in the sequences of four different nucleotides that make up our DNA. Human DNA is composed of more than three billion pairs of nucleotides. Some DNA provides a code for the construction of proteins, some seems to have a little understood regulatory function, and some may have no coding function at all. Even if we figure conservatively and assume that only one-twenty-fifth of the DNA is significant, the number of possible combinations of just that "significant" DNA is four to the power of one hundred twenty million. That is approximately ten to the power of seventy-two *million*. When the estimated number of atoms in the universe is "only" 10^{70} one can appreciate how unimaginably huge such a number really is.

This gives some idea why Darwinists are so careful to specify the *gradual* accumulation of *small* changes. Large leaps, involving sizable amounts of information, quickly become prohibitively improbable if *chance alone is operating*. Unfortunately for the Darwinists, many of the transformations required by the theory of evolution seem to demand such wholesale changes. That is because a single individual trait is typically part of a larger integrated system and a change in one part cannot be functional without changes in many other parts of the system. Look again at the sentence in the example on page 201. What if we tried to gradually transform this simple sentence (infinitely simple compared with even a bacterium) into another sentence? Each change must produce a functional whole: the sentence must be "fit to survive." Considered in isolation, short words present little problem because there are relatively few possible combinations of two or three letters and a large number of them are actual English words. "In" could become "an" or "it," and "the" could be transformed into "she" or "tie." Unfortunately, such changes would not improve the meaning of the sentence: they would not be "fit." And what about the word "beginning," the only word over four letters long in the sentence? How many reputable English words could be made by changing just one letter? The only one apparently is *beginnings*, which does not get one very far. Most long words, as well as nearly all sentences, are "isolated"—they either cannot be modified into anything else meaningful in a single unitary step, or the number of such possible transformations is extremely limited (which, incidentally, is why the spelling checker for a word processor can work). Michael Behe uses the term "irreducible complexity" to describe systems that are completely isolated in this fashion. His claim is that at the level of biochemistry, the work of life is carried on by innumerable molecular "machines" that are "irreducibly complex." That is, they are composed of several parts, all of which are necessary for proper functioning. Missing a single part, the molecular "machine" would be useless not only for its known biological function but for any other imaginable function as well. It is thus impossible to imagine how it could evolve in small incremental steps.

When critics challenge the randomness of Darwinism, they are not claiming that Darwinism is an entirely random process (as they are accused of doing); they are questioning whether, given the rarity of viable changes that can be made in a complex system, such variations could arise by chance within the necessary time. They also question whether *gradual* changes could ever account for the *systematic* changes evolution seems to demand.

To understand such systematic changes, one can take an example from the world of machines. Since humans design and build machines, we understand them better than organisms, so it is easy to imagine what would happen if aircraft, for example, "evolved" through gradual changes. It is not difficult to picture how the shape of the wing or of the fuselage might gradually change. But how could it gradually move from a piston-driven propeller engine to a jet engine? Any imaginable small steps to get from one to the other would not be functional. The system has to change as a whole. Intermediate steps would not be, in Darwinian terms, fit to survive. Denton provides numerous examples of analogous transformations necessary in animal evolution. A particularly intriguing example is the difference between the lungs of birds and those of other vertebrates. Our own lungs are constructed of a system of branching tubes that terminate in tiny air sacs called *alveoli*. Air is sucked into those sacs and then forced out again, the same way that it came in. It is an inefficient process because it is impossible to get all the old air out before the new air is brought in. The lungs of birds are constructed on an entirely different plan. The air moves in one direction only, so that it passes all the way through the lung before it is expelled. The lungs of other vertebrates are operated with relative simplicity. Like a bellows, we open them to bring air in and squeeze them to push it out. Birds require a more complicated mechanism to keep the air moving along. Denton observes: "Just how such an utterly different respiratory system could have evolved gradually from the standard vertebrate design is fantastically difficult to envisage, especially bearing in mind that the maintenance of respiratory function is absolutely vital to the life of an organism to the extent that the slightest malfunction leads to death within minutes" (211–12). The logic of the paradigm demands gradual changes, but the facts suggest large leaps. Everywhere researchers look in the family tree of life, they see complex systematic transformations that demand explanation, yet they insist on chance as the sole determinant of new variations and consequent gradualness of change.

As Kuhn predicts, the evolutionary biologists who study the question make no attempt to subject Darwinism to "falsification." They are interested only in "articulating" the paradigm, finding ways to show how it can be made to account for various biological phenomena. Attempts to demonstrate the failure of the paradigm are greeted with angry denunciation, not with thoughtful appraisal of the facts and arguments. If science actually worked the way the myth declares it to work, the scientific consensus would be that while there are serious flaws in the argument for Darwinism, the truth cannot presently be known: too much about the nature of genetic variation and how it arises is not known. The intransigence of liberal Darwinists like Gould can be understood in Kuhnian terms: they simply wish to preserve their central paradigm, to which they have devoted their careers. But from their point of view, committed Darwinists like Dennett and Dawkins actually do have reason to believe that Darwinism is inescapable and necessary regardless of the evidence. *Given their mechanistic materialistic assumptions,* they reason that Darwinism *must* be the case. No alternative seems possible. Since they "know" the universe to be nonteleological, the fact that life *appears* to be teleological can be explained only by Darwinism. Shaw's quarrel was thus not really with Darwinism as such but with the metaphysical basis of Darwinism, or more precisely with the metaphysical system Darwinism purports to justify.

The mechanists see Darwinism as the linchpin of their philosophy, but it may be its Achilles' heel as well. They maintain that the laws of physics, more or less as they are presently understood, are sufficient to account for every event in the universe. There is no "higher," teleological causation. But how can physics account for consciousness and, in particular, the consciousness of value? If the laws of physics and chemistry account for all of biology, it is hard to see why consciousness would even be necessary. Science rejects the idea that, for example, gravity can be understood as a stone's "desire" to be reunited with the earth. Scientific law says nothing about "awareness" or value; it is concerned strictly with rules that govern how matter moves through space. There is no provision in physics for molecules to move in such a way as to avoid pain or seek pleasure, so it is hard to see how physics and chemistry alone could ever explain awareness and desire. If known physical law accounts for everything in the universe, why are not all animals, ourselves included, merely unconscious automata? Since human beings, at least, are not automata, the materialist position appears absurd.

There is an alternative, the one proposed by Huxley: epiphenomenalism. One could continue to maintain that physical laws account for everything in the universe but that, in addition to producing changes in physical states, under certain complex conditions, they produce states of awareness: mind. Mental states, however, do not change physical ones. Although it would be necessary for the materialists to admit a degree of ignorance— they would have to concede that they know nothing about how consciousness is produced—there would be no need for a new, "higher" theory of causation. They would thus concede that there are *effects* (the multiple aspects of awareness) that are as yet not understood, but they could maintain that there are no new *causes*. If one accepts the commonsense view that physics cannot explain awareness, Darwinism is forced to accept epiphenomenalism. But if epiphenomenalism is true, Darwinism becomes incoherent. Our mental states are extremely complex and could be created only by the very gradual operation of natural selection, which weeds out unadaptive traits and reinforces adaptive ones. But if mental states cannot *cause* anything, they are adaptively neutral. Natural selection must be indifferent to them. So if epiphenomenalism is true, Darwinism is false. So Darwinism implies epiphenomenalism, but epiphenomenalism implies that Darwinism is not true; thus Darwinism is false. The only way out for the Darwinists is to deny the commonsense observation that mind cannot be reduced to matter. For Darwinism to be viable, it becomes necessary to insist not only that science has the answers to everything but that nothing really exists except matter. Mind is just something matter does. So orthodox, contemporary scientism insists not only on banishing purpose but mind as well. To a degree even Butler could not have imagined, they have truly pitchforked mind out of the universe. Any attempt to establish a place for purpose in the cosmos must begin with the repatriation of the mind.

CAN SCIENCE BE PURGED OF MATERIALISM
AND STILL BE SCIENTIFIC?

Before we examine the vexed question of the relation of mind and matter or the virtually unasked question of how to establish a science that recognizes teleology, it is well to remember that, as Shaw always insisted, arguments are not settled by reason and facts but by the fears and desires of the disputants. No one will ever convince the mechanists without assuring them that their fears are unfounded. Scientists see materialism as the necessary foundation of science. Attacks on materialism are attacks on science and are thus intolerable. This is true even of the liberal, religiously inclined scientists; that is why they insist on divorcing religion from science: they feel they can protect religion only by isolating it from the necessary materialism of science. Are they right? What is necessary to science, and could a science stripped to its essentials really have room for religion? In the case of Shaw's religion we can be more specific: can science find room for a teleological principle operating in the universe?

As was observed earlier in the discussion of George Eliot and the nineteenth-century rationalists, the thing valued most by the scientific mind is order. Scientists insist on a world that is orderly and knowable. Their most telling criticism of vitalism and any metaphysical system that includes teleology is that these are vague and ambiguous, operating according to fuzzy and indistinct principles. As was observed earlier, a teleological universe need not be an indeterminate one, but scientists want more than determinism; they want a knowable, predictable world. They want something like Popper's "falsifiable" scientific theories: hypotheses that make precise predictions that can be tested, which means that the events predicted would not otherwise be highly probable. Although Kuhn was right—science does not actually deem a theory "falsified" because of a single counterexample—the kind of hypothesis Popper describes is indeed necessary to science because the ability to make accurate predictions is what allows the paradigm to accrue authority and its accumulated failures to produce the crises that precipitate revolutions. So any theory of mind and teleology—of final causes—must be capable of specific predictions. It must concern itself with things that are observable and subject to analysis. The last point is important. There is a sense in which teleology is certain to be intrinsically holistic; it must deal with wholes that are more than the sum of their parts. But too often when antimaterialists take refuge in holism, they retreat into a vague and airy world in which nothing can be pinned down. Even if one insists that a particular "whole" is more than the "sum of its parts," one must be able to itemize those parts and precisely specify what "more" appears when they become a whole.

Another concept dear to the hearts of scientists is sometimes called the "unity" of science and sometimes "reductionism." The latter term has been freighted with unpleasant semantic cargo because of its association with the starker forms of materialism, whose advocates are called "NothingButters" by opponents because of their constant refrain ("the brain is nothing but a computer made of meat," "the mind is nothing but firing neurons," and the like). It is not surprising, given the materialistic assumptions of science, that reductionists attempt to explain everything in materialistic terms, but the concept of "intertheoretic reduction," as it is called, does not in itself demand materialism. It is, in essence, merely an application of Ockham's razor, an attempt to find a single set of coherent rules that governs everything. Or at least it would be if those who call themselves reductionists really sought to understand different phenomena and looked for a common explanation. In fact, reductionism is in practice usually only a rather crude example of Kuhn's "articulation" of paradigms. They do not seek a common explanation; they merely assert the sufficiency or their own paradigms. So computer scientists just declare that the brain is "nothing but" a computer, and to the neurological scientists, the mind is "nothing but" the brain. But there is no reason why that set of laws must be mechanistic—as long as it meets the other requirements mentioned above. So a science of spirit, a science of purpose or will, must be deterministic, subject to observation and analysis, and capable of predicting events that would not otherwise be likely. Preferably, it would also be capable of integration into a larger conceptual framework: a Theory of Everything, as it were. Conventional wisdom has it that notions like mind and purpose invariably fail such tests, while matter passes them easily. In fact, one of the ironies of the success of materialistic science is that it has cast doubt on the very reality of matter. The nature of matter turns out to be as problematical as that of mind, and mind may be as susceptible to precise description as matter.

Mind, Matter, and Metaphysics

This dual perception of the relation of mind and matter has changed over the centuries. There was a time when the philosophers were divided between those who thought that the universe was composed of nothing but matter and those who were convinced that mind was the sole substance of existence. The proponents of matter were known as "realists" and the disciples of mind as "idealists." People who believed that both mind and matter exist and are yet quite distinct from one another (a group that, then as now, included most nonphilosophers) were "dualists." Nowadays, those formerly known as "realists" usually refer to themselves as "materialists" and their opponents as "dualists." Idealism, in its purest forms, is not much heard from, but its concepts are important in establishing the terms of the debate. Dualism is now usually associated with Descartes, who articulated an extreme form of the doctrine. Because dualism accords so nicely with unreflective common sense, most people probably just take it for granted that both mind and matter exist and are distinct entities, but an unintended consequence of Descartes' precise formulation of the theory was that he made clear its logical difficulties. In particular, it is difficult, given strict dualism, to understand how mind and matter can interact, as common sense and most philosophies say they must. But if dualism is rejected, there appear to be two absurd (to common sense) alternatives. One leads to the conclusion that minds do not really exist and the other to solipsism: the doctrine that only "I" exist. Specifically, that only the present contents of my awareness exist. The materialists had to explain the first absurdity and the idealists the second. Idealism was once marginally favored by philosophers and realism by scientists—on the rare occasions when scientists thought about philosophy. Nowadays idealism is hardly ever mentioned, and "realism" (that is, materialism) is—at least by the materialists, who have a solid hold on orthodoxy—held up as the opposite of dualism. Dualism is often equated with "Cartesianism"—as if any dualistic philosophy must be identical to Descartes's. The contempt for Descartes so blatant in materialist writings is both ironic and unfair. The strict separation of the material from the spiritual helped protect an infant material science from the censorious attentions of a zealous church. That may have been its purpose. Now that science and the materialistic viewpoint are triumphant, Descartes is condemned for allowing a role for spirit at all. He could hardly, given his historic circumstances, have done otherwise.

Shaw's condemnation of the scientist for failure to live up to his own myths may have been vindicated by the acceptance of Kuhn's version of scientific progress, but Shaw's rejection of materialism is unquestionably not in keeping with present orthodoxy. The nineteenth-century materialism of George Eliot and John Tyndall which Shaw dismissed as passé would be derided by contemporary materialists as vitiated by timorous concessions to theistic authority. To a very large degree, philosophers have been converted by the scientists to the materialist way of thinking. The turning point that led to the present dominance of philosophic materialism may have been the publication, in 1949, of Gilbert Ryle's *Concept of Mind*. Nearly all contemporary defenses of materialism bear at least traces of ideas first elaborated by Ryle (1900–1976).

Ryle endeavors to exorcise what he calls the "Ghost in the Machine." That is what our "concept of mind" really is, he says. The discussions about minds and matter have been contaminated by what he calls a "category mistake." A category mistake can best be understood as the substitution of one level of abstraction for another. The first and most famous example he gives is of a visitor to a university who is shown buildings, offices, fields, and laboratories and then asks, "But where is the University?" The belief that minds are something distinct from bodies, he says, is a category mistake of that sort. Or rather it is a "family of radical category-mistakes" similar to that one (18). Ryle is not as specific as one might wish, but the tenor of his arguments is that while it is sensible to talk about minds just as it is sensible to talk about bodies, "minds" are concepts at a higher level of abstraction than bodies. Minds are not "objects"; they are dispositions, tendencies, and behaviors. When we talk about minds, we are really talking about certain things that bodies do.

The mechanists, who want to describe the world entirely in mechanical terms, find this idea eminently sensible. Others are distressed that it eliminates entirely the notion that there is such a thing as an "inner life." For there is, maintains Ryle, no such thing as a "private" life. "The sorts of things that I can find out about myself are the same as the sorts of things that I can find out about other people, and the methods of finding them out are much the same" (155). Everything we call the mind is only a matter of tendencies, dispositions, and behaviors. I observe these things in me just the same as I observe them in you.

There is a curious if superficial similarity in these ideas to Shaw's own rejection of "idealism." If the ideal of "justice" is illusory to Shaw as long as it means something other than certain persons wanting good things to happen to some people and bad things to happen to others, the notion of "mind" is to Ryle nothing but behaviors and dispositions to behaviors that we can observe in others. For Ryle and his followers, the mind is just an abstraction of certain aspects of the things people do. Contemporary materialists would say that "the mind is merely what the brain does" in the way that a dance is something that dancers do. It would be foolish to imagine that a dance is a "thing" like a table or a vase, but that is what people do when they imagine that minds are distinct from bodies or that mental events need to be discussed in terms different from those used to discuss bodies. One can speak of minds just as one can speak of dances, but to think that mind is something that has properties and attributes apart from the behavior of brains is equivalent to thinking of dance as something independent of dancers. The materialists are convinced that their opponents are misled by their inability to face the harsh truth of materialistic determinism. They have their own fears, of course. To them, the insistence that mental events have qualities unaccounted for by physical law is an invitation to chaos. A notion of the mental as something distinct from the physical is an open door into vagueness and fuzzy thinking.

If Gilbert Ryle is the exemplary champion of materialism, George Berkeley (1685–1753) is the most famous, and perhaps the most thorough, of the idealists. Berkeley's arguments, although they seem bizarre to most people now, as they did then, were meticulous and well thought out. That was probably because he was responding to the challenges of a nascent scientism which he regarded as dangerous and oppressive: the very scientism that culminated in the ideas of people like Ryle. The "new philosophy" of his time, inspired by the fascinating and revolutionary discoveries of Galileo, Newton, and others, was increasingly mechanistic and analytical. The investigations of the scientists had an unexpected consequence: it became increasingly apparent that if the new scientific theories were true, then the world as it actually exists is markedly different from the world as it appears to our minds. This observation leads naturally to questions about how it is possible truly to know anything about the external world. Thus the new philosophy raised the specter of skepticism as well as those of materialism and atheism. Science seemed to be suggesting that the universe was just a giant machine operating under fully deterministic laws, and there appeared to be little room in such a scheme for God. If He existed, at any rate, there was little for Him to do. The philosophy of Deism attempted to make room for a deity in a mechanistic cosmos: God is seen as the Divine Watchmaker who created the universe, wound it up, and has left it alone ever since. But the very insistence on the essentially mechanistic nature of the universe had the effect of highlighting those qualities of mind that common sense declared to be incapable of mechanistic explanation. That would imply some form of dualism: the idea that mind and matter are distinct and separate. The difficulty for the materialists is that their investigations lead them to the conclusion that only the material world is "real," yet it can be known only indirectly, through the mental world of sensation and perception. They rejected the idea that we can directly "know" the material world—the concept known as "naive realism"—and espoused instead something known as the representative theory of perception or representative realism. We do not, according to this theory, directly perceive the outside world; we only experience sensations presumably caused by that mind-independent world and transform those sensations through perception into what John Locke called "ideas." The act of perception is analogous to inference in that it is indirect and subject to error. We do not perceive material objects themselves; we perceive "ideas" that represent those objects.

When presented in this fashion, materialism reveals an obvious weakness: contending that only matter really "exists," it concedes that matter can be known only indirectly, through mind, which alone can be known directly. What is known does not exist, and what exists cannot directly be known. Berkeley's system of idealism begins with an attempt to exploit that apparent contradiction. He proposed to reconcile philosophy with common sense by asserting the reality of our perceptions and sensory experience but defied common sense by denying the reality of matter. In a sense, he affirmed the primary idea behind naive realism—that we can directly apprehend reality—while denying the secondary idea that what we directly apprehend is the physical world. The mind alone—all of our thoughts, perceptions, sensations, memories, and the rest of our awareness—really exists. We do apprehend reality directly, and it is entirely mental in nature. Berkeley did not, it should be stressed, endorse solipsism, the doctrine that the contents of *my* mind alone exist. Reality, for Berkeley, consisted of the contents of all minds, everywhere. We are not isolated inside the shells of our individual awareness, for the consciousness of individuals overlaps. It makes sense to speak of physical objects such as pencils and tables, but such things exist entirely as perceptions. "Their *esse* is *percipi*, nor is it possible they should have any existence, out of the minds or thinking things which perceive them" (25). But surely such perceptions have causes. We cannot will them in or out of existence, so the causes must be independent of our own minds. For Berkeley it is obvious that the cause cannot be material objects, which he argues do not exist, and just as obviously must actually be God. His argument against the existence of the

physical world is elaborate and more insightful than is often acknowledged, and many of his observations seem more discerning now, in light of
twentieth-century quantum mechanics, than they appeared to his contemporaries. They certainly are not conclusive, and few (but not no) philosophers today find them persuasive. His notions appeal to like-minded souls,
those horrified by the notion of being only a cog in a vast, pointless cosmic
machine. God is not an unnecessary hypothesis but an absolutely essential
premise. But those who love the image of the machine for its accessibility
to our understanding, its ability to yield to analysis, find Berkeley's world
of spirit repellent. It is unscientific, unaccessible to rigorous and systematic
study, and immune, in Popper's terminology, to falsification. It cannot be
tested; it must be accepted on faith.

There are logical objections to all these theories: Ryle's materialism,
Berkeley's idealism, and the dualism implied by representative realism.
The most telling criticism of idealism is that it conspicuously fails the test
of Ockham's razor, at least as a scientist would interpret it. Berkeley's form
of idealism is simple in that it poses a single cause for everything—God—
but such an explanation leaves much unexplained: specifically, why God
arranged things in the fashion we observe, which seems both unnecessar-
ily complex and distinctly unsatisfactory. In other words, using God as a
single explanation demands many more explanations for what we actually
observe, much as Ptolemy's circular orbits demanded the addition of innumerable epicycles to make them harmonize with observation. Most people
reject Berkeley merely because the existence of matter seems to them obvious and its rejection absurd. If, however, one accepts the rejection of naive realism and its conclusion that the physical world can be known only
indirectly, in a manner analogous to inference, idealism becomes plausible.
The case for the existence of matter comes down to its providing the best
available explanation we have for much of our mental lives: our sensations
being caused by interactions with matter.

One objection to Ryle's theory that mind is an illusory concept is simply that we have distinct experiences that belong to us alone. If we accidentally touch a red-hot stove, we will probably exhibit behaviors that will say
to those around us that we are in extreme pain, but none of them, however
sympathetic, will experience what we experience. The pain of a severe burn
may be evident to all present, but only the victim knows what it "feels
like." None of this matters to Ryle and his followers. For them, conscious
experience is "invisible." We are aware of our pains and pleasures just as

we are aware of chairs and tables. It never occurs to Ryle that the fact of awareness itself demands explanation. Or rather, it is "explained" as behavior.

Another, more interesting objection is that declaring the mind to be illusory entails unavoidable circularity, since "illusion" is an inescapably "mental" concept. There is no room in the world of matter for illusion; things either are or they are not. The attempt to "reduce" mental concepts to the physical devolves into explaining them away. The difficulty is that genuine reduction implies deduction. That is, to say that we can reduce phenomena A through W to concepts X, Y, and Z means that given X, Y, and Z one could logically deduce all the rest. Modern science has actually made it more difficult to envision explaining mental concepts in material terms even while rendering the idea of matter as difficult and obscure as mind is traditionally thought to be. The philosophical dilemma of materialist science has actually deepened immensely since the time of Locke: as scientists become ever more convinced that nothing but matter exists, science has made it increasingly difficult to say just what matter is.

Materialism and Naive Realism

But the materialists, in their attempts to exclude everything from the universe except matter in motion, find themselves returning to naive realism, despite its having been discarded by so many philosophers as untenable. Representative realism, merely by declaring that the mind does not directly apprehend the physical world, must acknowledge that mind indeed exists. Naive realism would appear to bypass the need for mind at all: it puts the brain (a physical system) directly in contact with other physical systems. But it then becomes necessary to ignore entirely the question of how such a thing as awareness is possible at all. There is no reason to assume that any physical system, considered strictly as such, should ever be aware of anything. It just behaves. Just as Kuhn maintains, the materialists do not really attempt to understand consciousness on its own terms; they strive to bring it into the fold of their favorite paradigms. So the computer scientists promote Functionalism, which declares that mind is nothing but a computer algorithm, and the neurological scientists trumpet Identity Theory, which insists that minds are nothing but the activity of neurons. If considered honestly and logically, such theories reduce us all to unconscious automata. In any case, naive realism is logically incompatible with Functionalism and the Identity Theory, for if mind is "nothing but" an algorithm for firing neurons, it is impossible to imagine how such a physical system, as a physical system, could have direct contact with another physical system outside itself. The brain, they insist, is nothing but a chemical-electrical machine, yet magically it directly apprehends the world outside itself. Such absurdities are unnecessary. The abandonment of naive realism, as Bertrand Russell showed, does not entail the abandonment of science. Russell, who was wholeheartedly committed to science and the scientific way of thinking, provided the basis for an alternative to the conventional materialism of Ryle. The stupendous success of modern science conceals a startling paradox. As Russell put it:

> Physics assures us that the occurrences which we call "perceiving objects" are at the end of a long causal chain which starts from the objects, and are not likely to resemble the objects except, at best, in certain very abstract ways. We all start from "naive realism," i.e., the doctrine that things are what they seem. But physics assures us that the greenness of grass, the hardness of stones, and the coldness of snow, are not the greenness, hardness, and coldness that we know in our own experience, but something very different. . . . Naive realism leads to physics, and physics, if true, shows that naive realism is false. Therefore naive realism, if true, is false; therefore it is false. (*Inquiry* 15)

Physics has achieved its triumphant conquest of the material world by denying the truth of our awareness of that world. As Russell said: "Modern physics . . . reduces matter to a set of events which proceed outward from a centre. If there is something further in the centre itself, we cannot know about it, and it is irrelevant to physics" (*Outline* 163). The hardness, temperature, color, and taste which we imagined to be attributes of material objects are only the effects those objects have on our consciousness. The immediate objects of our perception are not physical objects in the usual sense but what Russell calls "percepts," and they exist in our heads, not the world outside:

> We do not know much about the contents of any part of the world except our own heads; our knowledge of other regions . . . is wholly abstract. But we know our percepts, thoughts and feelings in a more intimate fashion. Whoever accepts the causal theory of perception is compelled to conclude that percepts are in our heads, for they come at the end of a causal chain of physical events leading, spatially, from the object to the brain of the percipient. We cannot suppose that, at the end of this process, the last effect suddenly jumps back to the starting

point, like a stretched rope when it snaps. And with the theory of space-time as a structure of events . . . there is no sort of reason for not regarding a percept as being in the head of the percipient. . . .

It follows from this that what the physiologist sees when he examines a brain is in the physiologist, not in the brain he is examining. What is in the brain by the time the physiologist examines it if it is dead, I do not profess to know; but while its owner was alive, part, at least, of the contents of his brain consisted of his percepts, thoughts, and feelings. (*Analysis of Matter* 319–20)

This leads us to an astounding conclusion: one of the most important initial observations about the nature of mind is that, at least in our waking states, the bulk of it consists of a model of the world outside our brains. Our senses collect data that are transported to our brain, an organ that uses that data to construct a model of the world about us. The material from which the model is fabricated is the stuff of consciousness. Naive realism is the confounding of that model with reality. The model is actually all we know, and the irony is that we know nothing about the stuff from which it is constructed. Literally, nothing.

This is strong stuff for people who want certainty, because it seems to throw everything we have come to regard as most real and certain into hopeless doubt. The initial reaction of many is to reject it as a horrible doctrine. It is not so horrible if you can accept doubt and be satisfied with probability—which is supposed to be the way of science. A consideration of the careful, reasoned objections to this theory show why this is so. Those objections are essentially of two types: that it leads to the hopeless absurdity of solipsism and that it demands the existence of a homunculus, which leads to an infinite regress. These are important arguments and will be addressed shortly. First, we should try to clarify, in more prosaic terms, just what Russell is saying.

Imagine yourself the pilot of a strange science fiction vehicle which for some reason—say, because the terrain you must traverse is highly radioactive—has a cockpit deep inside a windowless chamber. You are able to control this conveyance because you are surrounded by television screens and speakers that provide you with a panoramic view of the outside of the craft. The accuracy is so great that you appear to be looking directly out windows. The television cameras that provide these views are even controlled by the movements of your head so that as you move your view changes, just as with a real window. Suppose further that some necessity of design required that this cockpit be situated so as to face backward. As you sat in the vehicle you were facing the rear, yet the television view gave the impression that you were seated normally, facing the front. You would operate this craft just as you would an automobile with windows surrounding you, yet you would not be looking at the landscape around you but rather at images on the screens of cathode ray tubes. True, the objects surrounding the vehicle "cause" the images, or rather light reflected off them and into the cameras produces the images. But the glowing chemicals on the screen are what you really see. Russell is saying that all of our images are like that. The picture of our world provided by our senses is just that: a picture, not the thing itself. What he means by "the causal theory of perception" is that what happens in our brains is at the end of a sequence of causally related events but that the cause and the effect are not the same.

Centuries ago people thought that when we saw things our eyes somehow reached out to capture their appearance. Contemporary science teaches that photons from the sun (or from artificial lighting) are reflected off of objects in many directions, including into our eyes. The lenses of our eyes bend the light in such a way that the only light to reach a given point on the retina comes from a single direction. It is sometimes explained that the lens projects an image onto the retina, but at this point the image does not exist as such. Individual receptor cells convert the energy of the photons into electrochemical energy that sends signals along individual nerve fibers to the visual cortex. Only there, in a manner that remains totally mysterious, are the many signals from the eyes brought together to form the image that exists in our consciousness. So far as we know, all of the nerves that bring signals from our senses to the brain are pretty much alike. We have no idea why some signals result in the sensation of color and others the sensation of sound. We certainly have no idea how all this neural activity becomes part of a single, if ever-changing, awareness. Even the sensations of bodily awareness appear to be actually situated in the brain. This is the conclusion of the "phantom limb" phenomenon, in which amputees will report having sensation in limbs that no longer exist. There is much talk now about virtual reality: machines that can stimulate all of our senses in such a way as to make us imagine that we are visiting imaginary places and interacting with objects that exist only in a computer. Russell's thesis is that the only reality we know is such a virtual reality: a model of the world surrounding us rather than the real thing. He was convinced that the model was a reasonably accurate picture of the real world, but it was a model nonetheless. Indeed, because of the way our brains switch signals

from one side of the body to the opposite side of the brain, our consciousness may be sitting backward in our heads just like the pilot in the imaginary vehicle.

One objection to this idea is that it requires the existence of a homunculus, which in turn leads to an infinite regress. If there is an image in the
brain, the argument goes, there must by a conscious entity there to observe it: the homunculus ("little man"). But the consciousness of that
"little man" must now be explained. He (whatever "he" is) must be endowed with another "little man." And so on, infinitely. The answer to that
is that there is no need for a homunculus: all of our consciousness—our
sensory perceptions, both of our bodies and our surroundings, together
with our thoughts, emotions, ideas, and memories present to awareness—
constitutes a unified whole. Our sense of self, our awareness of our bodies,
our perceptions of the world, are all part of one thing. There is no need for
a homunculus and thus no regress. That is where the analogy to the pilot
of the strange vehicle breaks down. The television screens surrounding the
pilot are not actually like the images that are part of the brain's awareness.
The individual dots of glowing chemicals are not "aware" of each other;
they are not part of a "consciousness"—except, that is, in the mind of the
pilot. At least we have no reason presently to imagine that they are. What
we think of as an observer and the observed is actually all part of one thing:
a unitary awareness. And the only place where such awareness exists, to
the best of our present scientific knowledge, is brains.

A more serious charge for most people is that this leads to solipsism: the
doctrine that I alone exist. As A. J. Ayer put it: "The great difficulty with
any theory of this kind is to see how we can be justified in inferring that
any such external objects exist at all" (*Bertrand Russell* 84). Russell deals
with this problem extensively in his *Human Knowledge*. He points out
first that, however logical solipsism may seem to some people (it seems
absurdly paradoxical to others), it is psychologically impossible to believe.
Russell tells of receiving a letter from an eminent logician who said that
"she was a solipsist, and was surprised that there were no others" (*Human
Knowledge* 180). One can simply move from its psychological impossibil-
ity to a pragmatic position, maintaining that the external world exists in
roughly the way our perception says it does because that is the only theory
that seems to work. Even the person who swears he firmly believes that
Mack trucks exist only as images in his own mind still looks both ways
before crossing the street. Essentially, though, we believe in the reality of
the world outside our skins in the same way that we believe in any scien-

tific theory: by inference. Inference can never provide absolute certainty, and many find that unacceptable. But absolute certainty is a delusion. It is simply impossible to know with absolute certainty that life is not a dream. Yet what reasons do we have for believing that it is a dream? Apart from the fact that there are things we cannot explain, things we do not understand or fit into the current scientific paradigms, I know of none. Realism (philosophical, not Shavian) is the best explanation we know for our conscious experiences. While solipsism can never be absolutely ruled out, on the basis of what our best minds know, it is highly improbable. Even when probabilities can be precisely calculated, it is possible to feel very certain in what is strictly a uncertain world. According to contemporary science, which declares that all of the molecules in your body are in constant, random motion, there is a probability, which could be precisely calculated, that your body could spontaneously levitate and hover in midair. If you, however, reported that you had actually personally experienced such a levitation to a physicist who unquestionably believed in the theories that make that prediction and could calculate exactly the probabilities involved, she would (kindly, I hope) suggest that you seek psychological help. There is a point at which probability can be treated as certainty, even if philosophers and logicians might object.

The kernel of truth (and it is only a kernel) at the heart of solipsism is the fact that our own consciousness is the only reality that any of us can know *absolutely*. The model of the world that occupies the bulk of our consciousness is created through a process analogous to inference, which Russell called "physiological inference" (*Outline* 13) or "animal inference" (*Human Knowledge* 167). The truth of physiological inference, like that of any other inference, is tentative and conditional; it is a function of how accurately it predicts future events. Physiological inference is so accurate in predicting the way things will happen in our everyday experience that it allows us to behave just as if the model were the real thing. The new computer-based science of virtual reality has made us aware how artificial the model is. This amazing technology allows us to wrap a human body in a costume designed to stimulate the senses in a patterned manner, just as the real world does. Inside this wraparound machine, we are thrust into a new world, a world that exists only for us and is not shared with those around us—who, for now, do not exist for us. It is artificial solipsism. If we do not think carefully about it, we imagine that what we experience while we receive visual and tactile stimulation from the machine is an illusion, but what we experience otherwise is reality. There is no real difference between the two. We never do experience reality, only the models our brains have created. There is no theoretical reason why we could not some-day design a machine that would provide a virtual reality that would be indistinguishable from everyday reality. The only difference between the actual and the virtual would then be that the one is a more accurate model of what really exists.

This is known as the "argument from illusion." In essence, it reasons that the information provided by our senses, the images of reality our per-ception provides us, cannot be trusted. They could all be illusions. Yet those images exist. They lead us reasonably to infer a physical world which we believe in because we can make accurate predictions based on those "physi-cal inferences." Unfortunately, those inferences and the model of the world they create for us do not provide a clear understanding of the images as images. Where do they exist? Where could they exist but inside our brains? If you look at a familiar object, say a card table, the image you perceive is not the same as the dimensional object you "know" it to be. If asked to describe the tabletop you might say that it was brown in color and square in shape, yet the shape you actually perceive—unless you are look-ing at it from directly above—is some sort of parallelogram. The actual color will vary according to lighting conditions of intensity and direction. If the surface is shiny, parts of it may even appear white. A photograph, or even a painting, could provide you with a similar image. The image is not the reality, yet the image exists. Where could it exist except inside your brain? We never really "see" anything but the insides of our own minds.

What Is Mind?

Common sense tells us there must be more to mind than differences in time and distance, but common sense is not enough for the scientists. The greatest difficulty stems from the fact that mind and matter seem so im-possibly different that there seems to be no common ground on which to base a comparison. Even when philosophers attempt to analyze the specific qualities we know to characterize mind, the terminology is never as precise as that used to describe the mathematical world of physics. The two most important of these qualities, for our purposes, are "intentionality" and "unity." Intentionality refers to the fact that many mental states are "about" something; they refer to something other than themselves. Be-liefs, desires, and fears do not exist by themselves; they must be about something. I have a belief *that* the sun will rise in the east; I have a desire *for* a grilled cheese sandwich; I fear *that* the noise coming from under my car will mean a large repair bill. All meaning is a form of intentionality. The elements of physics, whether singly or in combination, are never "about" anything. The importance of intentionality for our concerns is clear: teleology is inconceivable apart from intentionality. Even when animals are taught to respond to visual cues, learning which ones produce food, several layers of intentionality are required, *if they are responding consciously* and not as automata. If final causes exist, if anything ever happens because someone or something wants it to, intentionality must be involved.

The other significant characteristic of consciousness is a unique form of unity.[4] Kant was the first to describe this distinctive aspect of the mind, but it is easily understood. This is how Searle describes it:

> I do not just have an experience of a toothache and also a visual experience of the couch that is situated a few feet from me and of roses that are sticking out from the vase on my right, in the way that I happen to have on a striped shirt at the same time as I have on dark blue socks. The crucial difference is this: I have my experiences of the rose, the couch, and the toothache all as experiences that are part of one and the same conscious event. (*Rediscovery* 129–30)

Not only are the inputs from our various sense organs (sight, smells, sounds, and so on) part of a single unity, but each of these is itself a unity of disparate entities. This is clearest in the case of vision. The perception of a couch in Searle's example is necessarily a unity of discrete entities. We can imagine our field of vision broken down, like a computer screen, into an array of pixels, each one corresponding to one of the rods or cones in our retinas. The perception of the couch requires some particular structure of such "pixels" in our consciousness; it requires a unity of disparate elements. This unity embraces elements across the dimension of time as well as space. The perception of movement, such as a flickering light, necessitates the unity of images through time. We do not simply see the solitary image of the present and "remember" the image that preceded it; we perceive it all together: a unity over differences in time and space. We do not see the light in a particular position and remember that it varied in position over the last few seconds; we see it "flicker."

Unity is thus the defining and essential characteristic of consciousness. There is nothing like it in the world of physical science. To expand your consciousness is to increase the number of different elements included in this unity; to diminish consciousness is to reduce them. If one imagines a series of such reductions, it becomes clear how they shrink awareness. Eliminate everything from consciousness except your visual field: all thoughts, physical sensations, all perceptions except the visual. You can merely *see* and cannot even think about what you are seeing. You are still conscious, but it is a reduced sort of consciousness. Reduce that consciousness even further to only the couch in the center of the field of vision, and then further still, shrinking it finally to a single pixel of visual information. Consciousness, at that point, would seem to have disappeared entirely, for without something to contrast it with a single bit of information is meaningless.

This "connectedness" of the contents of our conscious minds is not the only unique aspect of our mental lives. There is the whole array of atomic mental elements psychologists sometimes call "qualia": the various distinct sensation of consciousness, like the color blue and the sound of a single note of a flute. We know these things are attributes of our minds, not of the physical world, which has been deprived by modern science of all but mathematical characteristics. But there is no reason why the atomic (that is, irreducible) elements of the physical world might not have a one-to-one correspondence with the atomic elements of the mind. That is an unfamiliar concept, but it is not unreasonable—unless, that is, you assume that the material world can have no qualities that are invisible to us.

Something like that would have to be true if the materialist view of mind is even partly correct. On the materialist view, in a perfect neurological science a living brain could be examined (using some technology presently unimaginable), and scientists could say with perfect confidence, "This patient is thinking about a green two-story house." Not only that, the scientists would have to be able to identify the source of all of the various elements of that patient's conscious experience: each "pixel" (as it were) of information in the subject's mind. Yet even if they could achieve such an amazing feat, they would not be able to understand the peculiar structure of consciousness *because it is a structure alien to the conceptual world of materialist science.* The structures of the physical world—like the crystalline lattice of molecules in a solid—are all defined in time and space. The relationship of each molecule to the others, or of the atoms within the molecules, is strictly a matter of having a constant distance through time from the others. The elements of awareness are related in an entirely different way, a way that is unique and thus cannot be described by comparison to anything. All we can say is that the molecules do not have—or at least we do not imagine them to have—a similar relationship. They simply move, or do not move, in accordance with the forces acting on them. We have no reason to think that the molecules are "aware" of each other; they are simply "behaving" in ways that can be predicted by the laws of physics. A genuinely "perfect" neurological science would have to include a theory that allowed scientists to accurately predict the unique connections of mind from the outside.

The "connectedness" of mind makes intentionality possible. You cannot have a belief that God exists—or even that chocolate ice cream tastes good—without some concept of what God (or ice cream) means. A belief in God is not like a covalent bond between two atoms; it cannot be reduced to a simple formula of time and distance. It is intrinsically holistic. *Consciousness* is intrinsically holistic. It is more than the sum of its parts, for it is defined by the structure of those parts. That is why consciousness is important. The "qualia" could be ignored by the mechanistic materialists because outside of a structure of consciousness they would be meaningless. If every elementary particle in the universe were, in a presently unknown aspect of itself, a single pixel or bit of consciousness, the laws of physics would be utterly unaffected. If that were true it could be said that the entire universe was conscious (in an utterly trivial sense) but that it made absolutely no difference.

When Minds Change Bodies

When Ellie accuses Captain Shotover of not realizing that "we know now that the soul is the body, and the body the soul," she could be interpreted as a materialist, someone who imagines that what we call soul can be reduced to purely physical events (*Heartbreak* 5:145). Many today take that for granted; when mind and body are discussed now, it is often assumed that when you reject dualism, as Ellie does, you must espouse materialism. The idea that the elemental nature of the world could be closer to what we think of as mind is not even considered. People who seek to describe everything that exists in physical terms are called reductionists, but there is no reason why the basic set of rules to which everything is reduced could not be mental and spiritual, or at least like Bertrand Russell's "neutral monism." Neutral monism maintains that the ultimate reality is neither physical nor mental in the sense that we understand those terms but gives rise to both. Shaw never explicitly rejects dualism, but much of what he says about mind and body harmonizes with Russell's concept that mind and body, while distinct, are inseparable, like the two faces of a coin. If the universe is really constructed from a single type of building block, it must have characteristics that can give rise to what we understand both of body and mind.

Toward the end of their long debate, the Devil chides Don Juan for imagining a Life Force is necessary: "You think, because you have a purpose, Nature must have one," and Don Juan replies: "I, my friend, am as much a part of Nature as my own finger is a part of me" (*Man and Superman* 2:684). Don Juan's answer implies a pertinent question: how can purpose arise in a purposeless universe? Purpose entails desire, consciousness, and choice. If reductionism is true and a single set of rules governs everything in existence, those rules must provide for the three elements of purpose, or purpose cannot exist. Common sense says it must, but if every event in the universe is determined by the mindless, pointless laws of science, there is no room for choice. If my desires do not have the power, through my awareness of the world, to change events, both desire and consciousness are without point. Purpose is an illusion.

The issue is clear and momentous. If the mechanists are right, then all religion and morality are delusions. Shaw's entire philosophy must necessarily collapse: it is a house without a foundation. If Shaw is right, then will has the power to supersede mechanical causation, and the scientific view of the world is profoundly incomplete. If epiphenomenalism is true, and physical events cause mental events but mental events never cause physical ones, then the mechanical causal sequence of physics would be unaffected. True, we would still need new rules to derive the mental from the physical, but the laws of physics would still apply unchanged to the physical world. This is shown in the diagram below, where the sequence of mental events (a, b, c, . . .) is produced by the sequence of physical events (A, B, C, . . .).

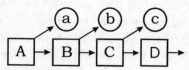

The sequence of physical events is exactly as it would have been if the mental events never occurred. But if mental events do cause physical events—if my desire for a sandwich and knowledge of the contents of my refrigerator influences subsequent events involving bread, lettuce, and cheese—then something radically different occurs:

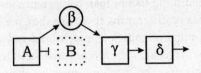

Here, mental event "β" produces a series of physical events (γ, δ, . . .) quite different from the one above. Bertrand Russell said that "modern physics . . . reduces matter to a set of events which proceed outward from a centre. If there is something further in the centre itself, we cannot know about it, and it is irrelevant to physics" (*Outline* 163). That is not quite true. If there is something "inside" that changes the behavior of those events, physics would need new theories to account for such behavior. In any case, we do know something of the "insides" of things: our own minds. We also have reason to believe that it changes things. That suggests that science is incomplete in a fundamental way. Science would correctly, as Russell implies, refrain from speculating about the "insides" of the "centres" that physics concerns itself with so long as such speculation explains nothing about what can be known in a simpler, more economical way. But science does posit theories about things it cannot know directly if those theories can explain observable phenomena. No one has seen a lepton or hadron, but their existence is inferred as an explanation for events that can be seen. If a simpler, more parsimonious theory comes along, they will disappear just as phlogiston disappeared with the advent of the chemical theory of fire.

The epiphenominalists might still argue that mental properties that appear to be the causes of our intentional, purposeful behavior are really just "tacked on" to purely physical processes that are as yet not understood, but the burden of proof would be on them to show how that could be possible. To the argument that merely asserting that organisms tend to seek pleasure and avoid pain is an assertion of mental causation that cannot be accounted for physically, the epiphenomenalists could answer that pain and pleasure could simply be "mental" manifestations of physical forces, possibly even physical forces we already understand: we are already familiar with forces that repel and those that attract. But desire acts through the complex of our united conscious awareness, which is an extraordinarily complicated occurrence. It is not enough to be hungry; we must also be able to recognize food and know how to obtain it. It is possible to program a robot to "recognize" images (although it is proving very difficult to achieve anything like human competence in that arena), but the computer does it very differently. If we are shown a series of unfamiliar photographs of familiar famous people we would probably have little difficulty making the correct identifications. It would be more difficult for the computer/robot because the machine must go about the process differently. We perceive the whole thing at once and say, "That's Bernard Shaw" or "That's Virginia Woolf." The computer merely processes numbers; or more literally, turns electrical switches on and off. It does not—it cannot— "see" the image as we see it. Each pixel is processed separately, one at a time. There is, so far as we can possibly tell, no time when all the electrically represented bits of information come together to create an image of Shaw or Woolf. Of course, we do not *know* that the computer does not "see" the image; we just have no good reason to suppose that it does. It has been designed to do the job of assigning labels to photographs without consciousness. Consciousness was left out of the design. It could not be designed any other way because we do not have the slightest notion how to produce consciousness. Our engineers cannot use what our scientists cannot comprehend. Yet our brains somehow go to a lot of trouble to provide us with images of our surroundings. If those images were not useful, if our brains could just as easily process the information as a computer does, why did evolution bother to produce awareness? If the brain is, in some sense, aware actually only of itself, why is so much of that awareness structured as a model of the brain's surroundings? Why is so much of our awareness devoted to a model of that which is outside of us? The implication is that our complex, fluid awareness is achieved at a high price and with much difficulty. It would not exist unless it were necessary. Teleological, purposeful, causation must exist. Don Juan was right.

This does not, however, necessarily imply dualism. Reductionism is still possible. The mental may not be capable of reduction to the physical, but the reverse is true: material causation could be a special instance of teleological causation. The key is awareness, made possible by those special connections of perception. Our experience suggests that a complex consciousness such as our own is achieved at a great cost and under special circumstances. Even if the entire universe is teleological, if the seed of purpose in the form of some elemental units of pain and pleasure somehow pervades it, events would still follow a mechanistic pattern without awareness. For purpose to appear purposeful, it must act through some sort of consciousness. Without that awareness the behavior of the elements of the universe is essentially mechanistic. Even if pain and pleasure, or some other basic expression of value, exists in every particle of the universe and has the power to act, without awareness the action would be random and mechanical. The Life Force, as Shaw always insisted, needs a brain.

A true science of the mind will come not by explaining away everything mental but by seeking to learn how the phenomena we call physical relate to the world of the mental. At present scientists are not even asking those questions. Instead of denying the existence of the mind, of subjective experience, as they do now, neurologists could search for the ways in which the two appear to coincide. How do the chemical and electrical properties of the brain reflect differences in subjective state? Is the observable state of the brain different when one sees the color red than when green is perceived? Are the nervous responses to visual stimuli different from those produced by sound (other than the part of the brain affected). Recent noninvasive procedures may make it possible to investigate such questions, but the questions must first be recognized as legitimate: the present materialist orthodoxy precludes them. It is possible that answers are inaccessible to us, but we will never know that unless we do all we can to seek them. But how much more would we understand our world and ourselves if we could discover a one-to-one correspondence between observable "physical" processes and mental states! If we made advances in that direction, we would be able to begin asking the next question: how does teleological causation work? Teleological causation, as has been noted, requires value (desire), awareness, and agency. If we could locate the "physical" correlatives of value and awareness, we would be in a position to learn about the nature of that agency: what Shaw called Will. It would then be possible to formulate respectable scientific hypotheses because teleological causation would produce outcomes distinctly different from purely mechanical causes. That is, predictions could be made that could be tested. We could actually begin to develop a true science of the mind. Many scientists now, fearful that mind is inaccessible to science yet deeply desirous of bringing all that exists under the sway of science, sweep the problem away by denying the reality of the mental.

Idealism, the theory that only mind exists, is just one of two classic answers to materialism. The other is pan-psychism, the belief that mind is in some fashion inherent in everything material. The vagueness of that definition will suggest to thoughtful readers why the idea has found relatively little favor. It seems initially an attractive alternative to materialism, idealism, and Cartesian dualism. Materialism, considered logically, reduces us all to unconscious automata; idealism provides no satisfactory explanation why we so persistently perceive there to be such things in our lives as tables, trucks, and tractors; and Cartesian dualism provides no way for two such unlike substances as mind and matter to interact. That is the appeal of Russell's "neutral monism," a form of pan-psychism that tries to avoid the logical difficulties that arise when one suggests that tables, rocks, and trees all have minds. Neutral monism is still vague, but we have seen how such vagueness could be remedied. An analytical approach to mind reveals that it is intrinsically holistic.

It also reveals how mind, or at least the building blocks of mind, could possibly be inherent in everything. It is not impossible to analyze mind; in fact, the analysis of anything at all is ultimately an analysis of mind: that is, it is an analysis of our mental representations of reality, not reality itself. We can think of our minds as analogous to the pixels on the screen of a computer monitor. More abstractly but in the same vein, we may view our minds as, to use a term from information theory, a matrix of differences. There are different types of differences. There are, for instance, spatial differences: each pixel occupies a unique position on the screen. There are also qualitative differences (which, on a computer screen, are given qualitative definitions) such as those of brightness, hue, and intensity. At any given moment, our minds contain a much more vast matrix of differences: color, sound, thought, taste, smell, and sensations that have no name. Of course, the whole universe can be seen as such a matrix of differences. What distinguishes mind is that the differences are united into a whole—the whole of our consciousness. Consciousness makes it possible to say that differences exist. The differences that constitute the matrix of the universe are not, so far as we know, "aware" of each other, and thus they do not know that they are actually "different." Only in the unity of consciousness can they be set side by side, to reveal that they are different. White only knows it is white when it finds itself next to black in some consciousness that can contrast them. So we can infer that the universe consists of an enormous number of differences and that each of our individual minds constitutes a tiny subset of those differences, set apart by the fact that they are bound together in something we call consciousness.

This observation suggests how the logical difficulties of pan-psychism might be overcome. Part of the appeal of pan-psychism is that it follows from the assumption, dear to scientists as well as many others, that there is a single set of rules governing the universe and that everything in it is composed of the same sort of "stuff." So if mind exists and arises out of what we call matter, all matter must have the potential, in some fashion, to produce mind. The differences that constitute matter are differences of time and space, but that does not mean that only such differences exist. If a completely color-blind person, one who perceives only light and dark, looks at our computer monitor, he would not see all of the "differences" associated with each pixel, but they would exist nonetheless. It is certainly possible that the differences of consciousness—color, sound, and other sensations—exist in some presently unimaginable fashion throughout the universe. What would appear to distinguish mind as we think of it is the element of unity: the bonding together of differences into awareness. Something more is needed as well. The structure of awareness must be meaningful; it must be such as to permit choice: meaningful action. It is of utmost significance that the bulk of the awareness our bodies provide for us is a model of the outside world, for that is a way of extending awareness beyond its "natural" boundaries. The brain, by creating a model of the external world, allows organisms to extend their "wills" into their environment.

We do not then have to assume that the consciousness of our bodies is limited to our brains. When the two hemispheres of the brain have been surgically separated for extreme medical reasons, studies of the patients suggest that two conscious entities are thereby created, each unaware of the other. A single body can thus contain more than a single consciousness. If teleological behavior is, as it seems to be, a trait in varying degrees of all living things, it follows that some degree of consciousness is to be expected in all life forms, including single-celled organisms. If that is the case, then it is not unlikely that there are independent pockets of consciousness throughout our bodies, all contributing to its proper functioning. The Life Force, the Will as a general principle of the universe, would indeed be, as Shaw insisted, the most important force in the cosmos. It would also be subject to analysis and scientific study. What is needed is for scientists to acknowledge that the question exists, to begin trying to understand the mind on its own terms, rather than vainly attempting to deny its existence.

THE REPATRIATION OF THE MIND

More than sixty years ago the noted physicist Sir James Jeans wrote:

> To-day there is a wide measure of agreement, which on the physical side of science approaches almost to unanimity, that the stream of knowledge is heading towards a non-mechanical reality; the universe

begins to look more like a great thought than like a great machine. Mind no longer appears as an accidental intruder into the realm of matter; we are beginning to suspect that we ought rather to hail it as the creator and governor of the realm of matter—not of course our individual minds, but the mind in which the atoms out of which our individual minds have grown exist as thoughts. (186)

Nothing has happened since in the realm of physics to give reason to change that assessment. However much biologists and psychologists may cling to old-fashioned materialism, physicists are acutely aware how untenable it is. Paul Davies and John Gribbin close their book *The Matter Myth* by referring to the phrase coined and made famous in 1949 by Gilbert Ryle, who has become something of a patron saint of contemporary NothingButters. Ryle derided the notion that there was anything in the universe except matter in motion as a fallacious belief in the "ghost in the machine." Davies and Gribbin wryly note that today "we can see that Ryle was right to dismiss the notion of the ghost in the machine—not because there is no ghost, but because there is no machine" (309).

If we are to believe, as the scientists are always urging, in the unity of nature, we cannot imagine that anything as complex as our consciousness appeared magically with the first homo sapiens. It must have developed out of some fundamental principles governing the universe. But you cannot build minds out of matter any more than you can build houses out of thoughts. The atomic elements of any structure must be appropriate to that structure. Bricks and mortar can produce houses because their nature is such as makes houses possible. We have made a tiny step toward identifying the mortar of consciousness when we noticed the *connections* that are the defining attribute of consciousness, but even more significant is the recognition that desire—will—is fundamental to the nature of the universe.

The assumption that has provided the foundation for so much of twentieth-century philosophy, that we are merely cogs in a cold, pointless universal machine that blindly and indifferently grinds away, is false. We are pilgrims on a long journey, the end of which is far beyond our ken. We are the soul of the universe, not its victim, and it is our frightful responsibility to guide it to its destination, a goal we can but dimly perceive. Science has not yet fully accepted this fact because individual scientists, like most of the rest of us, are conservative when it comes to relinquishing fundamental assumptions, but science must eventually come to see its truth. It must because the scientific ideal, the creed which scientists profess even when failing to practice, demands it. Shaw, dismissed even by many of his friends as a relic of the nineteenth century even as he claimed to be the prophet of the twentieth, will have the last word if, in the twenty-first, his stubborn and lonely proclamation finally becomes the new orthodoxy.

The Holy Ghost, he said, with astonishing accuracy and profound simplicity, is a scientific fact (Pref. *Back to Methuselah* 5:281).

IV

A Peroration

Catching Up with Shaw

Shaw proclaimed the coming of the superman; he did not claim to be one. He embraced realism and rejected ideals but failed as a prophet largely because when confronted with facts that fiercely challenged his beliefs he denied the facts rather than facing them and defeating them. The first half of the twentieth century was not a congenial epoch for one who insisted that all human beings are equally children of God. For Shaw the propensity to commit evil was a disease of the soul, not its natural state, and diseases have cures. He knew that the evil which spread throughout Europe during the world wars and the malignant interlude between them was the disease of Bill Walker's shriveled soul in an epidemic state, infecting whole societies and political systems, but he failed to see how virulent the cancerous malady had become. Wishing to win us over to Major Barbara's faith in evil's vulnerability to the curative power of good, he underestimated the difficulty of the obstacle. And ironically, the gulf between his understanding and that of the rest of the world that made him a prophet of such vision may have led him into the folly which Archer claimed was his natural condition: the blindness of apriorist thinking. The man who utterly rejected principles became so used to the idea that he was right and others wrong that he ceased to check the facts honestly. He had been right to dismiss as hysterical nonsense the stories of German atrocities spread by English propaganda during World War I; he dismissed similar characterization of the evils of Nazism, and he was wrong.

His glaring error in the specifics obscures the surprising fact that he was right about the general conditions that produce political evil: Nazism justified its evils with idealism and only thereby was able to infect an entire society. Shaw is still worth heeding, despite his mistakes, because the ideals that produced the Nazi atrocities—ideals he opposed—are still with us. Nazi racial concepts were built on Social Darwinism, and Social Darwinism is grounded in the metaphysics of scientific materialism, a philosophy that has become so pervasive its tenets are the unconscious and unexamined assumptions of most contemporary intellectuals. The deconstructing postmodernists of today who assert the relativity of all morality grow from the same soil as the Social Darwinists who delighted in the prospect of the weak being devoured by the strong. Progressives who frankly disbelieve in the possibility of progress offer little hope to oppose those who see progress in the annihilation of the "unfit," however that unlovely term might be defined. Shaw did offer an alternative, one based in reality and reason. The postmodern rejection of progress is a cogently logical extension of the assumptions of scientific materialism. Shaw's major achievement as a philosopher was to perceive that those assumptions are false. He did not make it clear *why* they are false or how logically compelling his alternative is. For those of us who despair of the impotent stagnation of progressive politics it is worthwhile to review just how compelling those arguments are. They are neither comforting nor soothing to the self-righteous, but they do provide a bracing, crisp challenge for those who seek to change the world rather than merely complain about it.

Shaw's scientific religion strikes many as neither scientific nor religious because it is based on the logical denial of the most cherished dogmas of each belief system. He found his faith by rejecting two great orthodoxies and embracing what remained. That would seem to leave a void indeed, yet what remains turns out to be not emptiness but profound and glorious truth. We have clung to those protective dogmas, flimsy as on honest inspection they are revealed to be, because they have shielded us from reality: the reality of our own responsibility.

The religious dogma denied is the faith in an all-knowing, all-powerful, and benevolent God. Leibniz put the argument as succinctly as anyone in his famous syllogism:

> Whoever does not choose the best course is lacking either in power, or knowledge, or goodness.
> God did not choose the best course in creating this world.
> Therefore God was lacking in power, or knowledge, or goodness.
> (377)

Leibniz offers to attack the second premise. Shaw dares to accept it and the inevitable conclusion, but he realizes that God's failure to choose the best course need not entail His lack of goodness, only His present deficiency in power and knowledge. Here too Shaw was heterodox: people find it easier to envision a cruel God than a weak or ignorant one. He answered that God would prevail in time; God did not create the universe: the purpose of the universe is to create God.

For the traditionally religious people an imperfect God is no God at all; for the scientific materialists Shaw's God-in-the-making is a cowardly evasion founded only in wishful thinking. Rejecting Nobodaddy, they fearlessly embrace NothingButtery. The scientific materialists believe they stand for logic, objectivity, and fact, but the refutation of Nothing-Buttery is as logically sound as the denial of Nobodaddy. It is, however, much less familiar. The Devil's position, sneeringly flung to Don Juan—"You think, because you have a purpose, Nature must have one"—is such a firmly entrenched orthodoxy that even opponents of materialism, such as Searle, stumble over it. If Don Juan's answer were reformulated as a syllogism, it would go something like this:

> I am part of the universe.
>
> I am aware, at least in part, of myself; I am not indifferent to my state; and I have some capacity to change that state.
>
> Therefore the universe is capable of being aware of itself, prefers some states to others, and is capable of changing them.

Nature does have a purpose, even if we cannot yet grasp what it is. Purpose cannot be reduced to purposelessness. A purposeless and mechanical universe could never give rise to values. That is the fallacy hidden within the naturalistic fallacy, which maintains that one can never derive *ought* from *is*. The fallacious hidden assumption is that values cannot be facts; that facts exist and values do not; that values are not an actual part of the universe but something imposed upon it. Imposed from where?

Contemporary materialists reserve their most withering contempt for Cartesian dualism, but their alternative is the utter denial of one-half of the duality rather than a genuinely monistic metaphysics. Mind, they say, is an illusion. Shaw would respond that that is nonsense. The materialist presumption that values are a completely arbitrary and accidental product of natural selection is untenable. Natural selection creates nothing; it selects only from that which has been created. It cannot create values from the pointless collisions, repulsions, and adhesions of atomic particles. To assume otherwise is like a parody of an elementary school problem in arithmetic: if you have six apples, eat two of them, and buy three more, how many pears will you have? No amount of adding and subtracting apples will tell you the first thing about pears. No amount of juggling molecules can tell you anything about values. The truth of the naturalistic fallacy is that one cannot derive value from a value-free context. If you assume the universe is intrinsically value-free, you must conclude that values do not exist. Values do exist; therefore, the universe is not value-free. You cannot argue that values are all derived from pain and pleasure, which are in turn the arbitrary and accidental product of firing neurons, because pain and pleasure are themselves elementary values and cannot be reduced to mechanics. The neurological system, conceived in exclusively mechanistic terms, must be strictly behavioral. It will be only about the movement of physical objects, purely by virtue of their physical properties, causing subsequent movement of physical objects. Once you suggest that neurons do something in order to avoid pain or seek pleasure and your premise dissolves like sugar in hot water. Purpose has entered the universe.

The mechanists could still argue that values have no effect on the behavior of the universe, that the behavior of every particle that exists is fully determined by mechanistic laws, regardless of how we or other sentient creatures might feel about it. It would then be incumbent upon them to explain how, in this mechanistic universe, such things as desires ever came to be.

The explanation they offer is Darwinism. The apparent purposefulness of biological systems, they assure us, is an illusion created by the purely mechanical process of natural selection. But Darwinism as the linchpin of atheistic materialism fails because even if *evolution* could be fully accounted for by natural selection, the purpose that we experience in our daily living, as Shaw repeatedly insisted, could still not be explained. The essence of teleological causation is value—desire—acting through awareness. Value and awareness acting together must have agency: they must be able to change things. Even if pain and pleasure are the building blocks of all value, they can be forces for change only if they act through awareness. An awareness that contains pain or pleasure must also contain an awareness of how to avoid pain and seek pleasure. Teleological causation rests on consciousness: a unity of differences that contains value (pain and pleasure or higher values), some kind of representation of the facts that stimulate those values (for example, what causes the pain), and a means to change those facts.

Science, unfortunately, is utterly at a loss to explain any of this. If the laws of physics and chemistry were sufficient to explain everything in the universe, awareness would not exist. All living things would be unconscious automata. Since that is patently absurd, the materialists are reduced to various attempts to explain consciousness away, to find elaborate schemes purporting to show that consciousness really is not consciousness. That is why they fall back on naive realism, even though the very science they idolize renders naive realism absurd. But the belief that their brains (purely physical systems) directly apprehend, through the senses, the physical systems around them allows them to force awareness into the background. Focusing on the physical, on matter in motion, which their dogma teaches them is all that can exist, they can squint their eyes and pretend that awareness does not really exist. But no matter how they equivocate and evade, an honest look at the logical implications of materialism always concludes that we are unconscious automata. And that is simply false. The more honest defense of materialism is the one endorsed by Huxley and Searle: epiphenomenalism, but epiphenomenalism destroys Darwinism as a keystone of mechanistic determinism. That defense provides a hole for the mechanists to crawl through, since it is at least conceivable that some other mechanistic explanation for conscious experience could be found. It is just extremely difficult to imagine what it could be.

Science fears teleology not only because it defies all accepted scientific paradigms but because the scientific mind dreads uncertainty and vagueness. Scientists shudder at the prospect of forces which they imagine must be capricious and incapable of analysis or scientific prediction. That dread, while understandable, is unfounded. Value exists, but there is not reason to imagine that it is random. Mind is certainly susceptible to analysis since if Russell's causal theory of perception is correct (and I am convinced it must be) all we ever can analyze is the contents of our own minds. Finding "falsifiable" (that is, testable) hypotheses that can explain teleology in its own terms is more problematical. It probably would involve new ways of correlating neurological systems with what we know of conscious experience, of mapping the united differences of awareness onto the molecular structure of the brain. I, of course, have not the slightest idea how that might be done, but since scientists presently refuse even to ask those questions there is no wonder that they have no answers. It is even possible, if teleological principles operate in some very diminished way throughout the universe, even in nonbiological systems, that physicists will find teleology useful in explaining the very weird things that happen at the subatomic level of the universe. But first the scientists must recognize that logic and the evidence insist that the universe is in some degree teleological. If they can only admit that, it is inconceivable that they should not want to investigate it. The universe has a will; how can we not want to know its nature?

Don Juan was right. Since he has a purpose, nature must also. The universe is groping, fitfully, part blindly and part sightedly, but steadily and progressively toward some end, of which we have only a vague and imperfect image. For Shaw, religion meant dedication to furthering that purpose in the best way that we know how, knowing all the while that we may be completely wrong; knowing that we may be one of the Life Force's inevitable "mistakes."

We do not know nature's purpose, but we know where to look for it. All values are to be found in our own souls. That implies an additional and awesome responsibility. Not only are we charged with creating—becoming—God, but we have no more certain guide than that fragile, flickering light from within. If we are to follow Shaw we must not take refuge in ideals, projecting our values and the responsibility that goes with them outside ourselves. Abstaining from idealism complicates our dealings with our fellow creatures; it certainly increases our responsibility toward them. As Shaw said, when you have finished with all of the labels with which we paste our values onto other people, "when you have called Helmer a selfish hound or a model husband and father, according to your bias, you have said something which is at once true and false, and in both cases perfectly idle" (*Quintessence* 198). That realization is, or should be, humbling. We all know, if we are honest, that we have both mean and lofty impulses, hateful and loving ones. When we reflect that our inclination to call someone wicked is merely a statement of our own ill-feelings toward that person, we should be less apt to justify harming that person. It is easier to brutalize people we fear and hate in the name of justice than in the name of our fear and hatred. Two wrongs, as Shaw was forever pointing out, do not make a right. Barbara Undershaft is correct: there are no good men or scoundrels, only children of one father.

That profound truth raises the question why we should have ill-will toward our fellows, why hatred and cruelty exist at all. Blanco Posnet says, "Theres no good and bad; but . . . theres a rotten game, and theres a great game," but that begs the question why the "rotten game" should exist (*Shewing-Up* 3:798). Shaw simply rejected the Manichean worldview without attempting to defend his monistic faith. While there is no strictly logical objection to the view that the world is intrinsically divided into light and dark, spirit and matter, and that these represent a cosmic struggle of good and bad, most people with a logical turn of mind usually prefer a monistic metaphysics to dualism of any kind. In that respect, the impulse that led Shaw to his belief in moral equality is not unlike that of the materialists in their quest to "reduce" the attributes of mind to the physical laws of matter: they seek a certain simplicity, elegance, order, and harmony in the world. That was probably not the deciding factor for Shaw; he just observed that most people had consciences that could be touched and roused, just as Barbara wakes Bill Walker's stultified soul by gentle yet insistent prodding. Fear and hatred are not the enemies of the Life Force, merely part of its defensive posture when under attack. Selfishness is only the result of the Life Force needing to satisfy the individual before that single consciousness can expand to an awareness beyond itself.

Of course, observation is apt to lead one to a monistic view of the moral universe only if one is endowed with the abnormally normal eyesight of a realist. When one can see the masks of idealism for what they are, it is easy to see how often they justify evil by disguising it as good. The diabolical engines and stakes of the Inquisition performed their evil in the name of religion and morality. The scientific materialists who see so easily through the wicked illusions of traditional religion are blind to the pernicious effects of their own ideals. The Nazi Holocaust, which Shaw almost predicted but could not see when it arrived, was arguably made possible by the perverted ideals of Social Darwinism—ideals that still thrive. The Nazi use of "eugenics" as an ideal to justify atrocity has caused the word to become so saturated in its evil association that it has become difficult to talk sensibly about the subject; it continues to be regarded idealistically, but now it is a negative, not a positive idol. And Shaw, who vehemently denounced the Social Darwinism that made Nazi eugenics such an effective shield for evil, is chastised for talking about eugenics without horror, although all he ever recommended was that the Life Force be allowed as much scope and freedom as possible to guide our breeding. Idealism clouds our thinking today as much as ever.

One of the effects of idealism is to allow us to worship an idea without the responsibility or inconvenience of practicing it. Shaw was, and is, deemed an impossible eccentric for treating two ancient ideals as practical programs for social organization: human equality and Christian charity. Suggest as Shaw did that a college professor and a janitor should be paid equally and you will be assumed to be joking. Many will not bother to argue with you; they simply "know" you are wrong. Yet point out that hierarchy has the advantage of having been thoroughly tried and tested, while equality remains only a sentimental hypothesis—that we know hierarchy works but equality is nothing but emotional dogma—and you will provoke shock or outrage. As for the Christian proposal to cure evil with good rather than more evil, politicians with better instincts assume without question that to take the Sermon on the Mount as a guide to social organization would be certain political suicide. Shaw did not see his proposals as outrageously idealistic but as sensible and practical. How else can evil be countered but with good? Whether in Ulster, the Balkans, or our own urban streets, the result of demonizing one's neighbors is tragically evident. Retribution is evil's means of reproduction. Act on the assumption that your neighbor is a devil and you are certain to become one yourself. The idea of equality may not be as old as the Sermon on the Mount, although Saint Paul insisted that we are members one of another. Many Christians who would not tolerate a word said against the Sermon on the Mount would be horrified at any attempt to put it into practice, and people who idealize equality usually assume that the social fabric would disintegrate were it seriously implemented. Much of the discussion of equality is muddied by confused ideas about what it means, but Shaw understood quite well that people vary enormously in talents and accomplishments. Equality in social discourse is a matter of value, not abilities. He insisted only that we *treat* people all the same. We speak of persons of exceptional talents as "gifted," thereby acknowledging that they are distinguished merely by good fortune. Do we wish to reward people for their good luck? Or punish them for misfortune? People are shocked to be told that they live in a society that punishes people—on principle—for their disabilities, but that is in fact the case. We simply do not have the courage to carry the policy to its logical extreme and condemn paraplegics and the blind to starvation. Modern liberalism is crippled by its acceptance of the idea that the more highly skilled "deserve" more than the less talented because once you concede that point, you effectively abandon equality; you must be satisfied only with mitigating the worst effects of inequality, a procedure that has the effect of shielding the evil doctrine from the examination it needs. Shaw assumed, probably correctly, that a strictly equal distribution of the national economic product would require distribution by a central bureaucracy, something that appears impossible in today's political climate. It is not true, although widely believed by reformers as well as reactionaries, that a centrally planned economy is unworkable, but its feasibility could be demonstrated only by a commitment to making it happen which is utterly absent today. If contemporary reformers accepted Shaw's belief in equality as morally imperative as well as his pragmatic concern with goals rather than ideology, however, there is much they could do.

Such goals could be simply stated, which conventional wisdom declares a necessity in the age of the sound bite. Here are a few:

Everyone willing to work for a living should be guaranteed a living wage.

No one should be allowed to partake of the national product without having contributed labor to create it.

No child should be punished for unwisely choosing her parents.

These should be catchy enough slogans, but they will not be used until those who would be reformers genuinely accept the idea of equality: that no one who helps to make the pie "deserves" a larger piece than anyone else.

One of the most important lessons we could learn from Shaw is that metaphysics matters. Our conception of the basic structure and principles of the universe must influence the way we choose to act in it. Scientific materialism has become so ingrained in our intellectual life that it has vitiated, almost to impotence, the liberal intelligentsia. Once accept that the universe is a cold, indifferent machine and that we are merely cogs, and you lose any foundation for ethics. You will accept, as fashionable liberal intellectuals now do, that no moral code is better than any other, even if you do not realize that such a position entails the abandonment of ethics altogether. Without a metaphysical basis for your ethics, you will be left to whine impotently about the cruelty of the powerful to the weak. The powerful, who have tacitly accepted Social Darwinism as the unofficial established religion of the West, cynically flaunt bumper stickers proclaiming, "He who dies with the most toys, wins." If we have become so mean, and so proud of our meanness, it is in large part owing to dereliction of duty on the part of the liberals—the would-be reformers—whose real functions were understood by Major Barbara and her father: they must supply gentle fans to awaken the embers of near-extinguished consciences and provide protecting shields to guard those embers from the destroying winds of hate and fear. The responsibility of creating Godhead is not one that can be undertaken without the firmest of foundations. Barbara has been accused of arrogance when she declares her intention to leave God in her debt. Whether or not she is guilty of hubris, such an assertion does require supreme confidence and a certain conviction of one's destiny. To take the terrifying responsibility of accomplishing the world's will, it is necessary to know with utter certainty that the world has a will.

If Shaw is remembered only as a dramatist, he will have made a substantial contribution to the cultural heritage of the human race, but he will have failed in his life's goal. His plays, like his politics and his daily life, are the product of his philosophy, his conviction that all men are his brothers and all women his sisters, a conviction that allowed him to present them from their own point of view, without judgment, a faith that let him learn from his own creations even as he invested them with his own wit and insight. Delightful as they are, the plays will truly serve their purpose only if they serve to shelter the spark of his most important insight, a spark that has failed so far to ignite the minds of women and men despite his own untiring efforts. If our civilization is to be saved, it must regain religion, a religion based on fact and science but that acknowledges the fundamental truth which Shaw never ceased to proclaim: that nature has a purpose which is truly ours and that we can find our own purpose only when we dedicate ourselves to fulfilling divine will. It is not "Thy will, not mine," but "Thy will is mine." That will come only when we know, thoroughly and completely, that divine will is as real and inescapable as gravity. The Holy Ghost, the Holy Will, is an undeniable fact. That is the central truth of Shaw's religion, his ethics, his socialism, his life, and his works. We still do not see it. As Ray Bradbury said, in the remarks that opened the introduction to this book, Shaw's spirit has been ahead of us all of our lives. It will remain so as long as we flatter ourselves that the difference in our perception represents our enlightenment and his delusion. Shaw opened his realist's eyes and saw the Holy Ghost. When, and if, we acquire the courage to open our own eyes so far, Shaw will finally make his mark.

Notes

Chapter 1. A Creed for Living: A Faith That Fits the Facts

1. *The Quintessence of Ibsenism* is most readily available to students of Shaw in two different collections of Shaw's writings: *Shaw and Ibsen,* edited by J. L. Wisenthal, and *Selected Non-Dramatic Writings of Bernard Shaw,* edited by Dan H. Laurence. These two volumes are not redundant, even with respect to the *Quintessence.* As is by now notorious, Shaw was an inveterate reviser of his own work. The Laurence collection is preferable if you want the original version of the work, while the Wisenthal edition gives a better view of how Shaw changed the book over the years. Both versions are available in *The Drama Observed,* a four- volume compendium edited by Bernard Dukore, but this useful yet expensive edition is less likely to be found in private collections. For the sake of clarity and convenience, references to the *Quintessence* will be to the Wisenthal edition unless otherwise noted.

Chapter 2. Realism

1. Since this is a book about Shaw's *philosophy* as well as his religion, it might be wise to forestall a possible confusion. "Realism" and "idealism" are standard terms in philosophy which are usually thought of as opposites, but while I refer to the fundamental Shavian view of the world as "realism," and will define it largely in terms of its contrast with what Shaw calls idealism, these are in no way the same as the realism and idealism of ordinary philosophical discussion. We will unfortunately need to use the terms in their philosophical sense in the final chapters. Despite the possibility of confusion, the terms are made inevitable by the way Shaw uses them.

Chapter 3. The Will and Its Responsibilities

1. There are two earlier versions of this passage and the paragraph in which it appears. In the original essay ("A Degenerate's View of Nordau" 359) it is simply the "cardinal Rationalist error." When it was revised and republished as *The Sanity of Art* in 1908 it became the "Rationalist-commercial error."

2. Others have seen this revision as the mark of a major change in Shaw's thinking, away from utilitarian values and toward a more positive attitude to ideals; see, for example, Wisenthal, *Shaw and Ibsen*, 36[1] and Turco, *Shaw's Moral Vision*, 96. I regard it as a minor change of view at most since Shaw had explicitly rejected the utilitarian position in the 1891 edition.

3. The similarity, both in language and concept, to the ideas of William James is remarkable. James's famous essay "The Will to Believe" appeared first as a lecture in 1896, five years after Shaw's letter, but James asserted the functional identity of will and belief in his *Principles of Psychology* in 1890. See Kaye's discussion of the similarities in the thinking of the two men, *Bernard Shaw*, 86–100.

4. "The man who cannot see that starvation, overwork, dirt, and disease are as anti-social as prostitution—that they are the vices and crimes of a nation—is (to put it as politely as possible) a hopelessly Private Person." Pref. *Mrs. Warren's Profession* 1:255.

"The Socialist is . . . in conflict . . . with the stupidity, the narrowness, in a word the idiocy (using the word in its precise and original meaning) of all classes." "The Illusions of Socialism" 418.

"No man can be a pure specialist without being in the strict sense an idiot." "The Revolutionist's Handbook" 2:784.

5. I am indebted to Michael Holroyd for the text of the letter in which this phrase appears. Shaw's correspondent is identified only as "Dear Sir." The letter, dated 11 August 1888, is in the Robert H. Taylor Library of Princeton University.

6. Freedom of the will has here the commonsense meaning which I take to be identical to that of Shaw and other Vitalists. It is not the same as the religious meaning, which maintains God made man "Sufficient to have stood, though free to fall," which has the effect of dooming man to fall while transferring responsibility for the fall to the victim. The latter concept entails its own logical difficulties.

7. Compare the preface with the first volume of *Plays: Pleasant and Unpleasant* 1:33: "There are certain questions on which I am, like most Socialists, an extreme Individualist."

Chapter 4. A Playwright's Progress

1. There should be here not a footnote but a simple citation. My discussion of the aesthetic of the well-made play owes more than I can distinguish from my own thoughts on the subject to an unpublished manuscript by Daniel C. Gerould. Professor Gerould is best known for introducing the plays of Witkiewicz to the English-speaking world, but he has written with clarity and insight on multiple facets of dramatic literature. He gives the well-made play the thoughtful attention it needs but never receives. Although it has been a term of contempt almost from the time it was coined, the expression "well-made play" epitomizes a view of the world that has saturated Western thinking for at least three hundred years and is vibrantly alive today.

2. In the preface and appendixes to the 1893 edition of the play. This volume is

difficult to obtain, but both preface and appendixes are reprinted in *Prefaces by Bernard Shaw* (1934). The preface, without the appendixes, is reprinted in Volume 1 of *Bernard Shaw: The Complete Prefaces*, Vol. 1: *1889– 1913* (1993), edited by Dan Laurence and Daniel J. Leary. The first appendix is reprinted in *The Drama Observed* (1:210–18), edited by Bernard Dukore. The second appendix, which I cite several times in the following paragraph, is a collage of excerpts from letters Shaw wrote to the press about the play, interlarded with additional comments by Shaw. The letters are reprinted in the first volume of *The Drama Observed* as "Bernard Shaw Replies to the Critics of Widowers' Houses" and "Unconscious Villainy and Widowers' Houses" (1:203–10). Since I cite material from both the letters and Shaw's comments, which are reprinted only in the 1934 edition of Shaw's prefaces, I have, for the sake of consistency, made all references to that volume.

3. Elle était une de ces femmes créées pour aimer et pour être aimées. Partie de très bas, arrivée par l'amour dont elle avait fait une profession presque sans le savoir, agissant par instinct, par adresse innée, elle acceptait l'argent comme les baisers, naturellement, sans distinguer, employant son flair remarquable d'une façon irraisonnée et simple, comme font les animaux, que rendent subtils les nécessités de l'existence. (My translation.)

4. Bertolini makes a similar point in his perceptive analysis of the play (*Playwrighting Self of Bernard Shaw*, 34).

Chapter 5. *Major Barbara*

1. A thorough and informative discussion of Shaw's numerous and substantial revisions of the play can be found in Bernard Dukore's Introduction to *Major Barbara: A Facsimile of the Holograph Manuscript*. Dukore's analysis details the many ways in which Shaw's changes improve the dramatic structure of the play.

2. Shaw implies at the end of the preface that the play should be considered as a parable when he "solemnly" denounces anyone foolhardy enough to claim it as a record of actual fact. Lest anyone miss the point, he made it utterly explicit for the British version of the film: "What you are about to see is not an idle tale of people who never existed and things that could never have happened. It is a PARABLE" (*Collected Screenplays* 485).

3. Shaw further emphasized the difference between Undershaft and his successor in his revision for the 1931 standard edition by changing "Six o'clock tomorrow morning, my young friend" to "Six o'clock tomorrow morning, Euripides." See Dukore, "Toward an Interpretation of *Major Barbara*."

4. In the Derry manuscript, Undershaft explicitly tells his daughter that the issue between them is whether or not he is, as Cusins had said, "a most infernal old scoundrel."

5. It is possible that Shaw got the expression from T. H. Huxley. In an essay called "The Struggle for Existence in Human Society," Huxley expresses very Undershaftian ideas. He discusses the difficulties in trying to achieve cooperation and

peace among citizens with conflicting interests: "The moral nature in us asks for no more than is compatible with the general good; the non-moral nature proclaims and acts upon that fine old Scottish family motto, 'Thou shalt starve ere I want'" (93). The actual motto, that of the family of Cranstoun from the barony of Midlothian, was "Thou shalt want ere I want." Huxley stresses the egoism of the sentiment and Shaw the extremity of need.

6. In his hysteria at the end of the second act, Cusins says, "Dionysos Undershaft has descended. I am possessed," but he also says that the Salvation Army "reveals the true worship of Dionysos" to "the poor professor of Greek" and that he worshiped Barbara because he saw "Dionysos and all the others" in her.

Chapter 6. Ethics, Economics, and Government

1. Shaw discusses economic theory at length in both *The Intelligent Woman's Guide* and *Everybody's Political What's What?*, but his most succinct presentation is *The Economic Basis of Socialism*, one of the *Fabian Essays in Socialism*. More can be found in *Bernard Shaw and Karl Marx: A Symposium*. Julian Kaye's chapter "Shaw and Nineteenth-Century Political Economists" provides an excellent summary of the influences on Shaw's economic thinking.

2. Many people find abstract mathematical concepts difficult, although those presented here are in some ways quite simple. I have borrowed Shaw's useful technique of providing concrete illustrations (in many cases using his own illustrations) while striving to make them clear to a contemporary audience.

3. See, for example, "The Illusions of Socialism" (413) and "The Simple Truth About Socialism" 173–74.

4. The success of Japanese industry in adopting the ideas of W. Edward Deming suggests one way this could be done. Much is made of the hierarchical nature of Japanese society, but the real difference is that Deming's management theories, as practiced by the Japanese, stress cooperation and mutual trust rather than internal competition and a system of rewards and punishments dictated form the top. See Deming, *Out of the Crisis*.

5. See Benno Müller-Hill, *Murderous Science*. This is a careful yet passionate book by a scientist (a geneticist) who came to the realization that scientists were profoundly implicated in the extermination policies of the Nazis. As a scientist, he was deeply disturbed by his conclusion that the scientific community of Germany, not just a handful of aberrant individuals, was greatly involved in the practice of mass extermination. These scientists not only justified extermination and made it respectable, but they were often involved directly, sending victims to the lethal chambers, vivisecting individuals who had been deprived of human rights, and organizing the slaughter. Müller-Hill argues that attitudes and assumptions typically held by scientists and inculcated in the teaching of science inclined these anthropologists, psychiatrists, and others to the murderous purposes of the Nazis. Most dis-

turbing, these attitudes have not changed, and the lessons of the past are being obliterated in a willful act of mass denial.

Chapter 7. The Marriage of Science and Religion

1. Kuhn has been done a great disservice by the postmodern critics who have misinterpreted his ideas to support their own brand of extreme epistemological relativism. The irrationality of these self-declared "Kuhnians" has led scientists to denounce Kuhn himself. Even those scientific critics who recognize that Kuhn did not support and in fact vehemently attacked such misuse of his ideas insist that he was wrong about the degree of irrationality in the scientific enterprise. Sokal and Bricmont, for example, say there are "two Kuhns": one moderate and acceptable, the other immoderate and wrong. Kuhn is acceptable when he says that there are irrational factors in science and that the strength of the evidence supporting scientific theories is often weaker than is supposed; he is wrong to say that irrational attachment to the "paradigms" ever outweighs reason and the evidence. They offer two arguments. They say that Kuhn's theory is self-refuting because if attachment to the paradigm always took precedence over the evidence the paradigm could never be changed (*Fashionable Nonsense*, 77). But Kuhn does not say that. The paradigm, he claims, does indeed accrue authority through reason and evidence, but once accepted it becomes increasingly like religious dogma so that when reason and evidence tend to refute it, the disciples defend it with a fervor akin to that which greets religious or political heresy. There is then a conflict between the scientists' emotional attachment to the paradigm and their emotional attachment to reason and evidence (and their own self-image as apostles of rationality). Revolutions in science come about as a way to resolve that conflict. The other argument is simply a flat denial that scientists ever put theory over observed fact (75–76). Unfortunately, the history of science is filled with easily "observed" instances that contradict this assertion, so the assertion that Kuhn is wrong is ironically an example demonstrating that he is right. Bertrand Russell famously observed that Aristotle held views about the nature of women that would have been refuted had he bothered to ask his wife. More germane to our inquiry is the way Darwinism and mechanistic theories of the mind are defended in denial of the most obvious facts of experience. Scientific denial of reason and fact in those areas are the subject of the remainder of this chapter.

2. Denton's book is excellent but relatively technical. Wesson is somewhat easier for those with limited knowledge of biology. More popular books presenting basically the same point of view are Phillip Johnson's *Darwin on Trial* (Washington, D.C.: Regnery Gateway, 1991), and Gordon Rattray Taylor's *The Great Evolution Mystery* (New York: Harper and Row, 1983). A standard on the challenges made to Darwinism by mathematicians is *Mathematical Challenges to the Neo-Darwinian Interpretation of Evolution*, edited by Paul S. Moorhead and Martin M. Kaplan (Philadelphia: Wistar Institute Press, 1967). A more recent and highly readable book is Michael J. Behe's *Darwin's Black Box* (New York: Free Press, 1996).

3. There is an simple error in Denton's calculations, which I have corrected. The error in no way affects his conclusion.

4. There are other distinct characteristics of consciousness: Searle describes a dozen. Only these two are significant to the question of integrating the mental with the physical and the teleological with the mechanical.

Works Cited

WORKS BY SHAW

The Adventures of the Black Girl in Her Search for God. New York: Dodd, Mead, 1933.

"The Author to the Dramatic Critics (Appendix 1 to *Widowers' Houses,* May 1893)." *The Drama Observed* 1:210–18.

Bernard Shaw and Karl Marx: A Symposium. New York: Random House, 1930.

The Bodley Head Bernard Shaw: Collected Plays with Their Prefaces. London: Bodley Head, 1970–74.

"The Case for Equality." *Practical Politics.* 122–44.

Collected Letters. Ed. Dan H. Laurence. 4 vols. New York: Dodd, Mead, 1965–88.

The Collected Screenplays of Bernard Shaw. Ed. Bernard F. Dukore. Athens: University of Georgia Press, 1980.

"The Conflict Between Science and Common Sense." *Humane Review* 1 (1900): 3–15. Reprinted as "Science and Common Sense" in *Current Literature* 29 (1900): 196–98.

"A Degenerate's View of Nordau." *Selected Non-Dramatic Writings.* 347–77. [This is a reproduction of an essay that appeared originally in 1895 and was revised as *The Sanity of Art* in 1908. It was further revised when it was included in *Major Critical Essays.*]

The Drama Observed. Ed. Bernard F. Dukore. 4 vols. University Park: Pennsylvania State University Press, 1993.

"A Dramatic Realist to His Critics." *Selected Non-Dramatic Writings.* 323–40.

"The Economic Basis of Socialism." *Fabian Essays in Socialism.* Ed. Bernard Shaw. London: W. Scott, 1889. 3–27.

Everybody's Political What's What? London: Constable, 1944.

"Fragments of a Fabian Lecture." *Shaw and Ibsen* 81–96.

"How to Become a Man of Genius." *Selected Non-Dramatic Writings.* 341–46.

"The Illusions of Socialism." *Selected Non-Dramatic Writings.* 406–26.

The Impossibilities of Anarchism. Fabian Tract No. 45. London: Fabian Socity, 1893.

"Imprisonment." *Selected Prose.* 857–924. [Taken from *Doctors' Delusions, Crude Criminology, Sham Education.*]

The Intelligent Woman's Guide to Socialism, Capitalism, Sovietism and Fascism. 1937. New York: Penguin, 1982.

London Music in 1888–89 as Heard by Corno di Bassetto (Later Known as Bernard Shaw) with Some Further Autobiographical Particulars. London: Constable, 1937.

Major Barbara: A Facsimile of the Holograph Manuscript. Intro. Bernard F. Dukore. New York: Garland, 1981.

Major Critical Essays: The Quintessence of Ibsenism; The Perfect Wagnerite; The Sanity of Art. London: Constable, 1932.

"Mr. Shaw's Method and Secret." *Selected Non-Dramatic Writings.* 438–41.

My Dear Dorothea: A Practical System of Moral Education for Females Embodied in a Letter to a Young Person of That Sex. New York: Vanguard, 1956.

Music in London: 1890–94. 3 vols. London: Constable, 1932.

"On Clive Bell's Article." *Shaw on Theatre.* Ed. E. J. West. New York: Hill and Wang, 1958. 150–53. [Reprinted from *The New Republic* February 22, 1922.]

"On Going to Church." *Selected Non-Dramatic Writings of Bernard Shaw.* 378–90.

Our Theatres in the Nineties. 3 vols. London: Constable, 1932.

The Perfect Wagnerite: A Commentary on the Niblung's Ring. 4th ed. 1923. New York: Dover, 1967.

"Postscript: After Twenty-five Years." *Back to Methuselah.* Bodley Head Shaw. 5:685–703.

Practical Politics: Twentieth-Century Views on Politics and Economics. Ed. Lloyd J. Hubenka. Lincoln: University of Nebraska Press, 1976.

Preface to *Killing for Sport. Selected Prose* 925–41.

Preface to *Three Plays by Brieux. The Drama Observed* 1188–1222.

Preface with Appendixes to the 1893 Edition of *Widowers' Houses. Prefaces by Bernard Shaw.* London: Constable, 1934. 667– 83.

"Realism, Real and Unreal." *Bernard Shaw's Non-Dramatic Literary Criticism.* Lincoln: University of Nebraska Press, 1972. 110–13.

"Redistribution of Income." *The Road to Equality: Ten Unpublished Lectures and Essays, 1884–1918.* By Shaw. Ed. Louis Crompton. Boston: Beacon Press, 1971. 195–278.

The Religious Speeches of Bernard Shaw. Ed. Warren Sylvester Smith. Foreword Arthur H. Nethercot. University Park: Pennsylvania State University Press, 1963.

The Road to Equality: Ten Unpublished Lectures and Essays, 1884–1918. Ed. Louis Crompton. Boston: Beacon Press, 1971.

Selected Non-Dramatic Writings. Ed. Dan H. Laurence. Boston: Houghton Mifflin, 1965.

Selected Prose. Ed. Diarmuid Russell. New York: Dodd, Mead, 1952.

Shaw and Ibsen: Bernard Shaw's The Quintessence of Ibsenism *and Related Writings.* Ed. J. L. Wisenthal. Toronto: University of Toronto Press, 1979.

Shaw on Theatre. Ed. E. J. West. New York: Hill and Wang, 1958.

Shaw on Vivisection. Ed. G. H. Bowker. Chicago: Alethea Publications, 1951.

"Shaw Reveals Who Was Candida." *Bodley Head Bernard Shaw* 1:603.

"The Simple Truth about Socialism." *The Road to Equality: Ten Unpublished Lectures and Essays, 1884–1918.* By Shaw. Ed. Louis Crompton. Boston: Beacon Press, 1971. 155–94.

Sixteen Self Sketches. New York: Dodd, Mead, 1949.

"Socialism and Human Nature." *The Road to Equality: Ten Unpublished Lectures and Essays, 1884–1918.* 89–102.

"Socialism for Millionaires." *Selected Non-Dramatic Writings.* 391–405.

"The Transition to Social Democracy." *Fabian Essays in Socialism.* Ed. Bernard Shaw. London: W. Scott, 1889. 161–87.

An Unsocial Socialist. Selected Non-Dramatic Writings. 3–203.

OTHER WORKS CITED

Archer, William. "The Psychology of G. B. S." *Shaw: The Critical Heritage.* Ed. T. F. Evans. London: Routledge and Kegan Paul, 1976. 300–304.

———. *Study & Stage: A Year-Book of Criticism.* London: Grant Richards, 1899.

———. *The Theatrical World of 1894.* London: Walter Scott, 1895.

Ayer, A. J. *Bertrand Russell.* Chicago: University of Chicago Press, 1972.

———. *Philosophy in the Twentieth Century.* New York: Vintage– Random House, 1984.

Baker, Stuart E. "Shavian Realism." *Shaw 9: The Annual of Bernard Shaw Studies* (1989): 79–97.

Becker, George J. Introduction. *Documents of Modern Literary Realism.* Ed. George J. Becker. Princeton: Princeton University Press, 1963. 3–38.

Behe, Michael J. *Darwin's Black Box: The Biochemical Challenge to Evolution.* New York: Free Press, 1996.

Bentley, Eric. *Bernard Shaw: 1856–1950.* Amended ed. New York: New Directions, 1957.

———. Foreword. *Plays by George Bernard Shaw.* New York: Signet Classics–NAL, 1960.

———. *Thinking About the Playwright: Comments from Four Decades.* Evanston, Ill.: Northwestern University Press, 1987.

Berkeley, George. *Principles of Human Knowledge and Three Dialogues.* Ed. Howard Robinson. Oxford: Oxford University Press, 1996.

Berst, Charles A. "*The Man of Destiny:* Shaw, Napoleon, and the Theatre of Life." *SHAW: The Annual of Bernard Shaw Studies* 7 (1987): 85–118.

Bertolini, John A. *The Playwrighting Self of Bernard Shaw.* Carbonbale: Southern Illinois University Press, 1991.

Blanchard, Brand. "The Case for Determinism." *Determinism and Freedom in the Age of Modern Science: A Philosophical Symposium.* Ed. Sidney Hook. New York: New York University Press, 1958. 3–15.

"A Book for Burning." *Nature* 293 (24 September 1981): 245–46.

Bradbury, Ray. "On Shaw's 'The Best Books for Children.'" *Shaw Offstage: The Nondramatic Writings.* Ed. Fred D. Crawford. SHAW 9. University Park: Pennsylvania State University Press, 1989. 23–24.

Bullough, Geoffrey. "Literary Relations of Shaw's Mrs Warren." *Philological Quarterly* 41: 339–58.

Butler, Samuel. *Luck or Cunning?* 2nd Ed. London: A. C. Fifield, 1920.

Carpenter, Charles. *Bernard Shaw and the Art of Destroying Ideals: The Early Plays.* Madison: University of Wisconsin Press, 1969.

Cazenave, Michel, ed. *Science and Consciousness: Two Views of the Universe: Edited Proceedings of the France-Culture and Radio-France Colloquium, Cordoba, Spain.* Trans. A. Hall and E. Callander. Oxford: Pergamon Press, 1984.

Chase, Stuart. *Power of Words.* New York: Harcourt, Brace, 1953.

———. *The Tyranny of Words.* New York: Harcourt, Brace, 1938.

Chesterton, Gilbert K. *George Bernard Shaw.* New York: John Lane, 1909.

Churchland, Paul M. "Eliminative Materialism and Propositional Attitudes." *Journal of Philosophy* 78 (1981): 67–90.

———. *Matter and Consciousness: A Contemporary Introduction to the Philosophy of Mind.* Rev. ed. Cambridge: Bradford–MIT Press, 1988.

Collier, Peter, and David Horowitz. *Destructive Generation: Second Thoughts About the Sixties.* New York: Summit Books, 1989.

Cosslett, Tess. *The "Scientific Movement" and Victorian Literature.* New York: St. Martin's Press, 1982.

Crompton, Louis. *Shaw the Dramatist.* Lincoln: University of Nebraska Press, 1969.

Damon, William. *The Moral Child: Nurturing Children's Natural Moral Growth.* New York: Free Press, 1988.

Davies, Paul, and John Gribbin. *The Matter Myth.* New York: Touchstone–Simon and Schuster, 1992.

Dawkins, Richard. *The Blind Watchmaker: Why the Evidence of Evolution Reveals a Universe Without Design.* New York: Norton, 1987.

———. *The Selfish Gene.* Oxford: Oxford University Press, 1976.

Deming, W. Edwards. *Out of the Crisis: Quality, Productivity, and Competitive Position.* Cambridge, England: Cambridge University Press, 1986.

Dennett, Daniel C. "Darwin's Dangerous Idea." *The Sciences* May–June 1995: 34–40.

Denton, Michael. *Evolution: A Theory in Crisis.* London: Burnett Books, 1985.

Dietrich, Richard Farr. *Bernard Shaw's Novels: Portraits of the Artist as Man and Superman.* Gainesville: University Press of Florida, 1996.

Dukore, Bernard F. *Bernard Shaw, Playwright: Aspects of Shavian Drama.* Columbia: University of Missouri Press, 1973.

————. Introduction. *Major Barbara: A Facsimile of the Holograph Manuscript*. By Bernard Shaw. New York: Garland, 1981.

————. "Toward an Interpretation of *Major Barbara*." *Shaw Review* 6 (1963): 62–70.

Edey, Maitland A., and Donald C. Johanson. *Blueprints: Solving the Mystery of Evolution*. Boston: Little, Brown, 1989.

Eldredge, Niles, and S. J. Gould. "Punctuated Equilibria: An Alternative to Phyletic Gradualism." *Modern Paleobiology*. Ed. T. J. M. Schopf. San Francisco: Freeman, 1972.

Eliot, George. *Essays of George Eliot*. Ed. Thomas Pinney. New York: Columbia University Press, 1963.

————. "The Influence of Rationalism." [*Fortnightly Review* 1 (15 May 1865): 43–55]. *Essays of George Eliot*. 397–414.

————. *Middlemarch: A Study of Provincial Life*. New York: Signet –NAL, 1964.

————. "The Progress of the Intellect" [*Westminster Review* 54 (January 1851): 353–68]. *Essays of George Eliot*. 27–45.

Evans, T. F., ed. *Shaw: The Critical Heritage*. London: Routledge and Kegan Paul, 1976.

Gardner, Martin. *Logic Machines and Diagrams*. 2d ed. Chicago: University of Chicago Press, 1982.

————. *The New Age: Notes of a Fringe Watcher*. Buffalo, N.Y.: Prometheus Books, 1988.

Gassner, John. "Bernard Shaw and the Making of the Modern Mind." *Bernard Shaw's Plays*. Ed. Warren Sylvester Smith. New York: Norton, 1970.

Ghiselin, M. T. *The Economy of Nature and the Evolution of Sex*. Berkeley: University of California Press, 1974.

Gilligan, Carol. *In a Different Voice: Psychological Theory and Women's Development*. Cambridge: Harvard University Press, 1982.

Gould, Stephen Jay. "Just in the Middle." *Natural History* January 1984: 24–33.

————. "Darwinism Defined: The Difference Between Fact and Theory." *Discover*, January 1987: 64–70.

Grant, Verne. *The Evolutionary Process: A Critical Review of Evolutionary Theory*. New York: Columbia University Press, 1985.

Haldane, J. S. *Mechanism, Life and Personality: An Examination of the Mechanistic Theory of Life and Mind*. 2d ed. 1923. Westport, Conn.: Greenwood Press, 1973.

Hardison, O. B., Jr. *Disappearing Through the Skylight: Culture and Technology in the Twentieth Century*. New York: Penguin, 1990.

Hawking, Stephen W. *A Brief History of Time: From the Big Bang to Black Holes*. New York: Bantam–Doubleday, 1988.

Hayakawa, S. I. *Language in Thought and Action*. 2d ed. New York: Harcourt, Brace, and World, 1963.

Hobbs, Thomas. *Leviathan: Or the Matter, Forme and Power of a Commonwealth*

Ecclesiasticall and Civil. Ed. Michael Oakeshott. 1651. New York: Collier–Macmillan, 1962.

Hoffman, Paul. "Your Mindless Brain." *Discover,* September 1987: 84–87.

Holroyd, Michael. *Bernard Shaw.* 4 vols. New York: Random House, 1988–92.

Horgan, John. "A Modest Proposal on Altruism." *Scientific American,* March 1991: 20.

Hubenka, Lloyd J. Introduction. *Practical Politics: Twentieth- Century Views on Politics and Economics.* By Bernard Shaw. vii–xxv.

Hume, David. *Enquiries Concerning Human Understanding and Concerning the Principles of Morals.* Ed. P. H. Nidditch. Oxford: Clarendon Press, 1975.

Huxley, T. H. "On the Hypothesis That Animals Are Automata, and Its History." *Body and Mind.* Ed G. N. A. Vesey. London: George Allen and Unwin, 1964.

———. "The Struggle for Existence in Human Society." *Readings from Huxley.* Ed. and intro. Clarissa Rinaker. New York: Harcourt, Brace, and Howe, 1920. 79–112.

Jeans, James. *The Mysterious Universe.* Rev. ed. New York: Macmillan, 1932.

Jevons, William Stanley. *The Theory of Political Economy.* 4th ed. London: Macmillan, 1911.

Johnson, George. "Casting Their Neural Nets." Rev. of *The Improbable Machine: What the Upheavals in Artificial Intelligence Research Reveal About How the Mind Really Works,* by Jeremy Campbell. *New York Times Book Review* 24 December 1989: 12–13.

———. "New Mind, No Clothes." Rev. of *The Emperor's New Mind,* by Roger Penrose. *The Sciences,* July–August 1990: 45–49.

———. "What Really Goes on in There." Rev. of *Consciousness Explained,* by Daniel C. Dennett. *New York Times Book Review,* 10 November 1991: 1+.

Kagan, Jerome, and Sharon Lamb, eds. *The Emergence of Morality in Young Children.* Chicago: University of Chicago Press, 1987.

Kaye, Julian B. *Bernard Shaw and the Nineteenth-Century Tradition.* Norman: University of Oklahoma Press, 1958.

Kozol, Jonathan. *Savage Inequalities: Children in America's Schools.* New York: Crown, 1991.

Kuhn, Thomas S. *The Structure of Scientific Revolutions.* 2d ed. Chicago: University of Chicago Press, 1970.

Leibniz, Gottfried Wilhelm von. *Theodicy: Essays on the Goodness of God, the Freedom of Man, and the Origin of Evil.* Trans. E. M. Huggard. London: Routledge and Kegan Paul, 1951.

Magarshack, David. *Chekhov the Dramatist.* New York: Auvergne, 1952.

Marshall, Dorothy. *Industrial England: 1776–1851.* New York: Charles Scribner's Sons, 1973.

Maupassant, Guy de. *Yvette; Misti.* Paris: Louis Conard, 1910. Vol. 29 of *Oeuvres complète.* 29 vols. 1908–10.

McRory, Desmond J. "Shaw, Einstein and Physics." *SHAW: The Annual of Bernard Shaw Studies* 6:33–67.

Meisel, Martin. *Shaw and the Nineteenth-Century Theater.* Princeton: Princeton University Press, 1963.

Michod, Richard E. "What's Love Got to Do with It?" *The Sciences* May–June 1989: 22–28.

Midgley, Mary. *Evolution as a Religion: Strange Hopes and Stranger Fears.* London: Methuen, 1985.

Minsky, Marvin. "The Intelligent Transplant." *Discover: The World of Science,* October 1989: 52–58.

———. *The Society of Mind.* London: Heinemann, 1987.

Morgan, Margery M. *The Shavian Playground.* London: Methuen, 1972.

Moyers, Bill. *A World of Ideas: Public Opinions from Private Citizens.* Ed. Andie Tucher. Vol. 2. New York: Doubleday, 1990.

Müller-Hill, Benno. *Murderous Science: Elimination by Scientific Selection of Jews, Gypsies, and Others, Germany, 1933–1945.* Trans. George R. Frazer. Oxford: Oxford University Press, 1988.

Myrdal, Gunnar. *An American Dilemma: The Negro Problem and Modern Democracy.* New York: Harper and Brothers, 1944.

Nethercot, Arthur H. *Men and Supermen: The Shavian Portrait Gallery.* 2d ed. New York: Benjamin Blom, 1966.

Nicoll, Allardyce. *Late Nineteenth-Century Drama: 1950–1900.* 2d ed. Cambridge, England: Cambridge University Press, 1967. Vol. 5 of *A History of English Drama: 1660–1900.* 6 vols. 1952–67.

Ogden, C. K., and I. A. Richards. *The Meaning of Meaning: A Study of the Influence of Language upon Thought and of the Science of Symbolism..* New York: Harcourt, Brace, 1959.

Pearson, Hesketh. *G. B. S.: A Full Length Portrait.* New York: Harper and Brothers, 1942.

Penrose, Roger. *The Emperor's New Mind: Concerning Computers, Minds, and the Laws of Physics.* New York: Oxford University Press, 1989.

Pipes, Richard. Rev. of *Stalin: Breaker of Nations,* by Robert Conquest. *New York Times Book Review,* 10 November 1991, sec. 7: 14–15.

Popper, Sir Karl Raimund. *The Logic of Scientific Discovery.* New York: Basic Books, 1959.

Postlewait, Thomas. "Bernard Shaw and Science: The Aesthetics of Causality." *Victorian Science and Victorian Values: Literary Perspectives.* 319–58.

Priest, Stephen. *Theories of the Mind.* Boston: Houghton Mifflin, 1991.

Proctor, Robert N. *Racial Hygiene: Medicine Under the Nazis.* Cambridge: Harvard University Press, 1988.

Rawson, Claude. "Playwright Pleasant and Unpleasant." Rev. of *Bernard Shaw.* Vol. 3: *1918–1950: The Lure of Fantasy,* by Michael Holroyd. *New York Times Book Review,* 20 October 1991: 3+.

Russell, Bertrand. *The Analysis of Matter*. New York: Harcourt, Brace, 1927.

———. *Human Knowledge: Its Scope and Limits*. New York: Simon and Schuster, 1948.

———. *An Inquiry into Meaning and Truth*. London: G. Allen and Unwin, 1940.

———. *An Outline of Philosophy*. London: George Allen and Unwin, 1927.

———. *Philosophical Essays*. New York: Touchstone–Simon and Schuster, 1966.

———. *Portraits from Memory and Other Essays*. New York: Simon and Schuster, 1956.

———. "What I Believe." *Why I Am Not a Christian and Other Essays on Religion and Related Subjects*. Ed. Paul Edwards. New York: Touchstone–Simon and Schuster, 1957. 48–87.

Ryle, Gilbert. *The Concept of Mind*. London: Hutchinson, 1949.

Sapolsky, Robert M., and Caleb E. Finch. "On Growing Old." *The Sciences*, March–April 1991: 30–38.

Schrödinger, Erwin. *Mind and Matter. What Is Life? And Mind and Matter*. 1958. Cambridge, England: Cambridge University Press, 1967.

Searle, John R. "Is the Brain's Mind a Computer Program?" *Scientific American*, January 1990: 26–31.

———. "Minds, Brains, and Programs." *Behavioral and Brain Sciences* 3 (1980): 417–24.

———. *Minds, Brains and Science*. Cambridge: Harvard University Press, 1984.

———. *The Rediscovery of the Mind*. Cambridge: Bradford–MIT Press, 1992.

Silver, Arnold. *Bernard Shaw: The Darker Side*. Stanford, Calif.: Stanford University Press, 1982.

Simon, Herbert A. "A Mechanism for Social Selection and Successful Altruism." *Science* 250: 1665–68.

Smith, Warren Sylvester. *Bishop of Everywhere: Bernard Shaw and the Life Force*. University Park: Pennsylvania State University Press, 1982.

———. Introduction. *Shaw on Religion*. Ed. W. S. Smith. New York: Dodd, Mead, 1967. 7–16.

Sokal, Alan, and Jean Bricmont. *Fashionable Nonsense: Postmodern Intellectuals' Abuse of Science*. New York: Picador, 1998.

Standen, Anthony. *Science Is a Sacred Cow*. New York: Dutton, 1950.

Strindberg, August. "Naturalism in the Theatre" [Author's Foreword to *Miss Julie*]. Becker, *Documents of Modern Literary Realism*. 394–406.

Teilhard de Chardin, Pierre. *Christianity and Evolution*. Tr. René Hague. New York: Harcourt Brace Jovanovich, 1971.

———. *The Phenomenon of Man*. Intro. Julian Huxley. New York: Harper Torch-books–Harper and Bros., 1961.

Turco, Alfred, Jr. *Shaw's Moral Vision: The Self and Salvation*. Ithaca, N.Y.: Cornell University Press, 1976.

Walkley, A. B. Rev. of *Arms and the Man*. *Speaker* 28 April 1894. Reprinted in Evans, *Critical Heritage* 66–68.

Weismann, August. *Essays upon Heredity and Kindred Biological Problems.* 2 vols. Trans. Edward B. Poulton et al. Oxford: Clarendon Press, 1891.

Wesson, Robert G. *Beyond Natural Selection.* Cambridge: MIT Press, 1991.

Wilson, Colin. *Bernard Shaw: A Reassessment.* New York: Atheneum, 1969.

Wisenthal, J. L. Introduction. *Shaw and Ibsen.* By Bernard Shaw. 3–73.

———. *The Marriage of Contraries: Bernard Shaw's Middle Plays.* Cambridge: Harvard University Press, 1974.

Whitman, Robert F. *Shaw and the Play of Ideas.* Ithaca, N.Y.: Cornell University Press, 1977.

Yorks, Samuel A. *The Evolution of Bernard Shaw.* Washington, D.C.: University Press of America, 1981.

Young, Paul. *The Nature of Information.* New York: Praeger, 1987.

Zola, Emile. "Naturalism in the Theatre." *Documents of Modern Literary Realism.* Ed. George J. Becker. 197–229.

Index

Stuart E. Baker is professor of theater at Florida State University. He is the author of *Georges Feydeau and the Aesthetics of Farce* and many essays devoted to a multidisciplinary approach to theater studies.